SCHOOL PARTNERSHIPS HANDBOOK

How to Set Up and Administer Programs with Business, Government, and Your Community

Susan D. Otterbourg, Ed. D.

Foreword by P. Michael Timpane, President
Teachers College, Columbia University

PRENTICE-HALL, INC.
ENGLEWOOD CLIFFS, N.J.

Prentice-Hall International, Inc., *London*
Prentice-Hall of Australia, Pty. Ltd., *Sydney*
Prentice-Hall Canada, Inc., *Toronto*
Prentice-Hall of India Private Ltd., *New Delhi*
Prentice-Hall of Japan, Inc., *Tokyo*
Prentice-Hall of Southeast Asia Pte. Ltd., *Singapore*
Whitehall Books, Ltd., *Wellington, New Zealand*
Editora Prentice-Hall do Brasil Ltda., *Rio de Janeiro*
Prentice-Hall Hispanoamericana, S.A., *Mexico*

© 1986 *by*

PRENTICE-HALL, INC.
Englewood Cliffs, N.J.

Library of Congress Cataloging-in-Publication Data

Otterbourg, Susan D.
  School partnerships handbook.

  Bibliography: p.
  Includes index.
  1. Community and school—United States.   2. School
management and organization—United States.
3. Educational planning—United States.   4. Education—
United States—Aims and objectives.   I. Title.
LC221.087 1986   370.19′3   86-91526

ISBN 0-13-793852-7

Printed in the United States of America

Foreword

The reawakening of corporate interest in education has been a prominent part of the landscape in most states and localities in the nation in the past few years. However, the explosion of this interest has occurred at a pace and in a form that has left many educators perplexed or uncertain about how best to respond. Business leadership has been inclined, in various situations, to offer jobs and job counseling, to offer assistance in the solution of management and logistical problems, or to weigh in on political and financial issues affecting the schools. Always, people in business have been evidently eager to enter discussions and to act jointly with local school leadership. Out of some of these discussions and encounters have risen entirely new inventions as channels for collaboration, including local education foundations and adopt-a-school or join-a-school programs by the thousands.

In the past year or two, the business interest has taken a dramatic jump from these many involvements in local projects and programs to an important role in education policy developments at state and national levels. Business leadership has been prominent in the membership and sponsorship of educational reform reports and proposals throughout the nation. Their range of expressed interest has extended far beyond traditional business concerns about employability, to such matters as the management of the schools and the vitality of the teaching profession.

An overarching theme to all of these moves has been the theme of partnership; that is, the notion that business and education share an important self-interest in the success of the schools and that in this modern time they approach the business of improving education on an equal footing. It is no longer a case of *noblesse oblige* on the part of business, nor a chance for hard-pressed educators to cadge "freebies" of various description out of the public relations interest of a local business community. Businesses must be concerned that every student finishing school have sufficient skills to be productive in the swiftly changing American economy; and schools must be concerned that they enjoy the permanent support of the business community as a necessary underpinning of the political and economic prosperity of American education.

Sue Otterbourg's book is an impressive and encyclopedic guide for the interested educational leaders who must now consolidate and institutionalize the important additional assistance that the business community can give the schools. Dr.

Otterbourg speaks from extensive experience, both in developing the emerging business-education partnership in New York City, and in extensive work for the Education Committee of The White House Office of Private-Sector Initiatives. Working for that committee, Dr. Otterbourg has had an unparalleled opportunity to see the range of activities emerging at the grassroots level across the United States and to arrive at the wise assessment of how such partnerships may best serve legitimate and mutual interests of both parties. Readers should absorb what she has to say at two levels—with respect to the successful development and implementation of operating programs, *and* to an appreciation, which shines through every page, of the reasons why both business and education will see such carefully crafted solutions as the appropriate expression of a shared purpose.

P. Michael Timpane, President
Teachers College, Columbia University
New York City

About the Author

Susan D. Otterbourg's 30-year career in education includes work as a classroom special education, elementary, and high school English teacher, as a school district administrator, as a consultant to urban and suburban school systems, as an elected trustee of the Ridgewood (New Jersey) Board of Education, and as a national expert on partnerships in education.

Dr. Otterbourg received her bachelor's degree in English literature from Smith College (Northampton, Massachusetts). Along with masters' degrees in education from Queens College (New York) and William Paterson College (Wayne, New Jersey), she was awarded a master's and a doctorate in educational administration from Columbia University's Teachers College (New York).

In 1981, she founded Delman Educational Communications, a consultant firm that concentrates on staff development, organizational management, and program evaluation for school districts, teachers, and administrators. An outgrowth of this consultancy was a specialty in partnerships in education.

Dr. Otterbourg was the coordinator in 1984 and 1985 for the first and second National Symposiums, held in Washington, D.C., on Partnerships in Education, sponsored by the President's Advisory Council on Private Sector Initiatives. She is currently, working on the third National Symposium.

She has served for several years as the principal consultant on a staff development program for New York City high school principals and assistant principals that was sponsored by a local partnership, the New York Alliance for the Public Schools. Dr. Otterbourg is also a member of the Editorial Advisory Board of *ProEducation*, the national magazine about partnerships with education.

Acknowledgments

I would like to acknowledge the support and guidance of the following people in the writing and preparation of this book: Robert K. Otterbourg, Kimberly Smith, Judith Goldwater, Edward Stoeffels, Maryanne Taddeo—and all of the partnership leaders who graciously and openly agreed to share materials, information, problems, and achievements concerning their programs.

About This Book

It is clear by now that many Americans want schools to improve instruction and learning opportunities. Of particular interest is how concerns of the private sector complement those of educators at all levels.

These expectations for school improvement cannot be met through traditional approaches and channels such as the reorganization and mobilization of existing local, state, and federal sources of funding and technical assistance. The reality of rising costs, the pressures for tax reform, the burdens of escalating deficit spending, as well as competition from other social service areas, appear to preclude major governmental spending for education at any level. Public education must instead consider new methods of using its resources and find new channels of support for school improvement efforts. To effect change, public education will increasingly have to help itself.

Many educators are doing just that by mustering additional technical, financial, materials, and volunteer support for their students, schools, and staff. Within their local communities, alliances are formed as educators ask for and get resources from their civic, business, professional, and university neighbors.

Educators know that although such alliances will not necessarily pay for staff salaries and maintain school buildings, they can support and supplement staff development, student enrichment activities, basic skills programs, career education projects, and a myriad of other instructional, professional, and learning opportunities for their school districts. In addition, they view alliances in terms of their potential for securing strong political allies at budget time—no small consideration, particularly in times of shrinking resources and rising costs. For businesses, these cooperative arrangements provide opportunities to protect long-term employment interests by training well-qualified employees of the future; to show their communities a sense of social responsibility; and to take advantage of tax write-offs.

These alliances or mutually collaborative efforts are called partnerships, and are usually initiated by educators. Although school-community partnerships are hardly new (think about all past parent-volunteer efforts), the movement toward formal partnership arrangements has really grown since the late 1970s. While partnerships are still in their infancy, educators are asking such important questions as "It is just one more fad?" "Is it worth the effort?" "How can we start a partnership?" and "Where can we go for help in this venture?".

Current information about partnerships has been limited generally to articles on partnership activities and specific program descriptions of a variety of successful partnership formats. For the educator who wishes to consider, initiate, and develop a partnership, such information is interesting, but fails to provide the hands-on technical assistance necessary for effective decision making.

Educators want to form alliances with other members of the public or private sectors in order to extend their use of community resources to meet local educational needs. They need practical tools to address questions and problems related to partnerships and to help assure that effective partnerships are established. This handbook is the result, written in response to requests from principals, superintendents, and other educational leaders for assistance and information about how to initiate and develop school-industry-community partnerships.

The *School Partnerships Handbook* will also help business and community leaders learn more about their roles, responsibilities, and level or scope of participation in any partnership venture. This book will prove useful to students in leadership and management training programs as a supplemental text to school-community program development.

Part One, "Starting a Partnership," addresses the basic decision-making process confronting school and community leaders: whether or not to initiate a partnership. Leaders are guided in this process as they consider the purpose of partnerships; advantages, disadvantages, and obstacles to developing partnerships; and guidelines to consider when making such decisions.

Part Two, "Preparing for a Partnership Project," is a planning section focused on activities that will establish a firm base for long-term relationships with partners. Such activities include assessing needs and resources, soliciting commitment, forming committees and task forces, and determining workable policies and guidelines. This part concludes with an examination of the design and scope of current partnership formats, which should assist you in choosing a format that will best meet your partnership's needs.

Part Three, "Launching the Partnership," explains how to establish the necessary management components, then shifts to how the successful coordination of these components will ensure the support, development, and implementation of partnership activities. With efficient and effective functioning of the partnership as a major goal, it's critical to carefully organize and coordinate your management team, partnership staff, budget and fiscal procedures, fund-raising efforts, recordkeeping, communication, program activities, and evaluation and reporting to all parties involved.

Part Four, "Maintaining and Extending Successful Partnerships," examines the strategies required to maintain and extend an ongoing, consistently effective partnership—with a view toward developing future programs and their direction. Program leaders are (1) helped to achieve specific goals related to modification and change, and (2) introduced to activities and strategies related to sharing and networking with other regional, state, and national partnership resources. In addition, partnership practitioners from across the country reflect on the future of the partnership movement.

Concluding the handbook is the **Appendixes** section—possibly the best resource of all—including names and addresses of people involved in successful partnerships across the country. These program sources represent a sampling of the partnership expertise that is currently available—expertise that comes in all shapes and sizes: large and small programs; differing formats, procedures, and activities; urban, suburban, and rural areas; and at local, regional, state, and national levels.

I wish you success in your efforts to set up or enhance your partnership program.

Susan D. Otterbourg

Contents

PART ONE
STARTING A PARTNERSHIP • 1

PART FOUR
MAINTAINING AND EXTENDING
SUCCESSFUL PARTNERSHIPS • 269

PART FIVE
APPENDIXES • 303

PART ONE

STARTING
A
PARTNERSHIP

Why Start a Partnership?

There has been a growing realization in many school districts that traditional approaches and channels to local, state, and federal funding and technical assistance are not sufficient to meet community or public expectations for school improvement. As a result, educators are prompted to seek additional funding, equipment, materials, and human resources to provide long-range, consistent and formalized support to the school district, its staff, and its students. Such resources may be sought locally, regionally, or nationwide; such resources may be found in the business, civic, or general community; such resources may already be providing support to the school district in an informal way.

Businesses and other civic and community organizations have shown a growing interest in working with their local school districts. This interest stems from their desire to improve community relations and organizational images, a growing need for qualified human resources, the potential of tax benefits, and the general public reaction to nationwide reports about the "state" of public education.

To mobilize these resources, school districts usually, and business, and civic organizations sometimes, are initiating alliances called *partnerships*. As the possibility of such mutually collaborative efforts is explored, leaders in these initiatives will be making decisions based on understanding both the advantages of partnerships and the obstacles to developing them.

ADVANTAGES OF PARTNERSHIPS

Support for the Educational Environment

Partnerships will not pay for teachers or maintenance of buildings. However, alliances can stimulate and support staff development, enrichment programs, basic skills projects, career education activities, and many other programmatic efforts that face restrictions or cuts because of shrinking budgets and rising costs.

Political Allies

Partnerships can prove to be formidable political allies during budget time—to counteract negativism and criticism of district spending. In fact, many temporary alliances have grown into permanent coalitions committed to the support of public funding for public schools.

Good Education Is Good Business

Partnerships reflect an understanding that the economic well-being and vitality of a community are tied to the quality of its public school system—and a commitment to that end. In effect, good education is good for business: a public education system that is perceived as effective will encourage and contribute to a community's general stability. Prospective employees and consumers find such a community an attractive place in which to live, and in cases of planned desegregation efforts, partnerships help to stem middle class urban flight that could erode the urban center's tax base.

Partnerships can help provide human resources and shared services to extend effective and efficient preemployment training at a lower cost per student than post–high school business retraining efforts. Whether large corporations or small businesses (with little or no access to training opportunities once they have hired employees), partnership programs are one concrete method to help businesses recruit entry-level employees who have good basic vocational, communication, and problem-solving skills; work habits; and attitudes.

Partnerships improve public perceptions of the positive role of business in the local, regional, and national community. In addition to improved community relations and a positive corporate image, business stands to benefit from tax deductions. Employee participation in partnership activities also encourages positive company morale and provides additional valuable leadership training for employees who serve in a variety of volunteer capacities.

More obvious and tangible advantages of these alliances to business-community partners could range from technological training and writing institutes taught by education staff, to use of school sites, student entertainment, cultural and civic activities (art shows, landscaping, service projects, and others), English and foreign language instruction, and child-care assistance.

Learning Opportunities for All

Partnerships can help to extend the learning opportunities for students; staff; administrators; parents; and business-civic-community–higher-education partners. That potential for enriched and expanded learning is perhaps most important; all partners in a successful partnership give to and take from each other within a structure focused on sharing and caring.

OBSTACLES TO PARTNERSHIPS

The Perception of Cost-Effectiveness

Partnerships are often perceived as "fads" that have little or no chance of attacking a school district's basic needs such as more money, staff development, the improvement of the core curriculum, and the retention of districtwide programs. Therefore, many partnership initiatives are rejected by school districts on the basis that benefits the program would bring to the students and staff are just not worth the time and effort.

Breadth of Commitment

School districts are used to committing resources over long periods of time. Usually, resources are either added or maintained at current levels. Drastic cuts are reserved for budget defeats, school closings, or other catastrophes. On the other hand, most companies will not *or* cannot commit resources for extended periods of time, and may find many partnership agreements too binding. Lack of understanding of alternative partnership arrangements by *all* partners, can hinder the development of an alliance.

School Rigidity and Bureaucracy

Partnership program directors and their community-business partners cite the difficulties of forming partnerships with bureaucratic school districts. Rigid regulations and procedures cause delays in reaching agreement and obtaining approval on courses of action, in establishing operating procedures and bylaws, and, where applicable, in coordinating a multidistrict model involving separate boards of education and superintendents.

Conflicting Misperceptions

It is often difficult for the worlds of work and school to speak to each other. Schools, used to their established bureaucratic processes, fear the unknown. They perceive that business might meddle in affairs about which it knows nothing, or else look at public education in terms of limited corporate interests. They will manifest such suspicions through both passive and active resistance strategies.

Potential business-civic partners may fear contact with schools in general and urban schools in particular. In addition, corporate disillusionment and misunderstanding regarding the products of public education can result in alternative forms of foot-dragging behavior.

Competing Demands on Available Time

Educational leaders and their complements in other organizations have many responsibilities. Competing demands on time can result in apathy and impatience toward planning and development of vital procedures and organization for creating a partnership. For business managers, short-term profits and large staff turnovers can take priority over long-term community relations investments. For educators, the day-to-day running of a school and the myriad administrative reports and duties usually come before commitment to the pursuit of additional resources for program enrichment or staff development.

Quantity versus Quality

Partnerships are often developed in a topsy-turvy manner. People get an idea or a bit of funding, pounce on either or both, and then build on a rather shaky foundation. Those responsible for administering such projects find that they are forever trying to get them under control to meet the educational needs for which they were intended. Doing too much too soon can cause the partnership to lose credibility *and* the partners to reject continued participation.

Problems Specific to Foundation Partnership Formats

Foundations are intermediary units and, as such, have the potential for being independent allies of public education. This independence can be perceived as threatening or out of the control of the school system, with agendas not necessarily consonant with those of educators. Although foundations constitute only one area of support for schools, the need to consistently seek "legitimacy" in the eyes of all partners can prove an obstacle to any foundation's productive efforts on behalf of the schools.

Problems Specific to Rural Areas

All the obstacles to forming partnerships listed above are compounded in rural areas, where

- national committees and reports do not usually address rural needs.
- isolation is a prominent factor. Resources in general are more limited and, specifically, large corporations are not usually linked to rural school systems.
- dissemination systems are usually inadequate to meet the communications needs necessary in building a partnership.
- legislative representation is less, and thus schools have limited influence or impact on legislatures.

- educators have little experience in working effectively with other organizations.
- subaverage salaries, high teacher turnover, and shortages discourage school staff from working on projects in addition to usual instructional and administrative responsibilities.

Making the Big Decision

In addition to a review of advantages of and obstacles to the development of partnerships, there are guidelines to consider before a formal alliance is proposed between a school district and its community. A discussion of these guidelines completes the necessary first steps before a final decision is made about pursuing and preparing a new partnership project.

REVIEW OF THE GUIDELINES

Needs and Goals

Can a partnership project most effectively meet designated needs and goals? Using an elimination process, consideration must be given to alternative projects that could meet such needs and goals more efficiently.

Mutual Benefits to All Partners

Mutual benefits to all potential participants are also reviewed. The most successful partnerships appear to be those in which exchanges take place: all participating partners receive some benefit from the relationship, such as human services, materials and equipment, tax write-offs, professional staff development, and site use.

Quantity and Quality of Available Resources to Meet Needs

An assessment of available resources is made to determine whether these resources can substantively meet the needs of the partnership project. Do you have sufficient time, money, staff, and commitment to develop and sustain a strong (but not necessarily large) core group organization?

Feasibility of Potential Partnership Designs

Responses from partnership leaders about their programs' formats yielded clear patterns. Partnerships appear to be multidimensional, with a variety of program formats under some kind of umbrella organization. In rank order, the most common umbrella organizations used were: (l) adopt-a-school, (2) volunteer programs, (3) school-business-university-civic organization alliances, (4) community schools, (5) foundations, (6) clearinghouses, (7) countywide projects, (8) committees, (9) regional associations, (10) statewide organizations, and (11) others such as national organizations, lobbying groups, general associations, and the creation of new magnet schools.

WHY PARTICULAR PARTNERSHIPS WERE CHOSEN

The ranking described above suggests the popularity of particular partnership formats, but does not tell us *why* such partnership programs were chosen. Survey responses to this question reflected a variety of approaches to problem solving as related to needs, resources, and available opportunities.

• Attendance at local, regional, or national conferences, at which programs were presented and community experiences discussed, persuaded some people to begin such a venture. As an extension of this decision, internal needs assessments of school districts led to the determination of needs and available resources, which, in essence, dictated the direction in which such alliances might go.

• Some nationwide business, professional, and civic organizations have historically been involved in educational programs focused on entrepreneurship, better-educated and informed consumers, service-to-community orientation, and the development of qualified human resources. For these organizations, partnerships are a logical extension of already existing programs and activities.

• A growing awareness of the need for community agencies to work together to maintain existing services and community cohesiveness has encouraged the development of many partnerships, particularly those in which the local school district has allied with nearby universities, other community development agencies, and city or town governmental offices. In many communities, the realization that the majority of the community was no longer directly interested or involved in educating their children forced schools to reach out to form new alliances that would encourage the support for public education.

• Some business and civic organizations stated that for some time they had been searching for ways in which to "connect" with the school community from which they derived the bulk of their human resources. Concerns regarding the entry-level competencies of youth—particularly those from the inner cities—were related to this effort. In a number of cases, the partnership grew out of an identified career education need for student exploration and a desire of an industry-education group to undertake a particular joint project.

• Other businesses said that their local school districts had requested help and support and had a program already planned in which the business could participate in a variety of ways (one-on-one, districtwide, or other ways).

• Already-established foundations were often asked to become independent, intermediary groups as "bankers" and/or administrators of a partnership project.

• The realization that state education departments needed to join with the private sector to garner additional support for public education has evolved more slowly. National reports on education, plus the White House support for such private sector initiatives, are proving to be an additional impetus to both state and national governmental involvement. For example, in federal agencies and departments, presidential guidance supporting participation has resulted in the mushrooming of alliances between agencies and school districts all over the county.

• Some respondents indicated that the program they chose just seemed to be the best format to use at the time.

• Partnerships have also grown out of pilot research projects in connection with higher education. In these instances, universities might initiate projects based on funding through grants. The partnership is then in place and becomes a base upon which to build.

POTENTIAL IMPACT OF PARTNERSHIPS

The final guideline to consider before establishing a partnership is the impact this decision will have on students, on the school district and its staff, on business and other civic organizations, and on parents and the general community. The effect of the higher-education community on partnerships is also reviewed.

On Students

Partnership leaders state that their programs' impact has been greatest at the classroom level. In just over 100 programs around the country, at least 16 million secondary students and over 2 million elementary students have been involved in some level of partnership program. Numbers are, of course, important; more critical is *how* the project has affected students. Patterns emerge as follows:

1. Students' learning horizons were expanded, particularly in relation to awareness of and access to the worlds of work, science, technology, and the arts, as well as the practical application of school work to their employment as adults. Daily school work was enriched by traditional and nontraditional experiences ordinarily unavailable through regular school channels and schedules.

2. Students learned that adults cared about and had positive expectations for them. These adults served as successful role models, tutors, and confidants. Students, many of whom were considered "at risk," developed self-confidence as they experienced success in these programs. Others (and numbers are not available) credited these programs with encouraging them to attend and remain in school, to seek post–high school training and college opportunities, and to secure employment following graduation.

3. Students received basic skills help on a more personal basis. Scores on standardized tests indicated improvement that was at least partially attributed to involvement in such programs.

On the School District and Its Staff

In the functioning partnerships of the over 100 school districts surveyed, approximately 56,000 administrators, teachers, and support staff have been affected by their districts' partnerships. In most cases, the impact was limited, that is, to a school, to a specific project, to a group of students or teachers at certain grade levels. Only 25 percent of these partnerships reported that the impact on staff, thus far, had been districtwide.

What were the most important objectives achieved for school district staff through their partnerships?

1. The word "caring" arose often in the responses. School staff appear delighted and surprised that people and organizations outside the schools want to support them and are willing to back up this interest with action. Teachers perceive a new recognition by their communities of their talents and efforts—and of the challenges facing the teaching profession. Communication and trust between public education and the private sector have grown as a result.

2. The opportunity for access to previously unknown but available resources from the private sector and community organizations comes at a time when educational programs face rising costs and restrictions of traditional resources.

3. Direct interaction with the larger community provides opportunities to extend educators' professional self-improvement skills.

On Business

Through the questionnaire, program directors and their business partners reported that approximately 6,700 businesses were involved in over 100 partnerships. The business partners stated that they are achieving the following objectives through their participation:

1. Businesses are being portrayed in a more favorable light by both their immediate communities and, in some cases, the nation as a whole. The publicity they received reinforced usual corporate and organizational efforts in the area of community relations—particularly community service programs.

2. Partnerships are helping to improve the morale of company personnel at all levels of management and operations.

3. Partnerships are encouraging the development of leadership skills of business staffs.

4. Businesses expressed how these alliances had given them new understandings of their own resources, many of which they had previously taken for granted. At the same time, they had become aware of the available educational resources for business within their communities.

5. Interest in partnerships has had a domino effect; businesses do not want to be excluded when other organizations are becoming involved in this communitywide effort.

6. Awareness of the problems experienced by public education has given business a better appreciation of both strengths and weaknesses of schools today. This understanding is coupled with the satisfaction that some of these problems can be addressed successfully through combined efforts.

7. The growing concern of business to attract qualified future employees is widespread. Direct and indirect support for public education through partnerships is perceived to have the potential to affect the quality of graduates entering the workforce.

8. There are personal rewards—with and without formal recognition—in helping students, teachers, and the schools through the vehicle of partnerships.

9. Summer work forces have been developed. This part-time work force provides opportunities for pretraining experiences for post–high school employment.

On Civic and Other Community Groups and the Community at Large

In the over 100 partnership programs surveyed, more than 1,000 civic organizations are participating in these programs. A sampling of the range of these organizations includes service clubs; PTOs; professional associations; United Way; women's groups; church groups; neighborhood groups; Kiwanis; Jaycees; other youth leadership groups; Rotary; city, state, and federal municipal agencies; hospitals; senior citizens' groups; chambers of commerce; sororities and fraternities; mental health boards and agencies; teachers' associations; national alliance groups; advisory neighborhood councils; police departments; museums; arts groups; Masons; League of Women Voters; Junior League; adult and community learning centers; Girls' Clubs; and the Private Industry Council.

Urban centers were particularly aggressive in pursuing such alliances. Of course, the range of resources in urban areas is seemingly endless compared with those available in smaller, more isolated school districts. School districts in suburban and rural areas may have already established long-time informal relationships with local civic and community groups and there is reluctance to disturb what is already working. Whether such informal alliances should be coordinated under the umbrella of a formal partnership program is being debated around the country.

Respondents stated the following as the result of the involvement of civic and community groups in partnerships:

1. Members of the community had heightened their awareness, and the general public's, regarding the strengths of the community's public education system, the needs of schools and, more specifically, the active support and community resources available and necessary to help meet these needs.

2. Increased enthusiastic support and recognition of the communities' young people was related to partnership activities.

3. Such programs appear to enhance a spirit of cooperation and involvement just at a time when many citizens felt alienated from the public schools. For example, partnerships have been catalysts to promote positive race relations and to assist community efforts in the passage of tax levies.

4. Personal rewards for civic and community partners—although not always measurable—were particularly satisfying.

On Parents

Although most program leaders had not measured the impact of partnerships on parents, they noted the following:

1. If parents see that their children are benefiting from particular programs at school, their involvement in and positive attitude toward public education increases.

2. The wide communication gap that often exists between parents and students, and business and civic community representatives, is narrowed through mutual concern and support for public education.

3. Many parents have been served directly by adjunct partnership activities, for example, by health screening clinics.

THE IMPACT OF THE HIGHER EDUCATION COMMUNITY ON THE PARTNERSHIP

Higher-education (post–high-school) institutions have had an impact on local partnerships in about 50 percent of those partnerships who responded to the questionnaire. In some districts, schools are working with a variety of these institutions. Such alliances are deterred by concerns related to (1) program control and (2) the traditional isolation of public education and higher education from one another (except in the area of course work and certification). Currently, such partnerships appear to be growing and directed to specific needs for both the public schools and higher education.

1. Year-round staff development for practicing teachers is a major thrust, particularly in the areas of management, mathematics, science, and technology.

2. Deans of schools of education are actively participating on partnership committees. Other university staff act as teachers and mentors (to school

staff and students), as well as advisors and resources in partnership programs at school sites and at the district level.

3. Professional students (law, medicine, business, education, engineering) have become teachers, mentors, and tutors to public school students in a variety of programs.

4. Higher-education institutions also

- donate facilities in which to hold partnership activities and equipment for training and retraining school staff

- act as clearinghouses or resource centers for school district research and curriculum projects

- encourage young women and minority groups to pursue nontraditional career areas

- act as the catalysts for other partners in an alliance, thereby bringing people and groups together to work on research and other projects addressing mutual needs and goals

- provide high school students with college experiences, cultural programs, and role models for careers.

PART TWO

PREPARING FOR A PARTNERSHIP PROJECT

The Role of the Planning Team in the Preparation Process

Although some partnerships were started earlier, the partnership movement has really blossomed since 1979. Through the survey, a majority of program leaders stated that program development took from three months to one year and, in some cases, as long as two to three years. In general, planning and development efforts were not rushed; responders remarked that building a solid base for such programs required time.

Who takes the leadership in initiating partnership programs? Program leaders say that partnerships are begun primarily by public school educators—usually superintendents of schools, directors of vocational and community education, or grants office directors. Higher education institutions have also initiated action and support. In instances in which noneducators provide the spark for program development, leadership comes from business and professional organizations, chambers of commerce or Rotary, and nonprofit organizations (local, regional, and national). These early partners usually form a planning team. Some team members will be appointed by a superintendent or CEO; others will volunteer their services.

PLANNING IS THE KEY

If a decision is made to develop a partnership, planning becomes the key to this effort's success. Check sheets can be blueprints and aids for helping planners through all the beginning steps of program development. For example, the check sheets outlined in Figures 3-1 and 3-2 can help to organize a planning team and facilitate team meetings.

THE PARTNERSHIP PLANNING TEAM

Composition of the Partnership Planning Team

Who should be *members* of the partnership's planning team? Program leaders agreed that effective planning team members

- have recognized status in terms of an established base of community support
- have a track record in working their way through the red tape of school and/or business, government, and civic bureaucracies
- have demonstrated authority to speak for their organizations
- are usually chosen by the superintendent of schools and presidents or equivalent leaders from businesses, civic organizations, and other community agencies
- may well form the core group that eventually becomes the operations staff for the partnership project

Note: Planning team members should understand (*from the very beginning,*) that they are not expected to remain as day-to-day working members of the partnership—although they may continue in this capacity.

Effective planning team members bring particular *skills* to the task of preparing for the partnership. They communicate successfully to a variety of audiences and display sensitivity to the needs of all partnership groups. Organizational and coordination skills are, of course, critical at all stages of program development. Under stress, planning team members exhibit flexibility and the ability to remain undaunted by obstacles.

The *number* of members on the planning team will vary, depending on the format and size of the partnership under development. Be mindful, in all cases, to keep the group as *small* as possible—but large enough to get the work done—and as *representative* as possible. Planning team members should include

- *a central office school staff person* who has authority to make decisions and reports directly to the district superintendent or assistant superintendent on partnership matters. This person could assume the chairmanship of the planning committee and later become the director of the partnership program.
- *business-civic-community-professional people* who have the authority to make decisions and report to top level management in their organizations. The number of committee members in this category depends on the scope of the anticipated partnership and available volunteers. Representatives from all interested broad-based groups should be included.
- *a school site administrator* (if the anticipated partnership will be school-based).
- *other school district personnel* as appropriate (for example, a teacher, union representative, districtwide curriculum coordinator, or staff developer).
- *a school district business officer* or staff person.
- *the school district's superintendent* (on call).
- *a head of the chamber of commerce*, other *CEOs* (on call).
- *a secretary* (part-time only needed at this stage).

Responsibilities of the Planning Team

The planning team will be making specific recommendations to the governing council related to the partnership's format, goals and objectives, general program, staffing, and initial needs and resource requirements. How are these tasks accomplished? The planning team usually holds *exploratory meetings* at which members receive and review current partnership information and share ideas related to short- and long-term partnership plans. Outside consultants and advisors may be asked to participate in this process. These sessions generally result in agreements on

1. responsibilities of planning team members (for example, assessment of needs and resources and securing of necessary approval and cooperation of early program partners).
2. the planning process to be used.
3. potential partnership formats.
4. schedules and timelines for developing and establishing the partnership. Meeting timelines should be flexible, but in place to provide guidance and direction. A clear schedule of meetings takes into account other responsibilities of planning team members, the extent of initial project goals for launching the partnership, and contingencies that might present obstacles to orderly program development.

Careful minutes of these sessions should be maintained; flow charts are also useful tools during this period as are check sheets like Figures 3-1 and 3-2.

ACTION PLAN CHECK SHEET FOR
PLANNING TEAM: COMPOSITION AND RESPONSIBILITIES

MEMBER

Name _____

Title _____

Affiliation _____

Address _____

Phone Numbers _____
              (Office)   (Home)

Supervisor:

Name _____

Phone Number _____

RESPONSIBILITIES

1. _____

2. _____

3. _____

4. _____

Name _____

Title _____

Affiliation _____

Address _____

Phone Numbers _____
              (Office)   (Home)

Supervisor:

Name _____

Phone Number _____

1. _____

2. _____

3. _____

4. _____

Figure 3–1

20

ACTION PLAN CHECK SHEET FOR PLANNING TEAM MEETING

Date/Time _____   Place _____

TASK (exploratory meetings)   RESPONSIBILITY

1. Site arrangements   _____

2. Food arrangements   _____

3. Agenda   _____

4. Notification of participants _____

5. Meeting minutes   _____

   a. Record minutes   _____

   b. Prepare minutes   _____

   c. Distribute minutes   _____

PARTICIPANTS

CHAIR: _____

AGENDA

_____

_____

_____

_____

_____

_____

_____   Signature of Partnership Director

Figure 3–2

21

Assessing Needs and Resources

An assessment process is a practical and systematic method for gathering information and data. Once the composition and responsibilities of the partnership's planning team are established, the team should begin to plan and implement an assessment to determine

- the needs of the population to be served;
- the priority order of these needs; and
- the breadth and depth of human, financial, and material resources available within the immediate community that will meet these needs.

This section examines how to (1) design and disseminate assessment instruments; (2) analyze, interpret, and report assessment results; and (3) use the assessment data to develop and communicate partnership goals and objectives to the community at large. Consult the "Needs Assessment Action Plan" (see Figures 4-1 through 4-4) for guided assistance in surveying the population, interviewing, preparing and distributing questionnaires, and using the questionnaire results.

DESIGNING ASSESSMENT INSTRUMENTS

Step One: Which Population Will Be Surveyed?

Partnerships disseminate assessments to two major populations: staff of the school district (administrators, teachers, specialists, and support staff) and the rest of the community (businesses, civic agencies, and nonprofit groups). Occasionally, a separate assessment is distributed to high school students. It is recommended that surveys be sent to as many community groups as possible; a broad-based response will be most useful when developing partnership goals.

Of course, the number of surveys distributed will depend on the population of your community. Large urban areas will want to be more selective in this distribution; they may survey just organizations within a particular geographic radius of a school or a community school district, plus selective citywide organizations. Smaller cities, and suburban and rural areas, may need to survey all local community and business organizations in order to elicit both quality and quantity of response and commitment.

Step Two: What Information Needs to Be Collected?

Assessments to gather data should be straightforward, uncomplicated instruments. They seek to determine what organizations and people need and what organizations and people can give. Since partnerships are usually initiated by educators, assessments emphasize what students and school staff need to improve instruction, learning, and management. Yet *all* organizations have needs that can be at least partially met through community alliances. Therefore, for purposes of building a long-term, healthy relationship, *all* potential partners should be assessed for *both* their needs and their resources. With such an exchange

1. school districts have the unique opportunity to elicit a spectrum of community opinion about public education in general and partnerships in particular
2. school districts will not be perceived as beggar groups
3. there is the potential of greater breadth of communication and interaction between all partners
4. community groups (particularly smaller organizations and businesses) should feel more positive about committing themselves to partnership activities

Step Three: What Will Be the Assessment's Format and Content?

Assessment Formats. There can be both informal and formal assessments. In some communities, informal assessments include phone or personal interviews, discussions at town forums, parent meetings or administrative conferences, and random house-to-house or block-by-block interviews.

Let's talk about the use of the *interview* format as an assessment instrument. This format is used

- when there are limited numbers of resources available to exchange with the school district.
- when the available resources (organizations and businesses) are difficult to reach.
- when previous attempts to elicit information through written communication have proved unsuccessful.
- when further information is needed, in addition to that received through a written survey. For example, the Nashua (New Hampshire) School District (see Figure 4-5) has developed an assessment instrument combining a written response and an interview.

Assessments gathered through *discussion groups, forums,* or *conferences* are, in general, used solely as a starting point. Such meetings are often vehicles for planning the development of a more formal assessment instrument. Nevertheless, in some rural areas, this form of assessment appears to be a satisfactory method (1) to extract the needs and resources of the immediate community and (2) to solicit and reinforce community and/or educators' participation and cohesiveness. It is recommended that minutes be kept at these meetings for the record and that, if possible, a printed one-page survey be available for the audience. These surveys, to be returned at the meeting's end or by mail, would require only check-off and short-answer responses; they would include space for inserting basic contact information (name, address, phone number) for future use.

Partnership leaders say that the most comprehensive form of assessment is a one- to four-page *printed questionnaire* with *clear directions*. Such a questionnaire is usually distributed with a cover letter from the school district's superintendent.

The format for most questionnaires is brief. Respondents either check off information or have sufficient space (don't crowd the page!) to write in short answers to the questions. All identifying information is on the assessment, including the person and place to which the completed instrument is sent.

Some assessments request information through broad and general information categories. It is felt that this format allows for more creative, flexible responses. For example, the Tulsa (Oklahoma) Public Schools' "Adopt-a-School Program" instrument (see Figure 4-6) is disseminated to assess general needs at specific school sites.

Although many of the assessment forms are kept purposely general, others try to elicit more specific needs and resource information from respondents. Many business organizations are unaware of the resources they have at their disposal that would be useful in partnership programs. Suggestions are then very helpful to them. One example of this detailed format comes from the Houston (Texas) Independent School District (see Figure 4-7).

Content of Assessment. The content of any assessment is, of course, guided by its purpose. Therefore, any assessment, prepared as part of a partnership's development, should extract information from respondents regarding their needs, available resources, and interest in and ability to participate in a partnership program. Those preparing the assessment instrument must do some preassessment sleuthing to obtain information about

1. general district needs in programmatic, instructional, staff development, management, and materials-equipment areas. Often, superintendents', principals' and teachers' long-standing "wish lists" are helpful in this process.

2. the rising costs and shrinking resources that can or could restrict the school district's ability to meet these needs.

3. other avenues of support (besides the potential partnership arrangement) that currently do or could meet determined needs.

4. the form, content and effectiveness of partnership activities (informal and formal) already active in the community.

5. the resources (for example, cultural, staff development, site usage, technological) the school district could provide to community businesses and other organizations. What is the potential for an exchange of such resources between the school district and its larger community?

6. the partnership arrangements and activities of other school districts (with similar demographics).

This information is gathered and reviewed, and decisions are made regarding the purpose(s) of the assessment. The planning committee is then in a position to decide their instrument's contents. They can move ahead, pick a format, and design and prepare the instrument. The following examples indicate that a process similar to the one described above was used successfully to determine the content of the following instruments:

- a survey sent to the community from the Lancaster (Pennsylvania) school district (see Figure 4-8)
- a survey disseminated to students from Private Initiatives in Public Education (PIPE) in Washington (see Figure 4-9)
- a survey sent to the business community from the TwinWest (Minnesota) Chamber of Commerce (see Figure 4-10)

PREPARATION AND DISSEMINATION OF ASSESSMENT INSTRUMENTS

Preparation

Preparation of the assessment instruments is usually done in house. Occasionally, the school district receives funding and/or actual printing support for preparation and mailing costs from a partner. Don't depend on external support! Assessments need not be fancy to be effective. Useful suggestions regarding preparation follow.

- If the instruments can be printed with a colorful ink or on colored paper, they will be more eye-catching and less likely to be instant wastebasket fodder.
- Research has shown that individually signed cover letters command more attention than letters with printed signatures.
- It is, of course, more cost-effective to send this material by bulk mail.
- If you can afford to enclose a stamped, self-addressed envelope, this strategy has been shown to elicit a larger response.

Dissemination

To School Staff. Assessments should be disseminated through the mail to staff *districtwide* to solicit their recommendations regarding needs and resources. This original assessment becomes the foundation for staff commitment and participation. It helps staff (1) to understand the partnership concept, (2) to realize that consideration is being given to their ideas and concerns, and (3) to place the anticipated program in perspective in terms of time and scope. In this way, expectations will not be raised beyond what can realistically be accomplished and hopes—and morale—will not be dashed.

To Business and the Community at Large. In most smaller cities, and suburban and rural school districts, mailing lists and contacts are usually developed by central-office staff who are responsible for disseminating the assessment to all business-civic-nonprofit organizations in the community whose student population is served by the school district. In large urban areas, where coordination of school programs may be delegated by the chief superintendent to the district superintendent level, the audience surveyed may be located within regional boundaries. In *any* district where potential partners are large organizations, superintendents should personally contact and present the survey to the organizations' directors, or CEOs, or presidents. Follow-up support then comes from the partnership's planning team.

It is useful for school districts to use the mailing lists of local community agencies and organizations. Superintendents' offices often have such lists. Otherwise, contacting local agencies for mailing lists provides an additional opportunity to spark interest in the partnership. Community organizations might agree to print, prepare, and actually mail the materials for you to their membership; often they will include a cover letter from the agency's leader.

Another dissemination method is to present and distribute the survey at local organizations' monthly meetings, luncheons, or dinners. Organizations usually honor such requests, which are seen as opportunities to become more involved with the local community. At these functions, presentations, followed by dissemination of the assessment, can elicit immediate interest in the partnership.

ANALYZING AND INTERPRETING ASSESSMENT RESULTS

Assessment results are tallied and reviewed to determine trends in needs, and the breadth and depth of available resources. Priorities are set and determined on the basis of both quantity of assessment results *and* assessed available resources. Unfortunately, you may have needs for which there are limited or no resources. Consideration must therefore be given to: (1) needs that surface as the program develops, (2) needs that cannot be met until the partnership program is well established, or (3) needs that cannot be met through partnership programs.

REPORTING THE ASSESSMENT RESULTS

After needs are reviewed and ranked and resources are determined, assessment results are reported to the entire community through a school district newsletter or reporting form. The format of this communication is brief and clear and can include a copy of the assessment to community members who (1) may not have previously received the assessment or (2) may not have responded to the earlier request for information. Widespread communication from the school district regarding the assessment process

a. informs the community of needs and resources of both the school district and its larger community

b. provides recognition to and solidifies commitment of those who responded to the survey

c. encourages the participation of businesses and organizations who previously had not responded to the assessment.

DEVELOPING GOALS AND OBJECTIVES BASED ON THE ASSESSMENT

The assessment of needs and resources gives guidelines to the project, thereby helping to support partnership priorities. Information from the assessment is then used to develop program goals and objectives for the partnership.

Content of Goals and Objectives

Goals and objectives will ordinarily fall into such areas as identified school site needs, staff development needs, specific program needs, and districtwide needs. There may well be complementary site and staff development needs for potential school partners. In response to queries, and a review of partnership program literature nationwide, program goals and objectives appear to focus on particular common themes.

For the School District (Students and Staff)

- to encourage career awareness for both students and school staff, thereby introducing students to the "real" world
- to improve the academic and vocational preparation of students for the world of work
- to stem the high dropout rate
- to provide opportunities for school staff to update the content of the curriculum and their personal professional skills
- to improve the management and supervisory skills of school leaders
- to extend and enrich the educational experiences for students
- to secure funds to support and supplement existing educational programs
- to enlarge the constituency of community involvement in the schools
- to supply role models and provide motivation and upgrade expectations for disadvantaged youth
- to create more summer jobs and preparatory skill training
- to reduce the racial isolation of students from the larger community

For the Community at Large (School District, Business, Civic, and Nonprofit Organizations)

- to share community resources to the benefit of all groups
- to offer business employees opportunities for leadership and service to others through volunteer activities (and encourage positive morale)
- to increase communication and understanding between educators and business
- to improve public confidence in public education
- to raise the community's awareness level of the needs of public schools

Writing Goals and Objectives

Goals and objectives for partnership programs should flow naturally from data obtained through assessments of needs and resources. Goals should be general enough to become the umbrella for more specific objectives, yet focused enough so that partners clearly understand the direction in which the partnership will move.

COMMUNICATING GOALS AND OBJECTIVES TO THE COMMUNITY AT LARGE

Communicating goals and objectives of the partnership program to school district staff and the community at large is the next important step for the project's planning team. Effective communication tools include newsletters, reports, and brochures. Widespread distribution of these goals and objectives performs a multitude of functions:

- It tells the community that goals and objectives are related to the earlier assessment(s) of community and school needs and resources.
- Along with the assessment, project goals and objectives establish a sound base for the partnership project.
- It provides guidelines for the project, focusing on what is possible rather than a "wish list."
- It informs the community that the project has been initiated and is in the process of development.

NEEDS ASSESSMENT ACTION PLAN
Part I: Population to Be Surveyed

A. DISTRICT

No. of Administrators/Supervisors ———

No. of Students ———

No. of Teachers ———

No. of Others ———

B. COMMUNITY

No. of Businesses ———

Kind: ————————

————————

————————

————————

No. of Civic Organizations ———

Kind: ————————

————————

————————

No. of Nonprofit Organizations ———

Kind: ————————

————————

————————

————————

No. of Parents ———

No. of Community at Large ———

Kind: ————————

————————

————————

No. of Others ———

Kind: ————————

————————

————————

————————

Signature of Partnership Director ——————————

Figure 4—1

29

NEEDS ASSESSMENT ACTION PLAN
Part II: Collecting Assessment Data

INTERVIEW INFORMATION

Name _____

Address _____

_____

Phone Numbers _____ _____
(home)   (office)

Date/Place of Interview _____

_____

Special Arrangements _____

_____

_____

SUMMARY COMMENTS

_____

_____

_____

_____

_____

_____

_____

_____

_____

_____

_____

_____

_____

_____

_____

_____

_____
Signature of Interviewer

Figure 4–2

NEEDS ASSESSMENT ACTION PLAN
Part III: Preparation and Distribution of Questionnaire

TASK	RESPONSIBILITY	APPROVED (Date/Initial)	DISTRIBUTED TO (Audience/Date)
1. Prepare cover letter	_____	_____	_____
			_____
2. Prepare envelopes	_____	_____	_____
			_____
3.a. Design questionnaire	_____	_____	
b. Prepare questionnaire	_____	_____	
c. Distribute questionnaire (through the mail)	_____	_____	_____
(at meetings—list them)	_____	_____	_____
	_____	_____	
4. Follow-up phone calls re: return of questionnaire	_____	_____	_____
5. Process/analyze data	_____	_____ Completed: _____	
6. Prepare report of results	_____	_____ Completed: _____	

_____
Signature of Partnership Director

Figure 4–3

31

NEEDS ASSESSMENT ACTION PLAN
Part IV: Using Questionnaire Results

TASK	RESPONSIBILITY	APPROVED (Date/Initial)	DATE/TIME/PLACE	FORMAT	AUDIENCE(S)
1. Reporting results	_____	_____	_____	_____	_____
			_____	_____	_____
			_____	_____	_____
			_____	_____	_____

			DATE/TIME/PLACE	FORMAT	PARTICIPANTS
2. Developing goals and objectives					
a. Rank needs	_____	_____	_____	_____	_____
			_____	_____	_____
			_____	_____	_____
b. Rank resources	_____	_____	_____	_____	_____
			_____	_____	_____
			_____	_____	_____

			DATE/TIME/PLACE	FORMAT	AUDIENCE(S)
3. Communicating goals and objectives	_____	_____	_____	_____	_____
			_____	_____	_____
			_____	_____	_____

_____
Signature of Partnership Director

Figure 4–4

32

THE COMMUNITY AND BUSINESS RESOURCE MANUAL
NASHUA SCHOOL DISTRICT

<u>RESOURCE SURVEY</u>

Name of Business or Organization: _____

Business Address: _____

_____

Name and Title of Contact Person: _____

Telephone: _____

Area of Participation: (Please check off area(s) of interest to you)

_____ ADOPT-A-SCHOOL   _____ STUDENT SHADOWING

_____ FIELD TRIPS   _____ SPEAKERS

_____ MENTORS   _____ TUTORS

This Manual has been made available to the Parochial School system, Mount Saint Mary, Bishop Guertin, The Adult Learning Center, The Boys Club, The Girls Club and Mt. Hope School. May these schools and organizations also use you as a resource?

Yes _____ No _____

A Brief Description of Your Business or Organization: _____

_____

_____

_____

_____

_____

Please use the reverse side of this paper for any comments and additional information.

Figure 4–5

<u>INTERVIEW</u>

Name of Business or Organization: _____ Date: _____

Name of Person to Be Interviewed: _____ Time: _____

Name of Contact Person: _____

_____ ADOPT-A-SCHOOL

_____ FIELD TRIPS

    Size of group _____   Day of Week   M   T   W   T   F

    Time of day _____   Advanced Notice Required?

    How much notice _____   yes   no

    Instructions for teacher _____

    _____

    Grade Level _____

    What students will observe _____

_____ MENTORS

    Area of Interest _____

    _____

    Grade Level _____

_____ SHADOWING PROGRAM

    Careers Available _____

    _____

    Grade Level _____

Figure 4–5 (continued)

INTERVIEW

Name of Business or Organization: _____

_____ SPEAKERS

Subject Area to Be Covered _____

_____

Day of Week   M   T   W   T   F   Time of Day _____

Advanced Notice Required _____

Instructions for Teacher _____

_____

Grade Level _____

_____ TUTORS

Subject Areas of Interest

       Math _____

       English _____

       Science _____

       Social Studies _____

Grade Level _____

Overall Comments at Interview: _____

_____

_____

_____

_____

_____

Reprinted by permission of Nashua, NH Partnership-in-Education Program.

Figure 4–5 (continued)

TULSA PUBLIC SCHOOLS
ADOPT-A-SCHOOL
School Site Assessment

Name of School _____ Enrollment _____

Principal _____ _____ Tulsa Design

Secretary _____ _____ Tulsa Semi/Department

Address _____ _____ Junior High

Telephone _____ _____ Senior High

Hours: _____

   Lunch: _____

Federal Programs: _____
_____

Special Programs: _____
_____
_____

What skills do you need most by Adopters? _____
_____

How do you see Adopters working to the best advantage? _____
_____

What material resources does your school need? _____

Would you be interested in mini-courses (special six week course in how to)? _____

What is the preferred time of day for the Adopt-A-School Team to come to your school?
_____

Do you have an organized School Volunteer Program? _____

Figure 4–6

Houston Independent School District

Business/School
Partnership
Program

SCHOOL NEEDS ASSESSMENT

Area ____ School _____ Principal _____ Phone _____

BUSINESS and INDUSTRY PEOPLE

Please check appropriate box to indicate how your school would use volunteers on loan from the business world 1–2 hours a week. Give specifics when possible.

SMALL GROUP OR
INDIVIDUAL INSTRUCTION:

( ) Remedial Reading _____

( ) Remedial Math _____

( ) Bilingual _____

( ) Gifted and Talented _____

( ) Other _____

ASSISTANCE WITH:

( ) Career Field Trips _____

( ) Career Speakers _____

( ) Internships _____

( ) "How to Get a Job Skills" _____

( ) Supplementing Math/Science Courses _____

Please list below any unique needs not listed above, such as enrichment, job placement opportunities, people with special expertise, etc.

_____

_____

FUNDS

Please list items you would purchase. A brief statement of intended use will assist potential donors.

ITEM	NO.	UTILIZATION

Reprinted by permission of the Houston, TX, Independent School District.

Figure 4–7

IN-KIND DONATIONS

Check appropriate box and give specifics:

( ) Subscriptions (magazines, company publications, etc.) _____

_____

( ) Books _____

( ) Transportation for Field Trips _____

( ) Printing (school paper, flyers, etc.) _____

( ) Equipment (drafting tables, audio visual, typewriters, etc.) _____

_____

( ) Awards _____

( ) Other (specify) _____

LOANED EXECUTIVES

(For Principals Only)

Would you like expert help on problems of management and administration? Experts on communication, finance, delegation, etc.? If yes, please indicate area of expertise.

_____

_____

I am naming the following person to coordinate Business and Industry involvement in this school:

_____   _____   _____
      name   title   phone number

RETURN TO VIPS OFFICE, ROUTE #10   Signed _____
     before September 15   Principal

Figure 4–7 (continued)

RESPONSE FORM

PARTNER DATA

Name _____ Title _____

Firm _____

Address _____ City _____ State _____ ZIP _____

I. DISTRICT SERVICES REQUESTED BY YOUR FIRM

_____ Facility/equipment usage   _____ Citizenship training

_____ Computer literacy   _____ Training of clerical staff

_____ Speakers bureau   _____ Research resources

_____ Advisory groups   _____ Public relations assistance
with partnership involvement

_____ Adult education   _____ Other (please specify on
reverse side)

_____ Apprenticeship work

II. PROPOSED INVOLVEMENT BY YOUR FIRM

STUDENT LEVEL

_____ Resource persons   _____ Internship

_____ Volunteers   _____ Mentorship

_____ Tours of facilities   _____ Sponsorship
Type _____

_____ On-sight courses or   _____ Display space for student work
workshops

_____ Career shadowing

STAFF LEVEL

_____ Resource persons   _____ Consultants

_____ Staff internships   _____ Loaned executives

DISTRICTWIDE   OTHER

_____ Assist with public service   _____ Please describe on reverse side
functions

_____ Donate surplus materials

Type _____

Reprinted by permission of Partners in Education, Lancaster, PA.

Figure 4–8

PIPE SURVEY OF _____ STUDENTS

Dear Student: As you most likely read in the student newspaper, _____High
School has been paired with _____ Company in an effort to see that
students coming out of high school have a more realistic idea of what the business world
is like.

The PIPE Advisory Council is in the process of dreaming up a "wish list" of activities that
could be initiated with our students and the employees at _____ Company.
The business world would like to offer us some activities and projects that they are willing
to share with us. Listed below are some ideas. We would like to have your input and
reaction. Please check the ones that you feel would interest you (ranking them in
numerical order, 1 being the lowest interest), and that you might be willing to spend time
doing.

All the activities would be done during the school day.

1. Would you be interested in finding out what businesses can and will expect of you
   when you start a job?

2. Would you like to go through a mock interview with someone from the bank? Find
   out what it helps to know in order to have a good interview?

3. Would you like to know how behavior and dress make a difference in the job world?

4. Would you like to have a Career Fair here where you would have a chance to talk to
   a variety of business employees and training personnel?

5. Would you like information on how a checking/cash machine account is handled at a
   bank?

6. Would you like to find out about job areas in marketing and sales that do not need
   specific training but hire many people?

7. Would you like to spend a day "shadowing" someone at his or her job to see what it
   is like? (perhaps for half a day)?

8. Would you like to spend 3–4 hours a couple of days a week as an intern to a
   business employee gaining experience in the business work world?

9. What other interests can you think of that are not listed here but you would like to
   know about?

Reprinted by permission of Private Initiatives in Public Education (PIPE), WA.

Figure 4–9

BUSINESS-EDUCATION SURVEY

The following survey was developed in order to gather information on the business community's response to forming a partnership with education. The school districts of St. Louis Park, Hopkins, and Minnetonka along with the West Suburban Chamber of Commerce have selected 55 member organizations, who represent varying industries and sizes of organizations, to participate in this survey.

We plan to complete the survey by September, so that we may interpret our findings and implement programs by Fall or Winter Semester.

Thank you for your participation.

INSTRUCTIONS

The first page is devoted to the needs of students, the second page for teachers, the last page is to assess your needs where the school district can be of service. Please check the box(es) which correspond to the appropriate option (i.e. internships, mentorships, etc.) in the appropriate field of interest (i.e. sciences, business, etc.) given your organization and employees.

Figure 4–10

SERVICES THE COMPANY CAN PROVIDE THE STUDENT

	SCIENCES (Physics, Medicine, Chemistry, Botany, Biology)	MATHEMATICS (Engineering, Computer Science)	BUSINESS (Clerical, Management, Finance, Marketing, Accounting, Sales)	GOVERNMENT ECONOMICS (Law, Private Sectors, Public and)	SOCIAL SCIENCES (Public Health, Sociology, Psychology)	COMMUNICATION (Advertising, Media, Speaking, Writing)	FOREIGN LANGUAGES (Trade, Travel, Interpreter)	HOME ECONOMICS (Interior Design, Design, Clothing, Nutrition)	INDUSTRIAL ARTS (Graphics, Drafting, Carpentry, Auto, Electricity)	ARTS (Photography, Arts, Performing, Visual)	OTHER (Architecture)	COMMENTS
INTERNSHIPS — Long-term relationship between student and organization												
CAREER SHADOWING — Short-term (2–3 days) relationship: student and organization												
MENTORSHIP — Long-term, close relationship: student and organization												
EXPERT RESOURCE CONSULTANT — Employee-expert in field serves as ongoing consultant												
ASSIST WITH STUDENT PROJECTS i.e. Science Fair												
GUEST SPEAKERS IN CLASS												
ONGOING COURSE TAUGHT ON-SITE												
USE OF EQUIPMENT ON-SITE												
ON-SITE TOURS												
OTHER												

Figure 4–10 (continued)

SERVICES THE COMPANY CAN PROVIDE THE

TEACHER

	SCIENCES	MATHEMATICS	BUSINESS	GOVERNMENT ECONOMICS	SOCIAL SCIENCES	COMMUNICATION	FOREIGN LANGUAGES	HOME ECONOMICS	INDUSTRIAL ARTS	ARTS	OTHER	COMMENTS
	Physics, Medicine, Chemistry, Botany, Biology	Computer Science, Engineering	Clerical, Management, Finance, Marketing, Accounting, Sales	Law, Public and Private Sectors	Public Health, Sociology, Psychology	Advertising, Media, Speaking, Writing	Trade, Travel, Interpreter	Interior Design, Design, Clothing, Nutrition	Graphics, Drafting, Carpentry, Auto, Electricity	Photography, Visual, Performing Arts, Architecture		
INTERNSHIPS Summer												
TEACHER-IN-SERVICE (workshop to familiarize with subject area and opportunity to learn new developments)												
EXPERT RESOURCE CONSULTANT												
TOUR												
CURRICULUM ADVISOR Advisor to Curriculum Committee												
OTHER												

Figure 4–10 (continued)

43

SERVICES THE COMPANY CAN PROVIDE THE SCHOOL DISTRICT AS A WHOLE

AND/OR

SERVICES THE SCHOOL DISTRICT CAN PROVIDE THE COMPANY

CLASS OFFERED AT SCHOOL OR ON-SITE

HEALTH	PERSONAL PLANNING	SKILLS BUILDING	BUSINESS	FOREIGN LANGUAGE	COMPUTERS	MANAGEMENT	COMMUNI-CATIONS	AUDIO-VISUAL	OTHER
Stress Management Wellness	Pre-Retirement Programs	Writing Speaking Reading etc.	Investment Planning	English as a Second Language Travel	Computer Awareness, Programming	Supervision Management, Staff Development, Short/Long Range Plan	Business Communication, Community Relations	Community Relations Cable TV	Audio-Visual Tape Production Brochure Develop.

USE OF FACILITIES AND EQUIPMENT

GYM	COMPUTERS	CAREER CENTER	CHILD-CARE	CABLE TV	OTHER
		Vocational Interest Testing/Counseling	Latch-Key Preschool Drop-In	Audio-Visual Use of Studio	Conference Rooms Auditorium, Conference Site

COMMENTS:

Reprinted by permission of the TwinWest Business-Education Partnership, MN.

Figure 4–10 (continued)

Soliciting Commitment to the Partnership

Commitment to the partnership project is solicited at first under the leadership of the school district's superintendent with the support of the planning team—and later by the partnership's operations staff. The importance of this effort cannot be overemphasized! Program goals are usually unreachable without assessing needs and resources and obtaining selected organizational commitment.

The check sheet (see Figures 5-1, 5-2, and 5-3) outlines the process of soliciting district and communitywide commitment and participation. Planning team members can use this tool to determine (1) who will be solicited for project participation; (2) how to obtain broad-based commitment; and (3) the format and content of agreements between potential partners.

GENERATING SCHOOL DISTRICT–PRIVATE-SECTOR COMMITMENT

At the School-District Level

Encouraging commitment from all levels of the school district—from board of education through central office and school site administrators to teachers and other professional and paraprofessional staff—is a first step. Boards of education are extremely cautious regarding initiatives they perceive as possible encroachment on board perogatives. Therefore, superintendents must work with their boards (before beginning *outside* solicitation efforts) to allay concerns and encourage their cooperation. Boards look to partnership programs that have the *potential* to provide

- supplemental resources for the extension and enrichment of existing instructional, staff development, and management programs
- support for successful programs that face restrictions or cuts because of rising costs and shrinking resources
- new programs that could not be developed through the usual funding channels

• all of the above without intruding on the policy-making responsibilities of a school board

Once the board is convinced of the value of partnerships, it should publicly commit the school district to this program in the form of a policy statement or proclamation that is read into the board minutes. Public recognition by the local board of education is a signal to the community of the importance of partnerships in relation to school improvement initiatives.

Efforts to solicit commitment to the partnership concept flow from the superintendent and the board to school sites, where support must be obtained from both administrators and staff. Staff should be fully apprised of

1. how partnerships will be developed
2. what forms partnership activities can take
3. what options staff have for partnership support
4. how the program can supplement (not supplant) efforts to improve time-on-task and student achievement
5. what potential such alliances have for improving positive communitywide perceptions regarding public education.

At the Community Level

As school district commitment is solicited, the planning team uses complementary strategies to elicit communitywide involvement in partnerships. At this stage, solicitation is usually limited to locally based civic, community, and business groups; pursuit of this strategy provides boundaries that can be dealt with more efficiently and helps keep partnership goals in focus. Examples of organizations from whom to solicit commitment could include

small businesses	large corporations
hospitals	government agencies: local, state and national
Jr. Achievement	
arts groups	parent organizations
Rotary	chambers of commerce
religious organizations	community volunteer groups
life insurance companies	National Alliance for Business
Private Industry Council	universities and colleges
	technical and trade institutions

ROLE OF THE PLANNING TEAM

The superintendent and the planning team usually meet to expedite the process of soliciting commitment to the program. If the planning team's membership is broad-based, that group forms the nucleus from which arms can reach out for support to all areas of the community at large.

USING SCREENING TOOLS

The team begins to assess the quantity and quality of potential partners. Useful tools to assist in screening personal, business, and professional contacts include: organizational mailing lists, local *Yellow Page* directories, rosters of community groups, and, of course, staff lists from the school district and community agencies.

SPECIFICS OF WHOM TO CONTACT

Of critical importance is the decision about *whom* to contact. Should the solicitation process be selective or more widespread? For example, the planning team might choose to solicit commitment from (1) known quantities (personal contacts), (2) school administrators, (3) local businesses, (4) community volunteer groups, or (5) all of these groups. The team may decide to use particular mailing lists, or to "blanket" the entire community (through a household mailing).

Initial solicitation efforts, wherever possible, should be directed at leaders, within and outside the school district, who have the status, authority, and ability to make decisions, who are aware of community resources, who have experience in other community activities, *and* who can secure voluntary cooperation from other top leaders.

THE PROCESS OF SOLICITING COMMITMENT TO THE PARTNERSHIP

The process of soliciting initial commitment is multifaceted. Members of the planning team may well have their own personal strategies for achieving this task, but these strategies should be carefully coordinated to prevent duplication of efforts.

Pooling Information on Potential Partners and Assigning Areas of Responsibility

All team members pool their suggestions about individuals and organizations from whom they intend to solicit support. Team members are assigned areas of responsibility for contacting potential partners that are complementary to

- their individual, personal contacts
- their group, organization, or agency affiliations
- their responsibilities within the school district or within the community at large

Using the Assessment Instrument and Data

Team members decide how their assessment instrument will be used to support the solicitation process. This instrument

1. can accompany the superintendent's solicitation letter when sent to selective or broad-based mailing lists

2. can be part of a follow-up package, together with a letter and any other materials, distributed after a personal phone call from the superintendent or a member of the planning team

3. can be sent after districtwide and/or school site meetings that were held to provide information and elicit interest in the proposed partnership program

Solicitation Strategies

The strategies team members will use can take many forms, including letters, phone calls, brochures and other printed materials, and meetings. Partnership directors stated that no one tool was "best"; a combination of forms appeared most effective and efficient to encourage positive responses to a budding partnership project. The use of personal contacts plus broad-based community mailings (to school, business, civic, nonprofit, volunteer organizations) was one successful combination of strategies.

Note: Solicitations to large organizations take special handling. Large companies should be approached at more than one level: the CEO or president level and the community relations, urban affairs, or department manager levels. Initial contacts are best done through *signed* personal letters from the superintendent's office. A solicitation letter from Memphis, TN (see Figure 5-4) is a good example of such a form letter. Follow-up phone calls should come from planning team members who have established some personal or professional contacts with leaders in those large organizations.

Conducting Meetings

Meetings to discuss the proposed partnership and elicit interest can be held districtwide, at a school site, at corporate offices, or at agencies. During these meetings

- previous experience in informal or semiformal partnership arrangements should be reviewed

- boundaries of the proposed formal project are clarified so that there is no misrepresentation or misunderstanding regarding: (1) the proposal's breadth and depth *or* (2) the scope of the requested commitment

Meetings with School District Staff. Even if the partnership proposed will be only a pilot project (for one school, one group of teachers, particular administrators, or one grade level), all district or regional staff must be apprised of the plan. Such broad-based communication efforts can dispel, or at least control, rumors, petty complaints, and negative behaviors that often arise when new ideas are proposed. Presenters should explain current project limitations as well as long-range expectations for both support and activities. Questions are answered directly and honestly to allay understandable concern about perceived intrusion by the private sector into the process of instruction.

If these procedures are followed, there will be sufficient core commitment from staff districtwide to respond in depth and with enthusiasm to the assessment *even if* immediate partnership services are not forthcoming; at the same time, the assessment won't have to be repeated. The process discussed above will also pinpoint potential leadership in support of partnership activities in various school sites. Those leaders should meet—as is appropriate—with the planning team and later with the operations staff to provide guidance for the project.

Meeting with Business or Other Community Groups. Guidelines must also be clearly explained to the community at large to allay doubts related to (1) the anticipated scope of participation, (2) involvement in school business, and (3) ability to meet requested needs.

There can be two levels of meetings with business and other community groups to solicit their commitment to this venture. At one level, planning team members, who are familiar with particular community agencies, can gather together select groups of leaders. At another level, people who respond to the assessments are contacted to attend follow-up sessions that confirm their commitment. These meetings might take the form of informal coffees, luncheons, or receptions that include opportunities for roundtable discussion. No one should ever attend a meeting without receiving printed information about the proposed program. One good example is a handout from Richmond, VA (see Figure 5-5); the question-and-answer format responds to interest in the district's Adopt-A-School program.

Making Phone Calls

The telephone is a useful tool—particularly when it is used (a) as a follow-up to meetings and letters in response to expressed interest or (b) to contact potential partners who have already established personal or professional relationships with a planning team member, the superintendent of schools, or a board member.

Writing Letters

Letters inviting program participation

- can be sent by planning team members to personal and professional friends and colleagues, professional and civic organizational membership, and national or statewide affiliates
- can be sent by the superintendent to selected mailing lists
- can accompany the assessment instrument as cover forms explaining the purpose of the assessment—at the same time eliciting interest in the project.

One letter from Lancaster, PA (see Figure 5-6), recognizes previous district informal support and proposes an expansion of this support to a more formal relationship; note that a flier was attached to the letter to provoke added interest.

Having Social Gatherings

Social gatherings are structured get-togethers (receptions, breakfasts, coffees, luncheons, buffet dinners) at which guests dine, mingle and learn about the proposed partnership. At each gathering, and in a prominent place, be sure to have a sign-in sheet or book to record guests' names, titles, addresses, and phone numbers; this strategy yields helpful information about potential partners.

The Invitation. One informal, effective example of an invitation to a school's "recruiting coffee" comes from Tulsa, OK (see Figure 5-7). The invitation can also be adapted for use by an established partnership program as a solicitation to the community at large.

The Presentation. A short presentation, to introduce the idea of a partnership, either precedes or follows the reception activity. The presentation can include brief speeches by the superintendent, a prominent local community or business representative, the president of the board of education, or some outside celebrity who has had in-depth involvement in the partnership movement. Often a short slide presentation or videotape, focused on student activity, accompanies this presentation.

Those who attend should receive some printed information about the proposed partnership and/or a form on which they can respond to requests for participation. Lancaster, PA (see Figure 5-8), uses such a form; note particularly the "Collaboration Grid" that encourages community partners to outline their client group, type of service, geographic area, and other special information, and the "Proximity Grid" that provides information on the geographic proximity of the business or agency to a particular school—a helpful tool when coordinating volunteer and other direct services throughout a school district.

Organizing School Events

School events such as fairs and career days introduce business, community, and educational organizations to each other within an environment conducive to breaking down more formal barriers. Of course such activities should be followed up by letters, phone calls, and meetings arranged to discuss possible alliances.

Printing Brochures, Newsletters, Fliers, and Other Materials

Printed brochures, newsletters, fliers, and other materials are eye-catching tools to solicit commitment to the partnership. On *all* of these materials, be certain to include information about the contact person, office address, and phone number. Some effective examples of these materials include

- a solicitation coupon that is part of a newsletter from San Francisco, CA (see Figure 5-9)

- a "Wanted" school adopters flier from Chicago, IL (see Figure 5-10)
- a newsletter to teachers from St. Louis, MO (see Figure 5-11)

Content of Solicitation Tools

What should be the content of the tools (meetings, phone calls, letters, and other printed materials) that are prepared to encourage interest and participation in a partnership? Tools must explicitly *and* implicitly carry the following messages:

1. The *school district has the credibility* to form a partnership.
2. There are *high expectations* for community involvement and support for such an alliance.
3. There are *key leaders* both within and outside the school district who have the knowledge and skills to secure broad-based community interest and cooperation.
4. Those planning the partnership are *sensitive to the concerns of all potential partners* who will consider entering into such an alliance.
5. *A partnership* between the school district and its larger community (of business, civic agencies, nonprofit organizations) *can make a difference* in extending, enriching, and improving instructional and learning opportunities for students.

VERBAL AND/OR WRITTEN COMMITMENT FROM PARTNERS

It is always nice to have arrangements signed and sealed on the dotted line. Written contractual commitment from partners is usually impossible and unnecessary at this stage of the partnership. It is more important to have

- letters of commitment and support. Such letters can be reproduced and used to interest additional participants.
- verbal agreements specifying anticipated participation and/or willingness to provide resources. Often these early supporters will agree to speak before audiences composed of other potential partners.
- actual in-kind arrangements to help the budding partnership become a reality, including extra secretarial help, printing, mailings, funding, reception activities, or a part-time executive-on-loan.

ACTION PLAN CHECK SHEET FOR SOLICITING PARTNERSHIP PARTICIPATION
FORM A: SOLICITATION PROCESS

TASK	RESPONSIBILITY	SCHEDULED COMPLETION DATE	COMPLETION DATE	CRITERIA FOR EVALUATING RESULTS
1. Screen contact.	_____	_____	_____	_____
2. Pool contact information.	_____	_____	_____	_____
3. Prepare and use assessment instruments. (See Figures 4–1 through 4–4.)	_____	_____	_____	_____
4. Organize, analyze, and disseminate assessment data. (See Figures 4–1 through 4–4.)	_____	_____	_____	_____
5. Use solicitation strategies:				
a. letters	_____	_____	_____	_____
b. phone calls	_____	_____	_____	_____
c. brochures/fliers	_____	_____	_____	_____
d. meetings	_____	_____	_____	_____
e. social events	_____	_____	_____	_____
f. newsletters	_____	_____	_____	_____
g. other	_____	_____	_____	_____

Signature of Partnership Director _____

Figure 5–1

52

**ACTION PLAN CHECK SHEET
FOR SOLICITING PARTNERSHIP PARTICIPATION
<u>FORM B: SCREENING</u>**

<u>SCREENING</u>

Tools Used

Mailing Lists	Contact	Phone
1. _____	_____	_____
2. _____	_____	_____
3. _____	_____	_____
4. _____	_____	_____
5. _____	_____	_____

<u>Yellow Page</u> Directory	Contact	Phone
_____	_____	_____

Professional/Business Directories	Contact	Phone
1. _____	_____	_____
2. _____	_____	_____
3. _____	_____	_____
4. _____	_____	_____

Staff lists	Contact	Phone/Ext.
1. _____	_____	_____
2. _____	_____	_____
3. _____	_____	_____
4. _____	_____	_____
5. _____	_____	_____

Organizational rosters	Contact	Phone/Ext.
1. _____	_____	_____
2. _____	_____	_____
3. _____	_____	_____
4. _____	_____	_____
5. _____	_____	_____

Figure 5–2

ACTION PLAN CHECK SHEET
FOR SOLICITING PARTNERSHIP PARTICIPATION
FORM C: BASIC CONTACT INFORMATION

Contact: _____   Solicitor: _____

Organization: _____

Address: _____

_____

Phone: _____

Secretary/Ass't.: _____

Contact's Organizational Affiliation:

A. School district _____   B. Business _____

    principal _____   large _____

    supervisor _____   medium _____

    administrator _____   small _____

    teacher _____   product(s) _____

    aide _____   _____

    other _____   _____

    _____   _____

C. Nonprofit Community Organization   D. Civic Agency

    service(s) _____   service(s) _____

    _____   _____

    _____   _____

    large _____

    medium _____

    small _____

E. Parents' group   F. Community at Large

    school _____   Name of group _____

    districtwide _____   _____

                                          Function of group _____

                                          _____

Figure 5–3

Initial Commitment to Participate

    A. Verbal _____   Contact _____   Date _____

    B. Written _____

        Letter _____   Contact _____   Date _____
                                  (attach copy to this form)
        Formal
        contract* _____   Contact _____   Date _____
                                  (attach copy to this form)

      Contract approvals signed by:

        School district _____

        Partner _____

Initial Partnership Participation:

Date Initiated   Kind of Resources (briefly describe amount and activities):

_____   human _____

               _____

_____   in-kind _____

               _____

_____   materials/equipment _____

               _____

_____   financial _____

               _____

Efficiency note: Use a separate check sheet (Form C) for each individual/
                      organizational solicitation and then file alphabetically.

*Usually signed and completed at later date.

Figure 5–3

Memphis City Schools • 2597 Avery Avenue • Memphis, Tennessee 38112

Reply To The Office Of
Superintendent

Dear Friend:

YOU, AS A LEADER IN OUR COMMUNITY, ARE CHALLENGED TO JOIN US IN AN EXCITING EFFORT CALLED "ADOPT-A-SCHOOL."

This joint venture allows the community to see the schools in a new light. The partnership formed provides the schools an opportunity to benefit from the resources of the community, and the community the opportunity to become involved in its school system.

Memphis needs this kind of partnership. It is essential for the economic future of our city that the gap existing between the community and its schools be removed. This is a plan where you can get involved—contribute to a vital area of the community and, at the same time, improve your already excellent corporate image.

My staff and I are totally committed to the success of this important program and I urge you and your associates to make the same commitment.

Sincerely,

Reprinted by permission of Adopt-A-School, Memphis City Schools, TN.
Figure 5–4

QUESTIONS AND ANSWERS

Q: What is Adopt-A-School?

A: An Adopt-A-School program is a close relationship between a business and a school wherein the business provides a wide variety of supportive services and advice.

Q: When my group adopts a school, what have we signed up to do?

A: Your group has offered to help a school meet SOME of its needs. What you actually do for a school depends upon the capabilities of your individual group. You are NOT asked to fill all the needs of that school. Whatever the size of your group's contribution —in volunteers, funds, expertise, materials or other types of assistance—your help is needed, wanted, and APPRECIATED.

Q: What are some typical projects?

A: The answer to this question can be quite lengthy. Here are just a few ideas:

1. Employment readiness courses or workshops.
2. Technical advice and assistance for the school newspaper, yearbook or literary journal.
3. Company speakers for classes and assembly programs.
4. Time management sessions for all school personnel.
5. Provide display space at your corporate office or public outlets for student exhibits.
6. Provide release-time volunteers or recruit volunteers from among retired employees.

Adopting companies will receive a long list of ideas.

Q: Once my group adopts a school, who is the main contact at the school?

A: The principal of your adopted school will assign a staff coordinator to work with your group. Your own group should also appoint a coordinator to work with the school staff and to simplify communications. Typically, this person may come from your personnel or public relations department.

Figure 5–5

Q: Is Adopt-A-School a new idea?

A: While Adopt-A-School is new to Richmond, it has worked successfully in dozens of cities throughout the United States. Some of these locations include:

Atlanta, GA	Jacksonville, FL
Baltimore, MD	Miami, FL
Boston, MA	Minneapolis, MN
Cincinnati, OH	New York, NY
Columbus, OH	Norfolk, VA
Dallas, TX	Oakland, CA
Denver, CO	Oak Park, IL
Des Moines, IA	Philadelphia, PA
Detroit, MI	Pittsburgh, PA
High Point, NC	San Francisco, CA
Houston, TX	Washington, DC

Q: Who are typical adopters in other locations?

A: There is no typical adopter. Adopt-A-School participants range from national corporations to branch locations and "mom and pop" businesses. A few of the better-known adopters include:

Atlantic Richfield	Montgomery Ward
Boston Edison	Mountain Bell
Burger King	J. C. Penney Company
Coca-Cola	Pepsi Cola
Coors	Prudential Insurance Company
Dallas Power and Light Company	Sears Roebuck
Ford	Shell Oil Company
General Electric	Southwestern Bell Telephone Company
General Motors	Travelers Insurance Company
Honeywell	Western Electric
IBM Corporation	Westinghouse
McDonald's	Xerox

Q: How will my company benefit from participation in the Richmond Adopt-A-School program?

A: Aside from the good neighbor role that such participation enhances, there are several short-term and long-term benefits to be realized.

The preparation of students to enter the marketplace as both skilled workers and informed consumers benefits the entire community. Your involvement gives you an excellent opportunity to identify and attract part-time, summer, and permanent employees.

The support of the private sector through the sharing of good management techniques and by providing volunteers or raw materials helps keep the cost of education down. That can mean lower taxes.

Reprinted by permission of Adopt-A-School Program, Richmond Public Schools, VA.

Figure 5–5 (continued)

SCHOOL DISTRICT OF LANCASTER

225 WEST ORANGE STREET
P.O. Box 150
LANCASTER, PENNSYLVANIA 17603

DATE

Dear

The School District of Lancaster would like to express its appreciation for the expertise and resources you have shared with our staff and students over the past years.

Enclosed is a flier describing the District's Partners-in-Education program. Both the School District and the Lancaster Chamber of Commerce and Industry have joined efforts in developing a way to work more closely with community, businesses and schools. Through the partnership endeavor there can be a mutual sharing of resources.

Since at this time you may wish to expand the type of relationship you now have with the School District, we would like to extend to you the invitation to become a formal partner-in-education.

If you would like more information about the program, please contact me for a complete packet.

Thank you for your consideration. If you have questions, please call me at 291-6144. I look forward to hearing from you.

Sincerely,

Jane T. Pelland
Asst. to the Supt.
for Partnerships

JTP/lb

enc.

Reprinted by permission of Partners in Education, Lancaster, PA.
Figure 5–6

COME TO _____ NAME OF SCHOOL) _____ ON _____ (DATE) _____

IN _____ (PLACE) _____ AT _____ (TIME) _____ AND FIND OUT!

By becoming a School Volunteer you can be a part of your school's operation.

The many ways you can get involved in the education process will be explained if you will join us for coffee, punch, and goodies. Your presence does not obligate you to help but there will be an opportunity to sign up if you so desire. We just want to acquaint you with the great variety of significant volunteer jobs available—large and small.

Let's get together—parents, grandparents, friends, retired citizens—and hear about this exciting community involvement in our schools!

Sincerely,

School Volunteer Coordinator
At Your School

Let us know if we will see you there. Call. . . . (phone number).

Reprinted by permission of Tulsa Public Schools Volunteer Program, OK.
Figure 5–7

RESPONSE FORM

I would like to receive more information on the

PARTNERS IN EDUCATION PROGRAM

_____

(Name)

_____

(Address)

_____

(Zip)

I would like to speak with a representative of the

PARTNERS IN EDUCATION PROGRAM

_____ YES   _____ NO

RETURN TO:
    Planning Office
    School District of Lancaster
    P.O. Box 150
    Lancaster, PA 17603

Reprinted by permission of Partners in Education, Lancaster, PA.

Figure 5–8

PREPARATION FOR COLLABORATION AND BARTER:

What does business or industry <u>discard</u> or have surplus quantities of that may be of use to us?

What resources do we have that we might share?

Space:

Equipment:

Supplies:

Staff/Volunteer Training:

Reference Materials:

"Professional" Expertise:

"Personal" Expertise:

Contacts:

National or Other Affiliations:

Unclassifiable:

Figure 5–8 (continued)

COLLABORATION GRID

US	AGENCIES SHARING INTEREST	BUSINESSES SHARING INTEREST	OTHER LINKAGES
Our client group: _____ _____			
Our type of service: _____ _____			
Our geographic area: _____ _____			
Other special focus: _____ _____			

Figure 5–8 (continued)

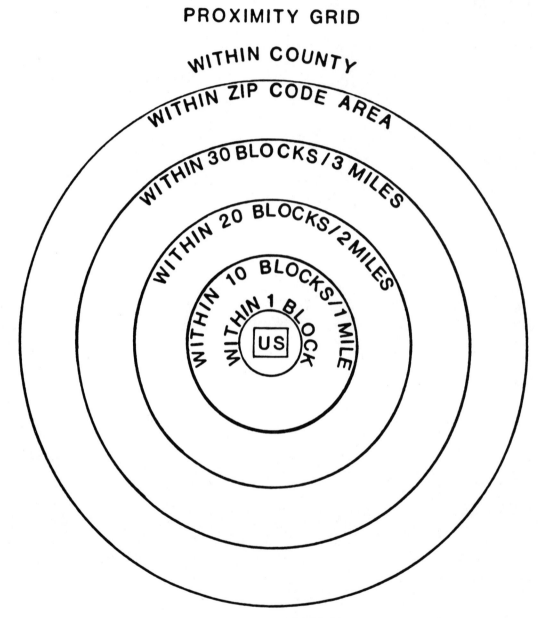

PROXIMITY GRID

WITHIN COUNTY

WITHIN ZIP CODE AREA

WITHIN 30 BLOCKS/3 MILES

WITHIN 20 BLOCKS/2 MILES

WITHIN 10 BLOCKS/1 MILE

WITHIN 1 BLOCK

US

Reprinted by permission of Energize Associates, PA.

Figure 5–8 (continued)

CURRICULUM: The Lens is Focused On Science

**By Sheila Brodie,
Evaluation Coordinator**

Students are singing new songs to old tunes. *The Lung Song* is a new version of *I've Been Working on the Railroad* with lyrics cleverly transposed to name the functions and activities of the human lungs. Kindergarteners are testing their lung capacities in science labs. First grade children are listening to stethoscopes they made themselves. Words such as ventricle, septum, artery and capillary are becoming the common "lingo" in elementary schools.

The number of grant proposals coming to the FUND for science projects, particularly from the elementary and middle schools, has increased tremendously. In the 1983-84 year, the FUND generated funds for 17 science programs, 12 made possible by a generous grant from Chevron USA, and 6 more programs began this fall.

The content of these programs ranges from dissecting a cow's eye to building a weather station. The walls of Miraloma Elementary School's Science Lab, for example, are laden with posters of animals, charts of the human respiratory system, a diagram of a skeleton that demonstrates all the human bones and joints and identifies their functions. On the counters are live animals: two rats, a pregnant mouse and a guinea pig, along with exotic equipment for these and other animals to play on. Visiting doctors, dentists and others in science-related professions serve as guest speakers, thus involving parents and other community members in the project.

Reach out—and touch somebody. Miraloma students get hands-on experience with the "equipment" in their science lab.

Paul Revere Elementary School's "Science for Everyone" taught by the school's librarian, Barbara Dahl, is received with active, enthusiastic student participation. Art is also incorporated into this science course. For example, students use their fingerprints, made during a lesson on skin, as bases for drawing elaborate and creative designs.

As our society becomes more scientifically oriented, educators realize the importance of developing new ways to teach science that will reach all children of all ages. Fifty-two middle school teachers eager to enrich their own scientific intuition participated in workshops at the Exploratorium taught by master teacher Chris de Latour

under joint funding from the Wells Fargo Foundation, Comdisco Financial Services Foundation and the FUND. The hope is that direct experience with the Exploratorium's exhibits, which emphasize experimentation, will encourage these teachers to create innovative science projects in their own classrooms.

Administrators and parents are expressing a strong desire to integrate and expand science programs into the regular school curriculum. The FUND encourages this process by facilitating larger programs and granting the funds classroom teachers need for smaller programs that, collectively, are an important step toward making it happen. ■

Help Wanted—Immediately, or Any Time Thereafter

Job Description: Fundraising, public information, publications, special events, office work, piecework, handwork—even homework!

Qualifications: Yours.

Hours: Any.

Location: Our place or yours.

Salary: Kudos, pats on back.

Benefits: Excellent—especially to our public school children!

Apply on this form or call the FUND.

☐ I WANT TO BECOME A FUND VOLUNTEER

☐ I WANT TO KNOW MORE ABOUT THE FUND

☐ I WANT TO SUPPORT THE FUND . . . Here is my check for

  ☐ $250   ☐ $100   ☐ $50   ☐ $25   ☐ $15   ☐ Other

Name _____ Phone _____

Address _____ City _____ Zip _____

☐ I attended the S.F. Public Schools.

☐ I am a parent of an S.F. Public School student.

San Francisco Education Fund ● 1095 Market St., #719, San Francisco, CA 94103 ●

Reprinted by permission of San Francisco Education Fund, CA.

Figure 5–9

WANTED

Adopters are needed for these Chicago public schools. Staff is available to assist organizations in developing exemplary Adopt-A-School programs. Call Adopt-A-School, Chicago Public Schools, (312) 890-8346, for further information.

Avalon Park Elementary School, 8045 South Kenwood Avenue
Need: program to provide students with greater awareness of and pride in Hispanic cultures.
Possible Activities: sponsorship of Spanish-language club, various activities involving Hispanic customs and traditions.
Adopting Organization: background, interest in Hispanic cultures.

Belding Achievement Skills Center, 4257 North Tripp Avenue
Need: program to improve student skills in reading and writing through marketing and advertising activities.
Possible Activities: setting up "companies" where students will become involved in various phase of marketing a "product."
Adopting Organization: advertising firm or advertising department.

Burley Elementary School, 1630 West Barry Avenue
Need: program to instruct students in operating mini computers.
Possible Activities: establishment of a school computer club, using four mini computers; field trips to department store to show how computers are used to maintain merchandise inventory.
Adopting Organization: department store.

Gladstone Elementary School, 1231 South Avenue
Need: program to demonstrate the use of math in science, computers, and the general business world.
Possible Activities: demonstrations for select groups of students on the use and importance of math in the "real world."
Adopting Organization: business.

Peabody Elementary School, 1444 West Augusta Boulevard
Need: program to serve above-average students.
Possible Activity: involvement of students in "hobby companies," to allow the young people to work on projects such as block printing, quilling, wood-working, etc.
Adopting Organization: arts and crafts company.

Phillips High School, 244 East Pershing Road
Need: program which relates math to the world of work.
Possible Activity: sponsorship of "development clubs," where company personnel provide students with activities involving computers, transportation, and legal, security, financial matters.
Adopting Organization: almost any company would be eligible for this activity.

Randolph Communication Arts Center, 7316 South Hoyne Avenue
Need: program in television production to help improve communication skills.
Possible Activities: instruction in the techniques of producing TV programs; activities in writing and producing "spots" for TV.
Adopting Organization: any local TV/radio station.

Reinberg Elementary School, 3425 North Major Avenue
Need: program to improve student math skills.
Possible Activity: sponsorship of a "banking club" which involves students in various banking procedures, including making sound investments and learning the differences between various investment options, i.e., CDs, savings accounts, etc.
Adopting Organization: any local financial institution.

66

Hibbard Elementary School, 3244 West Ainslee Avenue

Need: program to develop communication skills of students representing 32 different countries and speaking 32 languages other than English.

Possible Activities: production of school newspaper, role-playing, cultural sharing program.

Adopting Organization: any company with employees representative of various countries, cultures.

Hirsch High School of Communications, 7740 South Ingleside Avenue

Need: program to assist students in the development of computer skills.

Possible Activity: "real work world" situation with computer problems to be solved by students.

Adopting Organization: any company with computer/data processing division.

Lewis Elementary School, 1431 North Leamington Avenue

Need: program which will help increase school spirit by improving grounds and landscape.

Possible Activity: horticultural instruction which will enable students to design the landscape adjacent to the school building.

Adopting Organization: landscaping company or individual interested in horticulture.

Shakespeare Elementary School, 1119 East 46th Street

Need: program to develop music appreciation.

Possible Activity: development of a vocal, instrumental, or music appreciation program.

Adopting Organization: music department of a university or organization.

Taft High School, 6545 West Hurlbut Street

Need: program to provide students with techniques for producing and executing dramatic and artistic presentations.

Possible Activity: provision of staff to assist and critique students in staging dramatic and artistic presentations.

Adopting Organization: any organization involved with theater.

White Elementary School, Branch of West Pullman, 1136 South 122nd Street

Need: program to provide students with intensive reading and writing activities.

Possible Activity: creation of mini companies run by students in which they must develop and use reading and writing skills to accomplish a "successful business."

Adopting Organization: any organization with staff to serve in the program; Junior Achievement experience would be helpful but not necessary.

ADOPT
A SCHOOL
PROGRAM

OF THE CHICAGO PUBLIC SCHOOLS

Reprinted by permission of Adopt-A-School Program, Chicago, IL.

Figure 5–10

67

P A R T N E R S H I P :

![the Creative link - COMMUNITY RESOURCES FOR TEACHERS]

THE MAKING OF A PARTNERSHIP

October, 1984

The typical Partnership process

Have you ever wondered just what goes into making a School Partnership happen? Who takes care of the arrangements and paperwork? How is it organized? Who works with the sponsors? What do you, as teachers, need to do?

With school starting and your enthusiasm for the coming year at its peak, we thought now would be the perfect time to give you a step-by-step walk through what it takes to make a partnership, and hopefully entice you to give it a try.

1. Let us know you're interested.

The School Partnership Program is totally voluntary. A program usually begins when you let us know you are interested. Let us know of your interest by calling 361-5588. The divisional assistant responsible for your school will talk to you. There are three: Mary Ferguson, Helen Lynch and Vivian Ross-Mayo.

2. Tell us what you'd like.

A member of the Partnership staff sits down with you to discuss the goals and objectives for your subject area or the semester. We listen very carefully to what you want to achieve, what concepts you are having trouble teaching, what you would like to make more real for your students, or what you'd like an outside expert to teach that the textbook doesn't cover or is an area in which you are not as well versed.

3. Leave the paperwork to us.

We then draft a proposal with a list of sessions which we send back to you to review. We want to make sure it accurately reflects your ideas and goals.

4. We recruit a sponsor.

It is our job to find a community resource such as a business, university, governmental or cultural agency, or professional organization to be your sponsor for the program. Sometimes there is already a sponsor interested that we can

Discussing fall intra-city Partnership Programs are divisional assistants, (left to right) Mary Ferguson, Helen Lynch and Vivian Ross-Mayo.

immediately call. Sometimes it takes a bit more doing. Sponsor responses are often, "Yes, I can do it, but with modifications," or "yes, I can do part of it." These are usually resolved without any problems.

5. Bringing everyone together for final planning.

This meeting is usually the most crucial and creative part of the PARTNERSHIP process. You, your sponsor and divisional assistant have an opportunity to meet and discuss exactly what you want and can accomplish as partners.

6. We make sure it happens.

At this point, the PARTNERSHIP steps back and lets the sponsor prepare their program. Our job is to make sure everything comes together as planned. We arrange for transportation, see that times, places and dates are fixed, monitor the sessions, evaluate the program and assist if and when we are needed.

How city-county Partnerships differ

Since 1982, we have also included Partnership programs which bring students from city and county districts together. Last year Partnership programs included at least one class from all 23 county districts participating in the Voluntary Metropolitan Desegregation Plan.

Educating county districts about the program is a major goal for city-county divisional assistants, Shirley Brown and Shellie Hexter.

"A tremendous educational effort is necessary to inform teachers and administrators in the county about how the School Partnership Program works and how to use it," says Mrs. Hexter. "We initiate speaking requests through personal contact, letters and administrative meetings. We never turn down an invitation to speak!"

According to Mrs. Brown, "The response to the City-County School Partnership Program has been overwhelming."

After a county teacher becomes aware of the program and expresses interest, the Partnership staff begins looking for a city teaching partner. Once found, the two teachers meet with the city and county divisional assistants to brainstorm about the goals and objectives of their joint program.

Sharing the responsibility for all city-county Partnerships are divisional assistants, (left to right) Shirley Brown and Shellie Hexter.

As in a typical city partnership, the Partnership staff prepares the proposal and finds a community resource to sponsor the program.

A meeting between both teachers, the divisional assistants and the sponsor is the next step and is essential in having a clear understanding of what will be accomplished in the program.

An important aspect of the city-county partnerships is advance preparation by the teachers to insure a means for students to interact. This is accomplished in a number of ways. Letters between students and ice-breakers are effective, but team work

Figure 5–11

PARTNERSHIP:

Jerome Jones, Superintendent of Schools
St. Louis Public Schools

the Creative link
COMMUNITY RESOURCES FOR TEACHERS

Partially funded by Chapter II,
Education Consolidation and Improvement Act

activities have proven to the be least threatening and most successful method. This was the approach used in a partnership at KTVI and Double Helix. Students from both schools were dividied into "agencies," each of which worked together in competition with the other agencies to produce the best public service announcement, which aired on KTVI-TV.

Close monitoring is a key element in city-county partnerships to make sure both classes have a positive experience. City-county partnerships are typically three-session programs, meeting once at each school and once at the sponsor's location, unlike city school partnerships of six to eight sessions.

When the sponsor comes to us first

Quite often, sponsors will volunteer to become a part of the School Partnership Program before a teacher has asked specifically for a program in their area. We then contact teachers and schools who may be interested in the kind of sponsorship they are able to offer. This is often the case with cultural agencies.

Existing educational departments in the various St. Louis cultural agencies will often work with the School Partnership Program in tailoring one of their own educational programs or developing a completely new program to coincide with the curricular needs of the schools. Such was the case with the St. Louis Art Museum's ABC program (The Arts in Basic Curriculum) which involved 22 elementary city schools last year. The Muny Student Theatre Project plays are another example. Their performances specifically addressed the BEST objectives.

"One of my goals in having cultural agency Partnerships is to acquaint teachers with the vast educational resources and programs already in existance for them to use on their own," says divisional assistant, Mary Ferguson.

It's your move

It's been a busy summer. Many prospective sponsors are waiting in the wings, but the next step is up to you. In order to be responsive to your needs, we must know what they are. Get in touch with us now and let us help you bring something new and exciting to your students through a School Partnership Program. **361-5588**

PARTNERSHIP PREVIEWS AND HIGHLIGHTS

Planning for the mini Frontier Folklife Festival which was held recently at Carr Lane School are: (left to right) Hank Schafermeyer, SL/EAP; Mary Ferguson and Shellie Hexter, School Partnership; Jack Bang, principal and Marian Verbeck and Evelyn Gordon, teachers, Carr Lane; Marget Lippincott, Missouri Friends for Folk Art. Over 600 city-county students participated in the event.

U.S. Army Aviation Systems Command (AVSCOM) and **U.S. Army Troop Support Command** (TROSCOM) will sponsor programs in public relations, computers and federal law.

General Railroad and Equipment will sponsor programs on engineering, marketing and accounting at Sumner High School.

Metropolitan Sewer District will be sponsoring several programs in a variety of curriculum areas with an emphasis on science.

St. Louis Space Frontier will sponsor three space programs focusing on historical, geographical and cultural aspects of space.

Laclede Gas is expanding its sponsorship to include programs in physical science, video production, drafting and geology at Beaumont High School.

Washington University School of Fine Arts will sponsor an advanced art program with interationally-known sculptor, David Nash.

St. Louis Arts and Humanities Commission is sponsoring a series of programs for River Faces on mask construction, costuming and parading.

Care Unit Hospital will be sponsoring a drug program.

Gannett Outdoor and the **League of Women Voters** are jointly sponsoring a program on billboard design. The best design encouraging citizens to vote will be painted on a billboard and displayed the week of October 29.

London Brass Rubbing Centre and St. John's Episcopal Church will sponsor a series of programs on brass rubbings which will run through October 25th. Teachers interested in the program should call Partnership at 361-5588.

Bettye Collier-Thomas, executive director of Bethune Museum & Archives takes time after her lecture to speak with students. She and other distinguished lecturers such as author, James Baldwin, are part of a Black Studies Partnership Program with Washington University for 24 college-oriented students from Southwest, Northwest, Vashon and Sumner High Schools.

ANNOUNCEMENTS

Project Alpha will address adolescent pregnancy with adolescent males in a Partnership workshop Oct. 19, 20, 21 at Pierre Marquette. Teachers are asked to identify 14 to 18 year old black males with leadership qualities as confirees. Call Frederick Wright at 371-6500, ext. 46.

The Arts Resources Conference, an event co-sponsored by the Saint Louis Art Museum and the Partnership Program, will be held on Saturday, Oct. 20 from 2 to 5 p.m. at the museum. Displays and staff from St. Louis' visual and performing arts resources will be in the Sculpture Hall to inform you of cultural opportunities available to teachers. Performances will also be presented in the auditorium, and the event will end with a reception in the Cafe des Beaux Arts. Personal invitations are being sent to all teachers. If you do not receive one, contact Mary Ferguson or Hollis Heyn at the Partnership office - 361-5588.

**School
Partnership
Program**

5057 Ridge Ave.　St. Louis, MO 63113

Figure 5–11 (continued)

Forming a Governing Council or Central Committee

Leaders are unanimous in supporting an umbrella organization for a partnership project—no matter what the project's size or location. However, responses to the questionnaire indicated there is little agreement about the *kind* of governing structure needed for overall partnership program efforts. The most common format (and only 15 percent of the responses) was the central committee or council, of eight to twenty members, each of whom represented a particular sponsor group. Members included representatives of the school district (superintendent, board of education, community school coordinator, parent, union representative, principal, program coordinator-supervisor), of business (corporations, banks, and small businesses), and of community groups (chamber of commerce, Rotary, YMCA, religious organizations, private industry councils, hospitals, Red Cross, parent organizations, volunteer auxiliaries).

Over 12 percent of the respondents stated that they had originally had a central governing council or steering committee, but had changed that into an advisory committee that was convened and consulted occasionally throughout the year. Over 50 percent of the partnerships have no central committee. Instead, the partnership is controlled through an operations team at the school district level. Some of these programs indicated that a governing council or central committee format was not applicable to their kind of partnership; this was particularly true in partnerships limited to one company in alliance with one school.

The above data must be considered when discussing the potential role of a central umbrella structure to guide a partnership. Complementary to this discussion are the topics that will be examined in this section.

1. the advantages and disadvantages of having a central committee or governing council for the partnership
2. the governing council or central committee:
   * recruitment and appointment of members
   * composition of membership
   * council format
   * responsibilities of council members

3. recordkeeping for council activities
4. developing viable subcommittees and task forces:
   - format of subcommittees
   - membership of subcommittees
   - kinds of subcommittees
   - skills required of subcommittee members
   - responsibilities of subcommittee members

ADVANTAGES AND DISADVANTAGES OF A COUNCIL OR CENTRAL COMMITTEE

The planning team usually pulls together an advisory group that develops into the partnership's governing council or central committee. The format of these committees is variable and many partnerships have no central governing structure. Why is there such a dichotomy in this area?

Some school district staff—and community people as well—state that a central, semiformal or formal structure is unnecessary in developing a partnership program, particularly in smaller cities and suburban and rural communities where a tradition of informal partnerships provides a solid base for more formal alliances. In these districts, there were related questions about program control. Are partnership programs best managed by the school district? Many leaders voiced concerns about control of these programs by an outside agency (council or committee). They perceived that such an arrangement could lead ultimately to struggles over policy and guidance of responsibilities that traditionally belong to educators.

Other leaders appear to favor a partnership council or central committee as a governing organization to provide a coordinating function. They cite that it is easier to have such a structure in place *before* the program is launched than to impose one after the program has begun. As the partnership grows, this governing organization

1. restricts the partnership from developing into an unmanageable conglomeration of overlapping, disjointed activities.
2. guides the partnership's coordinating and accountability functions in the areas of policy and management.
3. represents "the partnership" as an institution to the entire community. If the committee is conceived as an umbrella organization, it is perceived to represent an independent point of view—the captive of no particular group.
4. builds support for local school improvement efforts, particularly when committee members represent sponsor organizations with status in the community.

THE GOVERNING COUNCIL OR CENTRAL COMMITTEE

Recruitment of Members

The office of the superintendent directs the recruitment of the governing council. A list of community leaders is drawn up. These leaders are contacted and then invited to a meeting (a breakfast session is nice) where they are introduced to the partnership concept; their interest in participation is elicited. A personal follow-up contact by the superintendent or appropriate designee is the next step.

Appointment of Members

Appointment of council members is usually made by the school district's superintendent together with a small group of advisors from the board of education and local community leaders. Those who agree to serve on the advisory council or committee at this beginning stage of the partnership understand that their guidance and expertise are required for a limited period of time; members are usually asked to serve for one, two, or three years. At a later date, if formal bylaws and partnership guidelines are developed, governing council members are nominated by a nominating committee and elected for one-to-three-year terms. Terms of appointment are staggered so that experience and expertise overlap from year to year.

Composition of Members

What should be the composition of these governing councils and central committees? Sometimes the planning committee and others developing the partnership are tempted to name only prominent community members. *Don't do it!* You will need a cross section of educational and private-sector leaders who will contribute time and effort—in addition to their names. Energetic participants are considered by many to be *most* important during initial partnership development.

Format

The format of partnerships' governing councils or central committees is essentially the same—no matter what kind of partnership is developed (foundation, adopt-a-school, or volunteer program). The governing councils and central committees are established as boards of directors. Information about the way different partnerships have set up their boards can be obtained by contacting programs listed in the appendixes of this handbook.

Members represent a range of community groups, businesses, and government agencies as appropriate to the goals and objectives of the partnership. Rules and regulations that govern the councils or committees are similar to those of other governing groups of nonprofit organizations.

Responsibilities

Governing council policies provide the overall direction for the partnership. General responsibilities are (1) to set policy, (2) to advise partnership operations staff, (3) to identify and recommend business and community resources, (4) to recruit new partners' active participation, and (5) to maintain and/or extend current partners' commitment to the partnership.

RECORDKEEPING FOR MEETINGS

Meetings should be scheduled at least quarterly (monthly during project initiation). Meeting reminders—together with agendas—are sent out well ahead of time. Remember, you are inviting *very* busy people to make a time commitment to your program. A secretary should be employed to keep and disseminate minutes of these meetings.

DEVELOPING VIABLE SUBCOMMITTEES AND TASK FORCES

When a central structure has been established, members determine their responsibilities and associated tasks. To expedite this process, subcommittees or task forces are developed.

Format of Subcommittees

Subcommittees are of no use unless they are working committees. Therefore, the purpose of the committee will dictate its tasks. In some smaller programs (for example, where one school or program is paired with one community partner), the governing council or central committee may be many subcommittees rolled into one—operations as well as advisement, guidance, recruitment, and policy-making.

In other partnership programs, there are two structures: a governing council or central committee and an operations or steering committee. There are no subcommittees in the formal sense; an individual within either larger group has particular responsibilities and—as an individual—*is* the committee.

In most of the partnerships, the governing council, with the planning team, initially develops the number, format, and scope of the subcommittees or task forces. The framework determines how the partnership will be governed as well as the number of subcommittees. As purposes and needs change, new subcommittees are created and others deleted.

A member of the governing council is usually appointed by the council to chair a subcommittee. People with particular expertise, who are not members of the council, may be asked to lead a particular subcommittee on an as-needed basis. A chairperson fills a term of one, two, or three years. Chairs rotate as do subcommittee members, thereby anticipating the need to change.

Membership of the Subcommittees

Membership in each committee should include representatives of the community *and* the school district. Whenever possible, these representatives should be perceived as leaders in their particular organizations—including personnel from administration, teaching, management, and operations.

There is one sensitive issue when discussing the balance of educators and community members on a subcommittee. Should there be more educators than other community members? It depends on the purpose of the committee. For example, where there is a review committee, set up to approve proposals by teachers or administrators for curriculum improvement projects, usually only one *inside* educator sits on that review committee—and only as an advisor. On the other hand, where a subcommittee is expected to work at schools to expedite a project, there will most probably be more school staff than community participants on that committee.

Kinds of Subcommittees

Subcommittees appear to fall into the following general areas: (1) program planning, development, and maintenance, (2) finance and budgeting, (3) resource allocation, (4) nominating, (5) monitoring and evaluation, (6) fund raising, (7) public relations and communication, and (8) staff development.

Skills Required of Subcommittee Members

Members of subcommittees should (1) be fully and consistently committed to the program; (2) understand the partnership concept and be able to translate program guidelines into effective operational activities; (3) have excellent communication skills; and (4) have both the sensitivity and time to act as liaison and catalyst with a variety of school and community groups.

Responsibilities of Subcommittee Members

Responsibilities are assigned to different subcommittees based on specific goals and objectives. Guidelines for committee members' responsibilities are set by the governing council. Some committees will focus on day-to-day operations; others will offer counsel and support to the partnership program in general and to the program's governing council in particular.

Programs assigned to each committee for development and implementation may begin immediately or at a later date. As the program develops, these subcommittees will submit interim and final evaluation reports to their governing council and, in return, receive assistance and guidance.

Determining Workable Policies, Guidelines, and Agreements

How formal should an alliance be between a school district and its community at large? In Section 6, you learned that some partnerships do not develop any central structure to provide guidance or set overall policy; however, it was suggested that, over the long term, it is advisable to establish a central committee or governing council whose goals and objectives are stated clearly and publicly, whose policies provide guidelines for the program, and whose alliances with partners preclude legal and tax entanglements.

This section, therefore, examines suggested partnership guidelines and policies, potential contractual arrangements between partners, and required legal counsel.

PARTNERSHIP GUIDELINES AND POLICIES

Guidelines and policies will set the overall direction for partnerships. The governing council or central committee usually develops and establishes policy with the help of the planning team and the guidance of the superintendent of schools. Policy guidelines are based on the individual partnership's purpose. Whether formal or informal, bylaws and guidelines ordinarily include the following components:

1. name of partnership
2. mission statement or purpose
3. membership
4. officers
5. selection, term (including filling vacancies), and duties of officers
6. composition and responsibilities of committees
7. meetings: annual, special, notice of meetings, quorum
8. administrative and financial provisions
9. amendments

Excellent samples of bylaws and policy guidelines can be obtained from Private Initiatives in Public Education (PIPE), WA; the Adopt-A-School Steering Committee, Nashua, NH; the San Francisco Education Fund, CA; the TwinWest Business-Education Partnership, MN; and the Adopt-A-School Council of the Los Angeles Unified School District, CA.

USE OF LEGAL COUNSEL

Consult frequently with your school district's legal counsel during the partnership's development stages. Early advisement will protect the school district generally and the partnership specifically from legal entanglements that could detract from program activities. What specific support can such counsel give to the partnership? Legal counsel

- can provide assistance and prepare formal articles of incorporation.
- can expedite professional service agreements, for example, for consultants who work on a project.
- can assess insurance coverage for partners who will be working in the schools or for students and staff who visit and/or work in partners' facilities.
- can review partnership guidelines and plans for activities. Such policies must not conflict with local, state, and federal laws, policies, and guidelines, some of which apply to private sector–public alliances.
- can prepare, together with the school district's business office, guidelines for receipt and expenditure of monies by the partnership.
- can advise planning team members regarding informal and formal partnership contractual agreements.

A special note on legal counsel for foundations: Figure 7-1, from Thomas Silk, Esq., San Francisco, CA, should prove helpful to those planning teams interested in establishing an educational foundation as their form of partnership.

CONTRACTUAL AGREEMENTS BETWEEN PARTNERS

Agreements between partners take many forms, ranging from legal contractual papers to ceremonial certificates. Once again, the purpose of your partnership will give direction to the form of your agreements. Examining the current agreements from partnership programs around the country provides some guidance regarding the variety of available alternative arrangements.

Approval for a partnership can be achieved in the form of a *board resolution*, informing the community at large that a partnership's development (1) has been recommended by the superintendent of schools and (2) officially sanctioned by the board of education.

Agreements can be in the form of *legal documents*, for example, the one between Private Initiatives in Public Education (PIPE) and the Seattle Chamber of Commerce, WA (see Figure 7-2). Note that the nonprofit corporation status of PIPE, *and* the exchange of monies as well as services, guides this form of agreement.

Partnership arrangements in the Dade County Public Schools, FL, consist of a welcoming *cover letter* (see Figure 7-3) *and agreements* (see Figure 7-4). Note that the agreement specified: (1) when the partnership was established, (2) the purpose of the alliance, (3) what services and resources the partner will give, and (4) what recognition the Dade County Public Schools will give to the partner in exchange.

Examples of less formal *agreement certificates* that could be adapted for any form of partnership arrangement come from the State of Pennsylvania (see Figure 7-5), from the Irvine Unified School District, CA (see Figure 7-6), and the San Diego City Schools, CA (see Figure 7-7).

Whatever format of partnership agreement is used, there should be a formal signing occasion (press conference, reception, breakfast, lunch, tea) in honor of the newly developed alliance.

FORMING AN EDUCATIONAL FOUNDATION

by Thomas Silk, Esq.
Silk and Marois
San Francisco

Once the decision has been made to raise funds to benefit the public school system, the next question is whether the public school system should be the direct donee or whether it makes more sense to set up a separate foundation to benefit the schools. For reasons varying from funding efficiency (establishing a foundation whose scope includes many school systems) to administrative simplicity (avoiding the burden on a particular school system that results from the receipt of many small amounts for a specific program), many supporters of the public school system have chosen to establish separate foundations to benefit the schools. Although there are many aspects to the formation and organization of a foundation, this paper focuses only on the legal.

The formation of a public school foundation requires selection of the appropriate legal form, formation of the entity chosen, and the registration and qualification of that entity with the various tax and regulatory agencies.

In most states the foundation will be formed either as a nonprofit corporation or as a charitable trust. Advice from local counsel should be sought to determine which form is most appropriate.

If a nonprofit corporation is selected, which would ordinarily be the case, your attorney will have to draft articles of incorporation and file them with the proper state office, often the Secretary of State. The articles should be drafted in such a manner as to give the foundation maximum flexibility in its operations, so that the articles need not be amended as the activities of the foundation change with time. The articles must comply with the state laws regulating nonprofit corporations and with the Internal Revenue Service requirements for exemption from income tax, as well as with the requirements of state tax authorities where applicable.

Once the articles are filed, the incorporators hold a meeting where they adopt the bylaws (which the attorney has drafted in conformity with state and federal laws), elect the board of directors and officers, authorize the opening of bank accounts and signatories to those accounts, and authorize the preparation and filing of the application for exemption from federal income tax and other exempt applications that may be required under law. You should note that many states require separate applications for income tax, property tax, local business tax, and sales tax exemptions.

Ordinarily the foundation will seek federal exemption as a nonprofit corporation organized for charitable and educational purposes under Section 501(c)(3) of the Internal Revenue Code. The exemption application, Form 1023, contains 41 pages, but is not quite so forbidding as it appears. Only a few pages apply to the sort of foundation we are discussing and most of the form may be completed by answering a few basic questions:

(1) The name and address of the organization;

(2) The name and address and any special qualifications of the members of the board of directors;

Figure 7–1

(3) The purpose of the organization;

(4) The proposed activities the organization intends to engage in to carry out those purposes; and

(5) A proposed budget for three years, including expenses by category and also receipts by category (e.g., foundation grants, corporate contributions, individual contributions, investment income, sales receipts, tuition fees, etc.)

Several points should be kept in mind in completing or reviewing the application for federal income tax. First, that the application should be mailed to the correct office of the Internal Revenue Service within 15 months from the date of the articles of incorporation are filed or the declaration of trust signed, if a charitable trust. If that is done, then the exemption, whenever it is granted, will be retroactive to the date of incorporation and, thereby, protect the organization and any contributors during that interim period. Second, be sure that all the required documents are enclosed with the application, including the articles or deed of trust, bylaws, and the proposed budget.

Third, study the instructions carefully concerning the private foundation/public charity distinction. What you want from the Internal Revenue Service is a ruling that the foundation is exempt under Section 501(c)(3) of the Code, but you also want an advance ruling that it qualifies as a public charity under Section 509(a)(2) or, better yet, Sections 509(a)(1) and 170(b)(1)(A)(vi) of the Code. Public charity status will allow the foundation a greater latitude in its operations, including the making of grants and, most important, it will allow contributors the maximum tax deductions available.

Fourth, many individuals and most foundations and corporations are opposed or reluctant to contribute to an organization until it has received its IRS exemption. While you may be able to interest another exempt organization in receiving contributions on your behalf until you receive your exception, this technique may also become awkward and it may be unsatisfactory to your funders.

Be sure to take into account in your planning the time that the formation process takes. You should expect that 6 to 9 months will pass from the date you first contact your lawyer until you finally receive your exemption.

State exemption laws must also be satisfied. Some states, such as California, require a separate application to the state tax agency to obtain an exemption. Other states require only a copy of the IRS exemption to be filed with that agency, and still others have no corporate tax from which to be exempt.

Only a few of the legal aspects of operating a foundation can be suggested here. State law will ordinarily specify the manner of election of directors, the duty of care and loyalty of directors, and the requirements of a quorum, meeting notices, and meetings themselves. Minutes of meetings must be kept. Reports are required of a foundation by various state tax agencies. Tax returns must be filed with the Internal Revenue Service within 4 1/2 months after the close of the foundation's fiscal year.

Finally, you should be careful to comply with the requirements for maintaining your foundation's exempt and public charity status under the tax laws so that the foundation may continue to offer contributors the maximum charitable contribution deductions available.

Reprinted by permission of Thomas Silk, Esq., CA.

Figure 7–1 (continued)

```
                     MEMORANDUM OF AGREEMENT
                            between
             PRIVATE INITIATIVES IN PUBLIC EDUCATION
                              and
                 SEATTLE CHAMBER OF COMMERCE
```

Memorandum of Agreement made this _1st_ day of _April_ , 1980, between Private Initiatives in Public Education ("PIPE") and the Seattle Chamber of Commerce ("Chamber").

RECITALS:

A.   PIPE is a nonprofit corporation formed under the laws of the State of Washington in 1979 for the purpose of developing a higher level of community involvement in the public schools and to provide additional resources for those schools.

B.   PIPE has a need for office space and support services and the Seattle Chamber of Commerce has agreed to provide such office space and support services in accordance with the provisions of this Agreement.

AGREEMENTS:

1.   Support Services Provided By Chamber.

(a)   The Chamber will employ the PIPE Executive Director ("Executive Director"). A preliminary position description is attached as Exhibit A. The Executive Director shall be responsible to the PIPE board for the program and activities of PIPE and shall be responsible to the Executive Vice President of the Chamber, or his designee, on personnel and administrative matters. Initially, the Executive Director will be an employee of the Chamber assigned on a full-time basis to PIPE. The Executive Vice President of the Chamber shall be responsible for making recommendations regarding the hiring, discharge and salary for the Executive Director and the PIPE board shall have the final authority on such questions. PIPE shall reimburse the Chamber for all costs associated with the employment of the Executive Director.

(b)   The Chamber shall provide office space for the Executive Director, including desk and file cabinets, without charge to PIPE.

(c)   The Chamber shall provide telephone service, secretarial assistance, stationery, xerox, printing, mailing and related services to PIPE on a cost-reimbursement basis.

Figure 7–2

(d)   Subject to approval of the Executive Vice President of the Chamber, the Chamber shall provide other staff support and facilities as may be needed by PIPE from time to time.

(e)   The Chamber shall provide bookkeeping and accounting services to PIPE without charge by setting up a separate account in its system. All revenue received by PIPE and all charges to PIPE will be recorded in such account and a monthly statement will be provided to PIPE. PIPE will maintain a separate bank checking account and check register for the payment of all charges. Receipts by PIPE shall be forwarded to the Chamber accounting department for deposit in PIPE's bank accounts (checking or savings, or both). Disbursements will be handled by the preparation of checks by the Chamber accounting department following approval of invoices received by PIPE in accordance with PIPE's approval procedures.

2.   Status Of PIPE.

(a)   PIPE will remain a separate entity with 501(c)(3) federal tax status. It will have its own board of directors, officers and bank account.

(b)   PIPE will implement its program and activities as generally described in the brochure attached as Exhibit B.

(c)   PIPE will raise funds from business and professional firms who are interested in its program and activities but will not, without Chamber approval, engage in a general solicitation of the business community or Chamber membership. In addition, PIPE will seek funds and in kind contributions from foundations, educational institutions, governmental organizations and other sources.

3.   Undertakings Of PIPE.

(a)   PIPE shall pay the Chamber for the support services described in Section 1 above as further described in the annual budget adopted by the PIPE board. The initial budget for the year ending August 31, 1980, is attached as Exhibit C. PIPE will make payments to the Chamber for the support services described in Section 1 on a monthly basis following receipt of a monthly statement from the Chamber.

(b)   PIPE shall conduct an annual evaluation of its program and activities, with the first evaluation to take place by September of 1980.

(c)   PIPE shall prepare an annual report which summarizes its program and activities and an annual budget and program plan for the following year. Copies of such

-2-

Figure 7–2 (continued)

annual report and annual budget and program plan shall be provided to the Chamber. In addition, PIPE shall provide such other information to the Chamber as may be requested from time to time.

(d) Any major changes made by the PIPE board to the program described in Exhibit B shall be reported to the Chamber.

4.   Term. This Agreement shall remain in effect until terminated by either party. Either party may terminate this Agreement as of the end of any calendar month upon giving sixty (60) days written notice of intent to terminate to the other party. Termination shall not affect PIPE's obligations to pay for support services provided by the Chamber through the date of termination.

5.   Chamber Participation In PIPE. The chairman of the Chamber's Education Committee, or other person designated by the Chamber, shall be invited to serve as a member of the PIPE board. In addition, the Executive Vice President of the Chamber, or his designee, shall be invited to attend all regular and special meetings of the board of PIPE.

6.   Liaison Committee. There will be established a joint committee of five persons to be called the Liaison Committee. The Chamber shall appoint two members, PIPE shall appoint two members (one being the President), and the four so appointed shall select the fifth member. The purpose of the Liaison Committee shall be to provide advice and assistance to the PIPE board and the Chamber as to details regarding the support services and changes thereto which may be made from time to time. This may include, but shall not be limited to, participation in the search for an Executive Director, employment arrangements and performance evaluation. It is not intended that the Liaison Committee will make policy decisions except as such policy decisions may be jointly delegated by the Chamber and PIPE. Meetings of the Liaison Committee may be called by the President of PIPE or by the Executive Vice President of the Chamber.

7.   Miscellaneous. It is understood that PIPE shall retain its separate identity and all of its corporate powers and privileges. Furthermore, nothing contained in this Agreement shall be construed as creating an agency relationship between PIPE and the Chamber or to affect PIPE's status as an independent nonprofit corporation organized under the laws of the State of Washington.

Executed as of the date first above written.

PRIVATE INITIATIVES IN PUBLIC EDUCATION

By _____

Its _____

-3-

Figure 7–2 (continued)

By _Dee Dickinson_

Its _Secretary_

SEATTLE CHAMBER OF COMMERCE

By _George Duff_

Its _Executive Vice President_

By _____

Its _President_

Exhibit A --
 Position Description
Exhibit B --
 Brochure on Program
Exhibit C --
 Budget for year ending 8/31/80

-4-

Figure 7–2 (continued)

DADE COUNTY PUBLIC SCHOOLS
ADMINISTRATIVE OFFICE
LINDSEY HOPKINS BUILDING
1410 NORTHEAST SECOND AVENUE
MIAMI, FLORIDA 33132

DR. LEONARD M. BRITTON
SUPERINTENDENT OF SCHOOLS

DADE COUNTY SCHOOL BOARD
MR. PAUL L. CEJAS, CHAIRMAN
MRS. ETHEL BECKHAM, VICE-CHAIRMAN
MR. G. HOLMES BRADDOCK
MS. JOYCE H. KNOX
DR. MICHAEL KROP
MRS. JANET R. McALILEY
MR. ROBERT RENICK

June 17

_____

Dear

As a result of our meeting, I am very pleased to welcome you to the ranks
of Dade Partners.

Please review the attached proposal, revise it if necessary, and return it to me
at:

      Office of School Volunteers/Dade Partners
      1410 N.E. 2 Ave.   Rm. 210
      Miami, Florida 33132

Welcome to Dade Partners!

Sincerely,

Gina Craig, Supervisor
School Volunteers/Dade Partners

GC/lb

Enclosure

Reprinted by permission of Dade Partners, FL.

Figure 7–3

INTRODUCTION

At a meeting on June 12, 1981, the principal and a staff member from Southridge Senior High, two executive officers from American Bankers Insurance Group, and two members from the Dade Partners staff met to discuss partnership activities. The following activities have been approved and as time passes and the partnership matures, additional items may be added to the proposal.

AMERICAN BANKERS INSURANCE GROUP WILL:

. Adopt Miami Southridge Senior High

. Establish a speakers bureau. Subjects might include marketing and promotion, computers or other subjects in the business field.

. Provide an area for a temporary student art work display.

. Sponsor an ad in the school publication.

. Sponsor a one-day insurance information seminar for business education teachers.

. Provide a "Shadow Day" for business classes.

. Participate in a career day and conduct tours of the plant.

. Provide some financial assistance to the school.

. Provide a school plaque for Teacher of the Year.

. Locate available space for meetings.

. Provide AMBI* courses for teachers (Listening skills, time management and stress management) after they have relocated in Cutler Ridge.

* American Bankers Management Institute.

DADE COUNTY PUBLIC SCHOOLS WILL:

. Publicize and promote partnership activities citywide in such publications as Dade Partners newsletter and Envoy.

. Publicize and promote partnership activities through the school newspaper or other school publications.

. Provide facilities for training sessions or classes.

. Promote the partnership through various activities in the school.

. Identify students to participate in partnership activities.

. Provide musical presentations during special events.

Figure 7–4

Southridge Adoption
Page 2

Once the business has relocated in the area, the following activities
may be added.

     . Provide fruit trees and vegetable gardens for agriculture
      students.

     . Sponsor band concerts.

     . Give in-house training for business students.

     . Provide employment opportunities to students on a part-
      time basis.

     . Provide assistance with audio-visual materials.

Reprinted by permission of Dade Partners, FL.

Figure 7–4 (continued)

Commonwealth of Pennsylvania

This is to certify that the

and

have entered into a
Partnership in Education
and have pledged to work together to improve
the quality of life and learning in their community

Dick Thornburgh, Governor
Commonwealth of Pennsylvania

Margaret A. Smith, Secretary
Department of Education

Robert B. Williams, Executive Director
Governor's Human Resources
Committee of the Cabinet

Partnerships in Education

_____
School Representative

_____
Partner

*Reprinted by permission of the Governor's Private-Sector Initiatives Task Force
and the Pennsylvania State Department of Education.*

Figure 7–5

Partnership
Promoting Educational Excellence

This Agreement joins the hands
of said business and public school in a uniquely
designed partnership. Both may pursue a mutually enriching
relationship with each other with full benefits
accruing in the Community.

In Witness, thereof, all parties execute this partnership on this

_____ day of _____, 19 _____

_____ Business Representative

_____ Community Representative

_____ Board of Education Member

_____ School Principal

_____ Student Representative

_____ District Superintendent

Irvine Education Foundation — Irvine Unified School District

Reprinted by permission of the Irvine Unified School District, CA.

Figure 7–6

Draft Copy--Not
for signature--
a final copy will
be sent to you
for signature.

SAN DIEGO CITY SCHOOLS
Office of the Superintendent

1985 - 1986

PARTNERSHIPS IN EDUCATION AGREEMENT

between

_____

and

_____

We agree to enter into a working partnership to attain the following goal:

_____

_____

_____

_____

In order to attain this goal, the following activities are planned:

1. _____

2. _____

3. _____

4. _____

5. _____

This is an ongoing project, subject to annual review. Both parties agree to
submit written evaluations of this agreement to the coordinator, Partnerships
in Education Program, in _____, 198_.
                              (month)

_____   _____
Name   (Signature)   **Name**   (Signature)
Organization   School
Phone   Phone

_____
Superintendent of Schools

_____
Date

ca

Reprinted by permission of San Diego Unified School District, CA.

Figure 7–7

Choosing a Partnership Format: Design and Scope

The scope of your project will depend initially on the breadth and depth of resources available to meet your most critical needs. If there are many quality human and material resources (not just buttons and T-shirts!), you can plan a more elaborate program.

Partnership leaders try to ensure that the partnership is under their control rather than vice versa. They want to avoid problems such as inappropriate demands on partners, the overtaxing of resources, communication lapses, dashed hopes, and the resultant poor morale. These leaders will try to overbudget resources to meet needs, thereby preparing to compensate for possible reductions or cutbacks.

CHOOSING YOUR PARTNERSHIP'S FORMAT

Some school districts already have a structure in place to deal with alliances between the school district and its larger community. Community foundations, for example, have long-standing experience in supporting local public education. The partnership either formalizes its already-established affiliations *or* extends, redesigns, or initiates a structure that is legal and workable, and with which it is comfortable. This structure then takes different effective forms.

The remainder of this chapter examines formats that leaders have found useful as they developed their partnerships. You will note that none of these structures are "pure," since they have been adapted to meet individual program needs. Additional contact information, to assist you in your decision to adopt or adapt a particular format, can be found in the appendixes of this handbook.

Adopt-A-School

The most prevalent form of partnership (nearly 50 percent of the questionnaire's respondents) is commonly termed *Adopt-A-School*. Sometimes, this format is labeled *Join-A-School*, *Partners in Education*, or just *Partnerships*. Whatever the name, a school is matched with one business, community organization, or civic agency; they become partners to support the improvement of education for students in that particular school. Sometimes, more than one business or community agency will be matched with one school. Multiple adoptions are solicited, for example,

- when the resources of the businesses or other organizations in the neighborhood of the school are limited.
- if the needs of a school require resources beyond the capability of one adopter.
- if all schools in a district are "adopted," but new organizations and businesses want to support public education through this program. Then additional adopters join forces with those already in place.
- if (for any reason) an adopter can or will no longer provide the needed level of resources or services to its adopted school. Other adopters then step in to maintain or extend the level of supplemental resources.

Adopt-a-school programs are usually administered from within a school district through offices connected with special or funded programs. Operations staff report directly to an assistant superintendent or to the superintendent of schools. Agreements between schools and their adopters are generally set for one year and then renewed each year thereafter. The success of this partnership format appears to stem from the following components:

1. There are specific program goals and objectives directly related to the needs of the individual school.

2. Emphasis is placed on the use of direct human resources and services. As a result, there is a high degree of personal satisfaction on the part of the adopter. For the adoptee, the opportunity to receive supplemental resources directly related to on-site needs supports basic curriculum and instruction *and* staff morale.

3. Although agreements between adopters and adoptees are informal and largely ceremonial, close bonding occurs as people from inside and outside the school ("their" school) work together.

What organizations "adopt" schools? Basically, any type of business, organization, or agency can adopt a school. The guidelines for adoption do not limit the *kind* of adopter.

The adopter's *location* is important. Proximity between adopters and adoptees encourages consistent contact and support and avoids the frustration of attempting to establish and maintain a long-distance relationship. This is especially true when human service–volunteer activities are part of the partnership program. Where city or suburban travel may pose problems, the adopter often runs a daily or weekly transportation service for volunteers.

Note: The adopt-a-school format has many successful variations, for example, in Wichita, KA; Rockville, MD; Cincinnati, OH; Memphis, TN; Los Angeles, CA; and Denver, CO.

Foundations

The foundation is another popular partnership structure used to garner funding support for schools in urban, suburban, and rural communities. Local foundations come in all shapes and sizes. Some function independently from the school district, and allocate funding directly to teachers, schools, and parent groups (with the approval of the board of education). More commonly, funds are elicited by the foundation and then placed under the jurisdiction of either a school board or a parent group.*

Foundations are ordinarily organized around a governing board of directors (usually at least one member of which is the school district's superintendent). Members of the governing council can include community leaders, educators who are not part of the school district, and business and labor representatives. Operations, such as reviewing proposals, monitoring projects, publicizing the program, and other general administrative activities, are carried out by a small staff plus volunteers. Operations staff reports to the governing council.

Note: Some examples of successful foundations are: the Educational Enrichment Fund in Tucson, AZ; the San Francisco Education Fund, CA; the Los Angeles Educational Partnership, CA; and the Allegheny Conference Education Fund, PA.

Alliances or Committees

Alliances are essentially umbrella organizations that coordinate a myriad of private-sector–public-education initiatives for a school district. These alliances may be (1) based within the school district, (2) purposely established independently off-site, or (3) located in the offices of some nonprofit, volunteer, or educational group such as a chamber of commerce, a Junior League, or a university.

Alliance membership can be as broad-based as the available local organizations, including representatives from the school district, business and industry, universities and colleges, local foundations, civic and volunteer groups, government and nonprofit agencies, public utilities, etc.

The governing structure of most alliances appears to be of a pyramid shape with

- a governing council at the apex
- an intermediary general administrative office (that coordinates alliance projects and reports to the Council)
- individual project staff units that administer the particular programs functioning under the alliance umbrella

Note: Following is a sampling of some successful alliances: The Philadelphia Alliance for Teaching Humanities in the Schools (PATHS), PA; the New York Alliance for

---

*Data from NASSP Special Report, *The Local Education Foundation: A New Way to Raise Money for Schools*, May 1983, by George Neill.

the Public Schools, NYC; the Peninsula Academies, CA; the St. Louis, MO, School Partnership Program; and the Atlanta Principals Institute, GA.

Volunteer Programs

Volunteer programs in support of schools are far from new. Parents, particularly, have been working for years at school sites, through federated parent organizations and on districtwide advisory committees; in these activities, parents have worked with both students and school or district staff. Community volunteer programs have also allied with schools on particular projects, linking the school district with its larger community. More formalized volunteer programs have, in recent years, been one effective format to support public education. Like alliances, foundations, and adopt-a-school programs, volunteer programs vary in form and size. Common structural elements are that

- the programs are usually school district based and managed
- the volunteers are recruited from communitywide businesses; nonprofit, government, and civic organizations; and other volunteer agencies
- the programs concentrate primarily, if not solely, on available *human* resources

Volunteer program leaders usually report to the superintendent of schools, and indirectly (periodically) to the board of education. In addition to a central, coordinating office, volunteer program staff are based at school sites to ensure program coordination at the individual school. Volunteers work under the direction of teachers, principals, and other school staff in three broad activity areas; supporting basic instruction to students, enriching educational experiences for students, and extending instructional time through assistance to professional staff in the areas of clerical and nonprofessional tasks. Volunteer program administrative activities focus on recruitment and training of a volunteer corps, matching of school needs to available human resources, and recognition of volunteers.

Note: Some exemplary volunteer programs include those in Tulsa, OK; Dade County, FL; Salt Lake City, UT; Houston, TX; and San Francisco, CA.

Clearinghouses

Clearinghouses are partnership structures that accomplish the following objectives:

- They elicit information regarding educational needs and available human, financial, and materials resources. This information may include local, regional, and national sources for partnership use.
- They seek out new resources to meet identified needs.
- They act as facilitators, catalysts, and networks for matching these needs to resources.

• They efficiently and effectively disseminate this information to the constituencies involved in the partnership.

Clearinghouses usually function organizationally outside the school district. If they are local or regional, they may be closely linked or provide services to one or more school districts. Like the other formats discussed in this chapter, clearinghouse partnerships take many forms.

Note: Some successful examples of partnership programs that act all or in part as clearinghouses are: The Cleveland Scholarship Programs, OH; the Corporate Action Committee (CAC), CA; Partnerships Data Net, Inc., DC; the National Association for Industry-Education Cooperation (NAIEC), NY; the American Newspaper Publishers Association (ANPA), DC; and the American Bar Association's Special Committee on Youth Education for Citizenship, IL.

PART THREE

LAUNCHING THE PARTNERSHIP

Developing and Managing a Partnership: Organization of the Management Team

You have assessed needs and resources; early partners have been solicited and committed to participation; governing councils, workable guidelines, policies, and subcommittees have been established; your partnership format has been chosen. Program development is now transferred from the planning team to an operations staff. This staff will be responsible for the day-to-day management of program activities as well as long-range planning, development, monitoring, and evaluation.

At this time, management procedures and components are established, based on guidelines initiated by your governing council and developed by your planning team. When these procedures and components are securely installed and capably coordinated, your partnership

- becomes an ongoing, consistent project effort
- has the flexibility to shift its activity structure from staff development to volunteerism to mentoring to career education, and so on
- can move from a cooperative venture to a collaboration in which all partners both give and receive
- will function efficiently and effectively
- elicits increasingly formal, and more dedicated commitment from all partners

Let's examine options for the management team as it sets in place its structure, procedures and staff. In the process, the team is challenged to respond to these questions:

- *Where* is the partnership's management team based?
- *What* kind of facilities are needed?
- *How* is the team organized?
- *What* are useful organizational timelines?
- *Which* procedures will successfully launch your partnership program?

Whatever the format of your partnership, no matter what its scope (number of partners, extent of activities, number of students and staff affected by the program), your partnership's organizational structure should be in place *before* you plunge into full partnership operations. If these structures and procedures are in place,

- you will not always be playing "catch up."
- you will not end up spending inordinate amounts of time and energy trying to expedite matters—time spent away from productive partnership activities.
- you will not lose credibility in your partners' eyes. Business and civic leaders *expect* organizational components to be in place.

WHERE SHOULD THE MANAGEMENT TEAM BE LOCATED?

Successful organization of partnership operations can be based at a school district's central office, off-site under the auspices of a foundation or a neutral agency, or on-site at the individual school. (*Note:* We are concerned in this guide only with school district–developed programs, not those initiated by state, regional, or national organizations). If the partnership is organized as an independent structure, the director is usually responsible to a governing council, board of directors, or central committee. If the partnership is *under* the direct supervision of the school district, the director reports to an assistant superintendent or superintendent and the board of education; any governing council, central committee, or board of directors then takes on an advisory role. Therefore, *where* the partnership is developed is closely related to *how* it is developed.

Outside the School District

Foundations

Your school board and administration may decide to set up an independent, tax-exempt organization (a foundation). In such cases, the school district should

a. retain the counsel of both lawyers and accountants to set up a foundation structure.

b. research and review the organizational components of current, successful local partnership foundations. For example, you could consult program leaders from The San Francisco Education Fund, CA; The Cleveland Scholarship Programs, Inc., OH; and the Montgomery County Foundations, MD.

c. seek technical assistance from national organizations like the Public Education Fund, PA. The Fund can help identify and secure start-up funding and local expertise as you develop your partnership.

Community Agencies

Sometimes a community agency other than the school district is asked to manage the partnership. These can be temporary or more permanent arrangements. Organizations such as local chambers of commerce, private industry councils, urban coalitions, or business-education councils often house or become bankers for a partnership; provide staff for program planning and implementation; lend executives as consultants and staff members as volunteer workers; and contribute start-up funding, facilities, and equipment. Information related to this form of support can be obtained from the Dallas Adopt-A-School Program, TX; the PIPE Program, WA; and the Peninsula Academies (Stanford Mid-Peninsula Urban Coalition), CA.

Alliances

Occasionally, an alliance of representatives from the private and public sectors is formed specifically to administer a partnership program *beyond* the direct supervision of the school district or any individual agency. Good examples to consult for technical assistance regarding this management structure include the Upper Midwest Small Schools Project, ND; and Senior Volunteers in the Schools, NY.

Within the School District

Most of the current partnerships (except for foundations) are organized and managed by a school district—regardless of their formats. Boards of education and school administrators prefer to control and set the guidelines for special district projects. In addition, ongoing commitment from school staff appears more easily elicited and retained if the partnership is district-based. Examples of successful partnerships that are under the supervision of their school districts are

- the Los Angeles Unified School District's Adopt-A-School Program, CA
- the Memphis, TN, Adopt-A-School Program
- the Volunteers in Public Schools Program of the Houston Independent School District, TX
- the Saturday Scholars Program of the Chicago Public School District, IL
- the Charlotte-Mecklenburg Schools' Community Resource Program, NC
- the St. Louis School Partnership Program of the St. Louis Public Schools, MO
- the Emeritus Teachers Project of the Washington, DC, Public Schools

OFFICE SPACE FOR THE PARTNERSHIP

The management team should be encouraged to look for available space to house the project. Of course, where the partnership is housed will be guided by whether the partnership is developed under the auspices of the school district *or* of an outside agency (for example, a chamber of commerce), and the format of the partnership (for example, independent foundations are usually located outside the district).

Often partnership programs are located in whatever space is available, for example, a vacant classroom in a school building, the site of the program's governing council, at the local chamber of commerce, or in the central office of the school district. The size or location of the office is not critical to the success of the partnership. It *is* important, however, that management team members be comfortable in their facilities and not too far removed from the partnership activities!

HOW IS THE MANAGEMENT TEAM ORGANIZED?

Basic Organization of Operations Staff to Accomplish Tasks

Responses to the questionnaire clearly indicated that there are no set organizational patterns for operating a successful partnership project. Many programs use organizational charts as tools to help outsiders *and* insiders determine the basic members of the management team, how the team is organized, and to whom the teams and team members are responsible. Most of these charts indicate levels of positions and chain of command. Some of the charts also provide extra detail on responsibilities of individual team members and interrelationships of members with partners both within and outside the school district. Figures 9–1, 9–2, and 9–3 illustrate the points outlined above; they can be adapted to meet a partnership's specific organizational need. These charts come from: the Denver Public Schools Partnership Program, CO (Figure 9–1); the San Francisco Education Fund, CA (Figure 9–2); and the TwinWest Business-Education Partnership, MN (Figure 9–3).

Management Team Positions

The management team is organized around certain basic positions. (*Note:* The responsibilities associated with these positions will be fully discussed in Section 10). A list of these positions includes

- an executive director or coordinator
- part-time consultants as needed
- business and community site-based coordinators or liaisons (as appropriate to the partnership's format)
- administrative assistants or program leaders
- secretarial support staff
- interns (as appropriate)

WHICH PROCEDURES WILL SUCCESSFULLY LAUNCH YOUR PARTNERSHIP PROGRAM?

The management team is wise to set up procedures that give direction to its partnership program. Procedures should be clearly defined and submitted for approval to the partnership's governing council, and to the district's administration and board of education as appropriate.

In the materials received from partnerships around the country, management guidelines were implied and, in some cases, defined through organizational brochures and "how-to" materials for partnership staff and participants. Examination of this information provides program management guidelines as well as direction in efficient and effective procedures to follow.

1. A project coordinator with clear responsibilities regarding program development, supervision, and general operations is assigned to administer and guide the partnership.

2. Staff roles are specifically determined, staff are assigned, and staff tasks and activities are monitored consistently.

3. An organizational timeline is developed for use by the management team. A program timeline is more than just a series of dates specifying when partnership goals should be accomplished. If it is well conceived, the timeline becomes a blueprint for program management and outlines: program goals and objectives; associated tasks and costs; staff responsibilities for accomplishing these tasks; an evaluation component; and dates for achieving stated objectives. Examples of planning forms that can be adapted as useful tools come from Nashua, NH (see Figure 9–4) and Houston, TX (see Figure 9–5).

   Other examples of scheduling forms that could be adapted to guide program management are a Recruitment Timetable from Charlotte-Mecklenburg, NC (see Figure 9–6), and a Start-up Timeline from Corporate Action in Public Schools (CAPS), CA (see Figure 9–7).

4. A process is developed through which the partnership continues an ongoing assessment to determine partners' needs and resources (an outgrowth of the assessment procedures outlined in Section 4).

5. Procedures for the following components are developed, implemented, and maintained:
   • budget and the finance process
   • recordkeeping and fiscal controls
   • communication
   • fund raising
   • public relations
   • reports
   • project activities
   • evaluation

The remainder of Part 3 of this guide discusses successful establishment and coordination of these management components.

ADOPT•A•SCHOOL ORGANIZATIONAL FLOW CHART

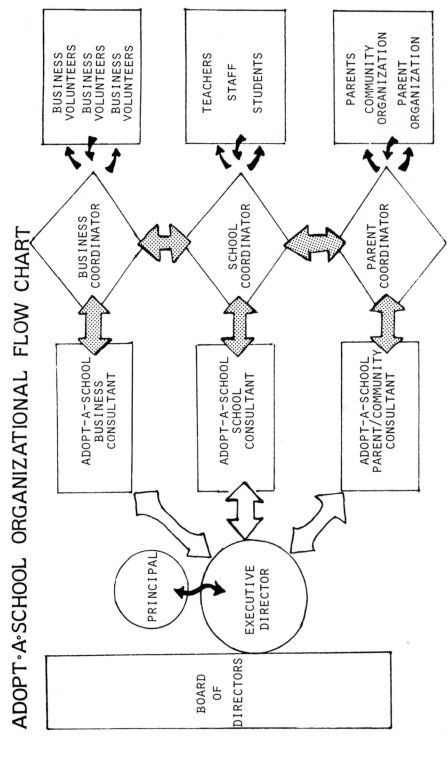

Reprinted by permission of Adopt-A-School in Denver, CO.

Figure 9–1

102

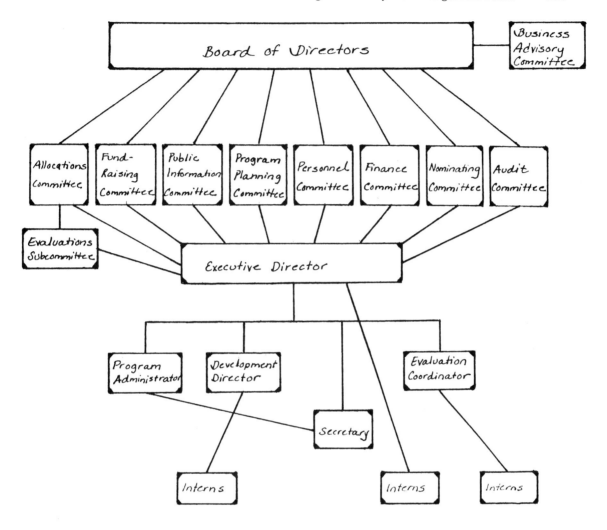

The Organization: An Overview

Reprinted by permission of the San Francisco Education Fund, CA.
Figure 9–2

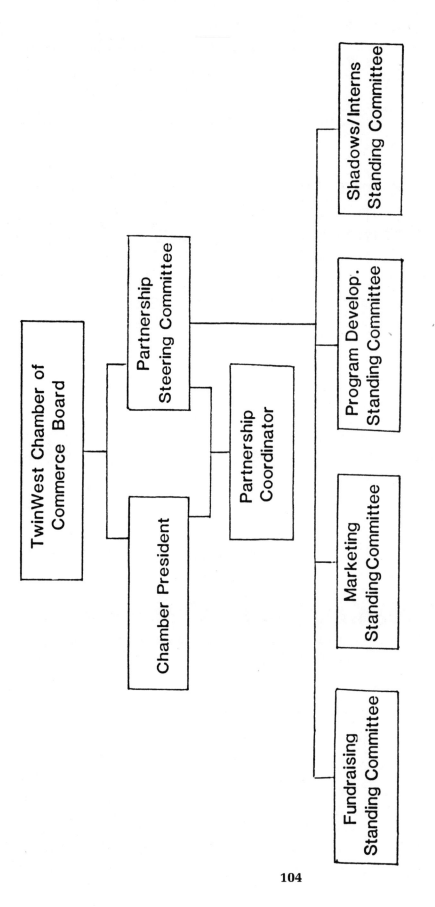

TwinWest Business–Education Partnership Organizational Chart

Reprinted by permission of the TwinWest Business-Education Partnership, MN.

Figure 9–3

ACTION PLAN

Description of Need: There is a need to provide career information to youth while either in school or participating in a youth agency using a variety of techniques.

Goal Statement: Establish a Community-Based Career Guidance System.

Objective	Activity(ies)	Person(s) Responsible	Resources Needed	Cost (Amount & Source)	Evaluation
1 Establish a process for a student career plan.	2.1.1 Subcommittee within School District has been formed to review best method of implementation.	2.1.1 Stanley Stoncius Principal, Nashua Senior High School.	2.1.1 On page 15 in the <u>Report of the Program Evaluation Study</u> establishes need for Career Planning.	2.1.1 None	2.1.1 Report.
	2.1.2 Agencies will review Career Plan document to determine their role.	2.1.2 To be determined.	2.1.2 Report submitted (<u>Report of the Program Evaluation Study.</u>)	2.1.2 None	2.1.2 Agency Report.
2 Establish a computer-assisted Career Guidance Network at Nashua High School, three Jr. High Schools, Boys Club, Girls Club and Adult Learning Center.	2.2.1 Research a number of computerized career programs.	2.2.1 John Cepaitis.	2.2.1 None	2.2.1 None	2.2.1 Report.

Figure 9–4

ACTIVITY TIMELINE

Activity	July	Aug.	Sept.	Oct.	Nov.	Dec.	Jan.	Feb.	Mar.	Apr.	May	June

Reprinted by permission of the Nashua, NH, Partnership in Education Program.

Figure 9–4 (continued)

HOUSTON INDEPENDENT SCHOOL DISTRICT
VIPS ADOPT-A-SCHOOL

DATE	COMPONENT	ACTIVITIES	RESPONSIBILITY
July 23, 19XX	Adopt-A-School Committee Meeting.	Plan August 5 meeting with principals. Materials in final form.	
July 24, 19XX	HISD trustee's meeting.	Identification of target magnet schools.	
July 29, 19XX	Chamber of Commerce Executive Committee Meeting.	Education committee, Chamber of Commerce, requests commitment to recruitment of corporations to adopt magnet schools.	
August 5, 19XX	Meeting with principals of targeted magnet schools, Chamber of Commerce representatives, and area superintendents.	Explain and sell Adopt-A-School idea. Agree on goals. Agree on needs assessment form and reporting. Get commitment of principals.	
August 13, 19XX	All magnet school principals.	See activities for August 5.	
August 14, 19XX	Chamber of Commerce.	See activities for August 5.	
August 15, 19XX	Needs assessments sent to schools.		
October 1, 19XX	Reporting system set up.	Reporting form developed in coordination with magnet school and O.C.E. staffs.	
October 6, 19XX	Needs assessments returned to VIPS office and analyzed.	School needs and commitment assessed.	

Figure 9–5

DATE	COMPONENT	ACTIVITIES	RESPONSIBILITY
December 1, 19XX	Individual corporate commitments brought in. Workshop on school contacts.	Chamber of Commerce has results of four months of recruitment of corporations. Degree of commitment is assessed.	
February 1, 19XX	Majority of targeted schools will have at least one business committed to adoption. Orientation for business contacts.	From Chamber of Commerce information, principal's needs assessments, consequent conversations with magnet school director, principals, and corporations, decide on matches and initiate contacts.	
October 1, 19XX through May 1, 19XX	Continued matching of businesses and schools and on-site orientation.	Continue above activity. Arrange meetings of volunteer corporations and school personnel at the schools. Orient both parties to other's commitments and restrictions.	
January 31, 19XX through May 1, 19XX	Follow-up.	Analysis of reports. Phone calls to contact persons. Visits to schools.	
April 19XX	Evaluation.	Develop with Department of Research and Evaluation.	
February 1, 19XX through May 19XX	Public relations.	With Information Services and IMS Task Force, distribute press releases, do talk shows, seize opportunities to speak to civic and business groups.	

Reprinted by permission of the Houston Independent School District, TX.

Figure 9–5 (continued)

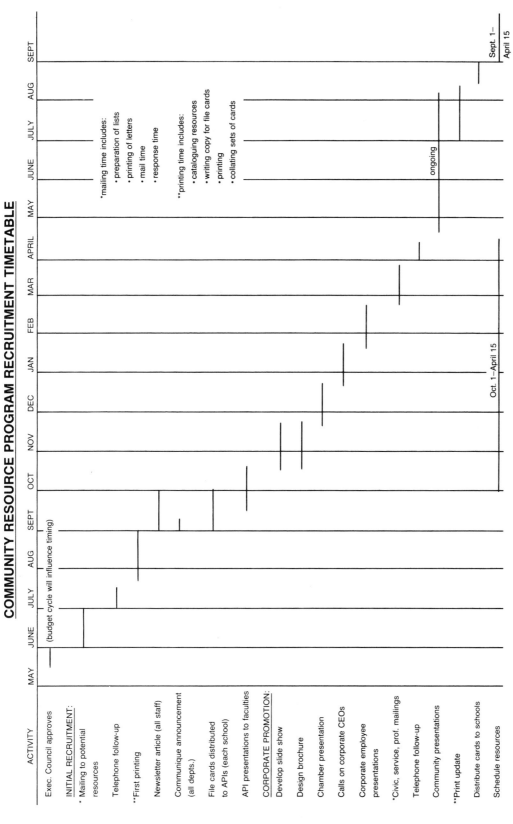

COMMUNITY RESOURCE PROGRAM RECRUITMENT TIMETABLE

| ACTIVITY | MAY | JUNE | JULY | AUG | SEPT | OCT | NOV | DEC | JAN | FEB | MAR | APRIL | MAY | JUNE | JULY | AUG | SEPT |

Exec. Council approves

(budget cycle will influence timing)

INITIAL RECRUITMENT:

* Mailing to potential resources

Telephone follow-up

**First printing

Newsletter article (all staff)

Communique announcement (all depts.)

File cards distributed to APIs (each school)

API presentations to faculties

CORPORATE PROMOTION:

Develop slide show

Design brochure

Chamber presentation

Calls on corporate CEOs

Corporate employee presentations

*Civic, service, prof. mailings

Telephone follow-up

Community presentations

**Print update

Distribute cards to schools

Schedule resources

*mailing time includes:
• preparation of lists
• printing of letters
• mail time
• response time

**printing time includes:
• cataloguing resources
• writing copy for file cards
• printing
• collating sets of cards

ongoing

Oct. 1–April 15

Sept. 1– April 15

Reprinted by permission of the Community Resource Program, Charlotte-Mecklenburg Schools, NC.

Figure 9–6

109

CAPS START-UP TIMELINE

MONTH(S)	ONGOING COMPANIES	NEWLY RECRUITED COMPANIES
• May/June	Preliminary school site assessment	
• June/Aug	Company contact	
• September	School site reassessment Company approval Recruitment, Orientation Selection of employees	
• October	School site orientation Placement	School site assessments
• Nov/Dec	Ongoing evaluation	Company contacts
• January	Team training/sharing sessions 1st semester evaluation Placement adjustments as needed	Company approval Recruitment of employees
• February	Ongoing evaluation	Orientation Selection of employees (mid-February) School site orientation
• March	Ongoing evaluation	Placement of corporate volunteers (early March)
• April	Ongoing evaluation	Ongoing evaluation
• May	2nd semester evaluation	Ongoing evaluation Semester evaluation
• June	Company sharing sessions Recognition	Company sharing sessions Recognition

Reprinted by permission of Corporate Action in Public Schools (CAPS), CA.

Figure 9–7

Staffing Your Partnership: Roles and Responsibilities

Your management team has found a home. The team's organizational structure and timelines for partnership development have been established. Now it's time to consider staffing your partnership program. Effective, coordinated staffing inspires credibility and respect for the program from all partners. During this staffing process, consideration must be given to

- how staffing will be structured
- roles and responsibilities of staff
- skills required for accomplishment of tasks
- the use of job descriptions as staffing tools
- partnership staff training

STAFFING STRUCTURES OF PARTNERSHIPS

Within or Outside a School District?

Partnership programs are relatively new phenomena, and few partnerships are established independently. When developed *within* a school district, many of these programs have evolved as arms or integral parts of the offices of grants, community relations, desegregation, or state and federal programs. Support staff within the larger office may be assigned either part-time to the partnership or on an as-needed basis. Integration of the partnership program with established programs may be successful or difficult, depending on (1) how programs complement each other and (2) whether there is sufficient staff to accomplish successfully tasks and objectives of *all* programs involved.

When it is developed *outside* the district (for example, under the auspices of a chamber of commerce, the office of a community agency or business organization, or foundation), the partnership has a more independent structure. Staff are assigned to the program from the school district or from a sponsoring agency; often staff are lent part- or full-time to the partnership for a specified period of time.

Staffing Structures

No matter what the partnership's location or format, staffing structures of partnerships do not differ markedly from one another. The management staff usually includes a director-coordinator–program administrator who has some support staff. This support staff can include administrative assistants or program leaders, secretaries, consultants, and evaluation specialists. Support staff can also mean coordinators and volunteers from both the school site (principals, supervisors, teachers, aides) and the community and business.

From the partnership survey, it was learned that most programs have two to seven staff members based at a central office; 73 percent of the staff work in these programs on a part-time basis. Sixty-five percent of those working in the programs are employed by school districts; the remainder are employed by the private sector. Most of the central partnership staff are paid. Workers in the field are nearly all volunteers.

ROLES AND RESPONSIBILITIES OF PARTNERSHIP STAFF

The Management Team

Members of the partnership team

- act as catalysts, thereby encouraging and facilitating relationships between the school district and the community at large
- solicit, coordinate, and assign resources (human, material, financial) to best meet identified needs and school improvement efforts
- take care of transportation, paperwork, and preparation and dissemination of materials relating to the program
- orient, train (as appropriate), and recognize human resources for their services to students and school staff

The Director

Partnership programs are led by people with such titles as director, executive director, coordinator, or manager. If the job of partnership director is only one part of a larger responsibility, the project director might also be the principal, assistant to the superintendent, coordinator of career education, community resource assistant, community school coordinator, or director of vocational education.

According to the survey, most partnership leaders function under the direct supervision of the school district; they may report to the superintendent of schools, an assistant superintendent, or an executive director of another department. Within these boundaries, the partnership's governing council performs a purely advisory function.

If they are based outside the school district, partnership leaders might report to the director of the local chamber of commerce, to another community agency, or directly to the partnership's governing council or board of directors. Occasionally, the partnership director is "split" and becomes responsible to both an outside governing council *and* the board of education.

Whatever the title, wherever the base of operations, the partnership's director has a broadly conceived role. The director must be proactive–the spokesperson, orchestrator, liaison, and leader of the project. Responsibilities of this leader are (1) to guide and manage the planning, development, implementation, supervision, monitoring, and evaluation of the project; (2) to recruit partners and staff; (3) to facilitate solutions to problems concerning staff, project activities, program image, fund raising (as appropriate) and relationships between partners; and (4) to establish and extend the necessary communications network between participating partners.

Assistants to the Project Director

In large partnership programs with many components (for example, volunteer, adopt-a-school, vocational, or mentoring programs), assistants are responsible for management of individual program areas as if each area were a minipartnership. In smaller programs, where there may be one assistant or a secretary-assistant, this person provides support to the director in *all* project areas.

The Secretarial Staff and Interns

Secretaries may be hired on a part- or full-time basis. Often these secretaries work for supervisors of other programs; they perform only selected tasks to assist with partnership activities. Whenever possible, it is better to have a part-time secretary with responsibility *solely* to the partnership than a full-time staff person who has divided loyalties among projects.

Secretarial responsibilities include the usual correspondence and clerical duties. This staff member is often the first line of communication (by phone, correspondence, or meeting) between outside partners and the partnership and should, therefore, *consistently* communicate positively with the partnership's public, be sensitive to the needs and concerns of all partners, and express enthusiastic commitment to the partnership concept.

Interns, whether on summer or regular schedules, whether paid or volunteer, will help (1) expedite program research; (2) facilitate the organization and implementation of meetings and other partnership events; (3) attend school advisory council meetings (and report and record proceedings); and (4) act as liaisons at a variety of partnership events.

School Site Staff

Partnership staff at a school site are drawn from the school's staff of principal, supervisors, teachers, and aides. Although these staff have primary responsibilities in the area of educational management and instruction, they make an additional commitment to act as the partnership's school coordinators or facilitators.

Usually, if a partnership program is based at a school, a coordinator is designated to administer and facilitate activities. The principal retains overall responsibility for the partnership as he or she does of *all* school programs.

The School Coordinator. Whether the site coordinator is the principal, another supervisor, or a teacher, the coordinator is the liaison for the partnership between staff members within the school, between the school and its partner(s), and between the school and the partnership's central office. The coordinator acts as a resource person and facilitator in relation to these partnership activities:

- conducting the school's needs assessment
- reviewing available resources
- matching needs to resources
- designing programs (with others) that meet identified needs
- setting up schedules and routines that are agreeable to both school and business-community partners
- arranging for (and sometimes conducting) orientation and training programs for partners and school staff
- monitoring and reviewing programs (as appropriate) and helping to adjust these programs as necessary
- keeping supervisors both in school and at the central office apprised—in a timely fashion—of the partnership's successes and problems.

The Teacher. What about the classroom teacher who participates in the partnership program, but is *not* the school's coordinator? Teachers are responsible to use available resources (school coordinator, central office liaison, partners, equipment) to meet class and student educational needs. If the program invites participation in professional self-development activities, teachers should avail themselves of this opportunity. Teachers should also make an effort to attend partnership events; this attendance publicly signals staff interest and commitment to the program.

A School Advisory Council. The advisory council is a support tool for the partnership at the school site level. These councils are usually composed of representatives from the following groups: supervisors, teachers, parents, students (as appropriate) and business-community partners. The chair of that council is the school partnership coordinator. If that responsibility has been delegated by the principal to another staff member, the principal sits on the council as a member.

The council meets regularly to solve problems and make decisions related to partnership policy, procedures, and activities (as appropriate). Meeting minutes are recorded, prepared, and disseminated in a timely manner to council members, to parents, to partners, and to the central partnership office.

Consultants

Consultants can be helpful, during the partnership's early development, in

- assisting the partnership staff in establishing program guidelines, structures, and procedures
- setting up communication networks
- researching, compiling, and analyzing data
- facilitating decision making

The independent perspective and outside support from consultants to the partnership can be extended (if appropriate) as the partnership grows; for example, consultants can help the program tap into wider regional and national resources.

The Superintendent, Board of Education, and other Central Office Administrators

The superintendent's primary responsibility is to display commitment to the program, consistently and visibly, through

- attendance at partnership events (including recognition and "adoption" ceremonies)
- meetings with business and community leaders
- presentations in support of the program at community events (Rotary luncheons, village and city council meetings, chamber of commerce activities)
- hiring practices that result in experienced staff
- behaviors that encourage partnership staff to extend their expertise in program management (regional and national conferences, visits to exemplary programs)

The superintendent is also responsible for obtaining the commitment of the district's board of education. This responsibility is something that *only* a superintendent can do! Once the board is committed, it articulates this commitment through such formal procedures as a board resolution in support of the program and attendance at various partnership events.

Partnership Liaisons: Widespread Involvement as a Critical Issue

Who acts as the liaison between the school district and its business partners? Anyone involved in a partnership program—central-office partnership staff, administrators (superintendent's office or school site), partnership coordinators (at businesses, in agencies, or in schools), the governing council, teachers and students—could be considered liaisons between the school district and its larger community. They are potential ambassadors of good will for the program, communicating the enthusiasm and commitment that must be present if the partnership is to maintain its momentum and flourish.

SKILLS REQUIRED OF PARTNERSHIP STAFF

All partnership staff should have excellent organizational and communication skills. They are in the service business and, as such, should demonstrate that

- they can effectively communicate the program to a range of community and school groups
- they are flexible and resourceful when administering a program that has many, often disparate, pieces to coordinate
- they can organize both tasks and people
- they know and understand the needs and resources of their particular community
- they enjoy what they are doing and are committed to the partnership concept

USE OF GUIDELINES AND JOB DESCRIPTIONS AS STAFFING TOOLS

Guidelines and descriptions are useful tools to define jobs and responsibilities for applicants. Decisions can then be made about employment and supervision related to needed staff skills, number of staff required, and responsibilities to be assigned. Some examples of job descriptions currently used to assist partnership leaders in managing, staffing, and supervising their programs come from the TwinWest Business-Education Partnership, MN (see Figure 10-1) and the Houston Independent School District, TX (see Figures 10-2 and 10-3).

PARTNERSHIP STAFF DEVELOPMENT

A major responsibility for partnership leaders concerns staff development programs for all partners—schools, and community-business. This responsibility falls under two areas—orientation and training.

Orientation

Yearly, biannual, or quarterly orientation activities (1) provide a program overview to partners, volunteers, and staff who are new to the partnership concept and program; and (2) give the partnership an opportunity to motivate and solidify commitment of all participants. In addition, orientations (3) provide guidelines for program activities for the coming months; (4) inform participants of schedules for activities and training; and (5) reacquaint partners with the organizational structure, objectives, staff and procedures of the program. An agenda, from an orientation meeting held by the Los Angeles Adopt-A-School Program, CA (see Figure

10-4), illustrates the plan and associated tasks of an orientation activity as do the comprehensive guidelines used by The Houston Independent School District, TX (see Figure 10-5), during orientation sessions for their business volunteers.

Many programs also prepare specific handbooks that provide such information for all participants; these can be updated and extended as the partnership grows and matures. Excellent examples may be ordered from Hudson, OH; Memphis, TN; San Diego, CA; PIPE in Seattle, WA; Richmond, VA; Chicago, IL; Tulsa, OK; and the Massachusetts State Department of Education. See the Appendixes for further contact information.

Staff Training

Staff training for all partners (school, business, civic) is a regular, ongoing responsibility of program leaders. Training sessions should be held on a regular basis—monthly or quarterly—with *activities planned well ahead of time* to facilitate the schedules of all partners.

Usually, more informal staff training sessions are held for particular groups (school and business coordinators, partnership staff, teachers, volunteers, and so forth). These small group sessions are held (as appropriate and convenient) at the partnership's central office, at a partner's office, or at school sites. Training activities are designed to improve partnership leaders' and their staffs' competence in such areas as

1. facilitation and management of the partnership program and its activities
2. development of group process and interpersonal skills
3. recruitment of partners
4. communication skills
5. fund raising
6. training of volunteers

One important training priority focuses on the training of school volunteers who provide regular assistance to school staff and students in such areas as tutoring, enrichment activities, and classroom "housekeeping" chores. Training sessions may be directed at staff who are using volunteers in their schools and classrooms, on volunteers who are assisting teachers and other educators, or on school coordinators who will be administering these volunteer programs at the school site. Susan Taranto's excellent book, *Coordinating Your School Volunteer Program* (VORT Corporation, 1983), gives extensive information regarding training specifically for school volunteer programs.

Training for partnership leaders and staff sometimes occurs through an alliance between the local district, the state department of education, local community groups, and colleges (if available). Such alliances, for example, provided local partnerships with extended support, experience, and expertise in Nashua, NH, and in school districts throughout Pennsylvania, Indiana, North Carolina, and Florida.

TwinWest Chamber of Commerce

POSITION DESCRIPTION: Coordinator for TwinWest Business-Education Partnership

ACCOUNTABLE TO: Assistant Director of the TwinWest Chamber of Commerce for daily operations and the steering committee of the TwinWest Business-Education Partnership for program model and philosophy.

I. Position Summary

To promote and foster new and existing relationships between business and education. To become a resource and key contact for business and education and to provide the link between the business and education communities.

II. Specific Responsibilities

A. Develop a networking system that identifies and creates an awareness of training, retraining, and educational programs being conducted through the Business-Education Partnership where schools and businesses share their resources.

B. Facilitate growth and development of programs serving students, teachers, and the school district as a whole as part of the Business-Education Partnership (i.e., student and teacher internships, career shadowing, leadership exchange).

C. Work with Committee on estimating budget of Business-Education Partnership.

D. Prepare support material as requested by the Business-Education Steering Committee.

E. Work with Committee in developing yearly program goals to be approved by the Chamber Board.

F. Coordinate the development of appropriate promotional materials for the Business-Education Partnership.

G. Coordinate special projects and programs sponsored through the Business-Education Partnership (i.e., special seminars and career shadowing for hearing impaired).

H. Publicize and promote partnership concept through presentations and written articles.

I. Other responsibilities as directed by the Chamber of Commerce or the Business-Education Partnership Steering Committee.

Figure 10–1

III. Qualifications

    A. Ability to assume initiative in program development and problem solving.

    B. Demonstrated strong communication skills (written, oral, and with groups).

    C. Strong organizational skills.

    D. A working knowledge of the business and educational communities and their programs.

    E. An understanding of the differences between such programs as internships, mentor programs, community involvement activities, and cooperative vocational education is desirable.

    F. B.A. Degree preferred with two years of related experience.

IV. Internal Relationships

Work with Chamber staff members as necessary to interpret chamber policy, publicize partnership, and produce support materials.

V. External Relationships

Work with schools and membership determining needs and encouraging involvement. Maintain contact with other districts, associations, and partnership projects.

Extensive work with volunteers.

Reprinted by permission of the TwinWest Business-Education Partnership, MN.

Figure 10–1 (continued)

Business/School
Partnership Program
Houston Independent School District

SCHOOL-LEVEL BUSINESS COORDINATOR
JOB DESCRIPTION

The principal of the school will appoint a school-level business coordinator to handle the logistics of business contributions of time and materials.

DUTIES

The school-level business coordinator will:

1. Assist the principal in conducting a needs assessment.

2. Once a business is recruited, attend all meetings of the Principal, VIPS, and corporate representatives to aid in working out details of the partnerships.

3. Conduct an orientation to school policies and the building for business volunteers. Give guidelines to the volunteers. Encourage them to work with the curriculum. VIPS will help with the orientation.

4. With the principal, match business volunteers and donations to individual teachers. Give guidelines to teachers.

5. Arrange initial contacts between teacher and volunteer. Make certain a starting date, time, and place are established and that the volunteer will have something specific to do, even if it is only observation the first time.

6. Follow up after the first appointment and see that the date, time, and place are determined for subsequent meetings.

7. Be the contact person for the VIPS office and the volunteers.

8. Record hours and contributions and report to VIPS office.

9. Arrange official school recognition of deserving business contributions.

10. Perform ongoing evaluation of the program and coordinate recommendations and requests for additional services or volunteers.

11. See that the business is officially reinvited in the fall or notify VIPS if this is not to be the case.

QUALIFICATIONS

The school-level business coordinator must possess knowledge of the school staff and be a respected member of the school team. This coordinator must

> be committed to the business partnership idea

> have a good mind for detail and follow-through

> be a person who can be counted on to do what is agreed upon

> have a telephone at the school

Suggested Candidates: Home School Community Agent, Counselor, Magnet School Coordinator, Vice Principal

Reprinted by permission of the Houston Independent School District, TX.
Figure 10–2

**Business/School
Partnership Program**
Houston Independent School District

COMPANY COORDINATOR

After executive approval has been given for the project, a coordinator within the company should be appointed. This person is the direct link between the school, HISD's VIPS staff and the company. The coordinator would be responsible for:

- Meeting with principal, school contact, and VIPS to determine needs of the school.

- Preparing recruitment materials.

- Informing and recruiting potential volunteers. A packet could be prepared with materials available from VIPS.

- Obtaining support and authorization of immediate supervisors for release of employees.

- Arranging orientation and other meetings.

- Facilitating transportation.

- Arranging for other resources and/or programs provided by the company for the school.

- Arranging for company recognition of its volunteers.

- Arranging a "rap" session in the summer for company volunteers, school contact person, and VIPS coordinator.

This person would facilitate communication between company top-level staff and its employees as well as between the company and HISD.

It is essential that the coordinator be well informed about the project and believe in the value of the program.

Having a committee rather than one person responsible for the project would give continuity to the Business-School Partnership in case of employee termination or transfer.

The company coordinator should be high-enough level to get things done.

Reprinted by permission of the Houston Independent School District, TX.
(adapted from a job description form of the SFEF, CA).

Figure 10–3

LOS ANGELES UNIFIED SCHOOL DISTRICT

Adopt-A-School Program

**MEETING OF ADOPT-A-SCHOOL CENTRAL STAFF
AND REGION/DIVISION ADMINISTRATORS**

Mayfair Hotel
September 4, 1985

GOAL: To Assure a Quality Program for Each Partnership

AGENDA

1. Welcome

2. Introductions

3. Breakfast Is Served

4. Adopt-A-School—Past, Present, Future   Bruce Schwaegler
Co-Chairperson
Adopt-A-School Program

5. Adopt-A-School Council Activities   Iris Hackett
Chairperson
Adopt-A-School Council

6. Annual Report

7. Expectations   Richard A. Ragus
Assistant Superintendent

8. First Actions

9. Questions and Answers

10. Announcements

11. Adjourn

Reprinted by permission of Adopt-A-School Program, Los Angeles Unified School District, CA.
Figure 10–4

Business/School
Partnership
Program

ORIENTATION GUIDELINES

Suggested information and procedures to be presented to business volunteers at the school

A. <u>BECOMING ACQUAINTED</u>

    1. Introduction to administration, staff, and pupils when appropriate.
    2. Description of school community.
    3. Tour of school plant (give a school map if available).
        —traffic patterns, entrances, exits
        —fire drill routes and locations
        —restroom locations (students and adults)
        —supply rooms
        —location and availability of instructional materials
        —eating facilities
        —parking facilities
        —smoking facilities
    4. Observation of classroom.
    5. Individual and family background (from the student's teacher when appropriate—information to be kept confidential).

B. <u>PERSONAL RESPONSIBILITIES</u>

    1. Absences (procedures to follow).
    2. Checking in and out (time sheet—where it is).
    3. Reading posted bulletins.
    4. Proper dress.
    5. Use of school equipment.
    6. Confidentiality of school records.
    7. Critical observations regarding students or staff should be taken directly to the teacher, the school coordinator, or the principal.

C. <u>SCHOOL POLICIES</u>

    1. Regular and Minimum Day Schedules (give an HISD calendar).
    2. Discipline.
    3. Releasing children to adults.
    4. Visitors.
    5. Students leaving classroom.
    6. Teacher leaving classroom.
    7. Use of school phone.
    8. Books sent home.
    9. Homework.
    10. Notes, letters sent home.
    11. School keys.
    12. Emergency calls during school hours.
    13. Use of custodial services.
    14. Lost and Found.
    15. Meetings.

Figure 10–5

D. ASSIGNMENT OF VOLUNTEER

Tell the volunteers you will make every effort to see that they are contented with their assignments. We believe this is essential for the welfare of the volunteer, the students, and the school staff. If for any reason their work is not satisfying, is nonproductive, or is not comfortable, they should immediately discuss a change with the school coordinator or principal.

Reprinted by permission of the Houston Independent School District, TX
(form adapted from NSVP, VA).

Figure 10–5 (continued)

Financing a Partnership: Budgeting, Expenditure of Funds, and Fund Raising

Although "quantity" doesn't necessarily mean "quality," it is helpful for a partnership program to have financial security. Traditionally, in supplemental programs (like partnerships), financial support to fund both current operations and special events comes from the school district and from federal and state sources. However, businesses, nonprofit and local governmental agencies, community and parent groups, and foundations provide additional financial support to partnerships through direct monies and in-kind resources. In-kind resources include:

- office space
- on-loan staff
- transportation
- postage
- tickets for events

- payment of administrative, accounting, and legal costs
- clerical and secretarial support
- printing and preparation of materials
- telephone
- materials and equipment

WHO CONTROLS THE PARTNERSHIP'S FUNDS AND HOW ARE THEY ADMINISTERED?

Funds Controlled Internally

There is usually some question whether it is easier or more efficient if the partnership funds are controlled by an outside agency or directly by the school district. Funds handled internally (as they are in most programs) are subject to a myriad of bureaucratic problems—particularly in larger cities where every program is treated the same; that is, *all* programs (regardless of their size and format) must use funds in accordance with standard operating procedures (SOPs). District regulations can be obstacles to expediting procedures related to (1) bidding for site

125

usage, equipment, and supplies, (2) fee payment for consultants, and (3) arrangements for additional stipends for district staff who work beyond the regular school day. The amount of time and energy partnership leaders must spend on processing and facilitating these SOPs diverts their energies (and strains their patience) from productive program tasks.

On the other hand, school districts usually feel more comfortable when the bulk of monies for any of their school projects is within their control. They may be right. Stricter district regulations provide guidelines to deter mismanagement of funds.

The partnership's project director is usually responsible to the district's business office, superintendent, and board of education for administering the funds in a fiscally prudent manner. Sometimes, major funding is managed by the partnership's director, while limited discretionary funds are given to individual schools or programs.

With such internal financial controls, the partnership leader has access to support and guidance from district business administrators and staff, who can help directors of special programs deal with day-to-day budget details and problems. Many program leaders are already familiar with preparing and dispersing monies associated with large budgets. *What differs in partnership programs* is that

- direct private funding is additionally involved.
- in-kind resources (human and material) must also be taken into account when partnership funding is discussed. For example, how do you determine that so many volunteer hours, or pieces of equipment, or tickets to events are equated to X dollars?
- solicitation of funding and in-kind resources can be assigned and then become an additional and time-consuming responsibility of the partnership staff.

Funds Handled Externally

Funding for the partnership may be managed and therefore controlled outside of the school district. Monies are placed in a separate account under the aegis of a governing council, a foundation, committee or community agency.

What does such external control mean? Budgets are then approved by the outside agency rather than the school district's budget office. Activities like payment of bills, transfer of monies from one account to another, and expenditures of funds are submitted directly to the person or office that makes accounting and budgeting decisions for that external agency. Advantages to this arrangement are clear: the partnership does not have to maneuver each budget task through the bureaucratic ladder for approval. Unfortunately, most school districts will not allow any programs connected with or under their jurisdiction to have any large amount of program funds placed outside of their control; state guidelines relative to budgeting and accounting in public school districts often further restrict outside control of school program funds.

Split Control of Funds

Partnerships often have affiliations with other organizations that have similar philosophies and goals and are in strong financial positions. In such cases, control of partnership funds is then split between the school district and an outside agency.

BUDGET DESIGN AND IMPLEMENTATION

What we are concerned about here is how funding can be effectively coordinated and efficiently administered by partnership staff. Understanding of budget design and implementation is a key objective.

Help in Budget Preparation and Implementation

Experience tells us that district business administrators can provide powerful support to the partnership as it develops and matures. It is important to note here that a constructive relationship between program and business administrators does not just happen; it must be nurtured in order to obtain the full benefit of these advisers' experience and expertise.

Partnership staff should not ignore the help available in budget preparation from their district business offices. Consultants from the business departments of partners, or lawyers and accountants from other nonprofit organizations, offer additional perspectives on setting up budgets and expediting financial recordkeeping when managing and administering special programs. For example, a detailed paper for reference on financial recordkeeping and control in relation to nonprofit organizations can be obtained from Harvey Schwartz, Hood and Strong, Certified Public Accountants (advisers to the San Francisco Education Fund, CA). *Note:* See the appendix for further contact information.

Budget Design

In answer to the question, "What budget format do you use?" partnership leaders supplied a range of alternatives in samples of their budget formats. In part, the budget categories they listed reflect two important considerations related to budget design:

• *The budget categories available to the partnership director.* An overwhelming majority of the partnerships used budget formats exactly like or complementary to the formats of the organization that controlled their funds; program leaders found it easier to be in step in this area.

• *The goals and objectives of the partnership program.* The budget is considered a planning tool; therefore budget categories that are listed indicate which program areas require funding in order to implement partnership activities successfully and to attain partnership objectives.

A list of program areas, drawn from the budget samples submitted through the survey, should be helpful to partnership leaders who are developing budgets for their programs.

LIST OF BUDGET CATEGORIES FROM SAMPLE BUDGETS

PERSONNEL

    ADMINISTRATORS

    COORDINATORS-PROGRAM LEADERS

    OFFICE ASSISTANTS

    SECRETARIAL-CLERICAL WORKERS

BENEFITS

    SOCIAL SECURITY

    RETIREMENT

    GROUP MEDICAL

    GROUP DENTAL

    GROUP LIFE

    VISION INSURANCE

    WORKMEN'S COMPENSATION

    UNEMPLOYMENT COMPENSATION

    EMPLOYEE COUNSELING

OTHER PROFESSIONAL AND TECHNICAL HELP

    CONSULTANTS

    RESEARCHERS

    INTERNS

EVALUATION

SPEAKERS

TRAVEL AND TRANSPORTATION (FOR STUDENTS AND STAFF)

    LOCAL—MILEAGE/CARFARE

    OUT-OF-DISTRICT

SUPPLIES (GENERAL, OFFICE, ACTIVITIES)

BOOKS

REPRODUCTION, PRINTING, BINDING

ACCOUNTING

LEGAL ADVICE

EQUIPMENT

    RENTAL

    REPAIR AND MAINTENANCE

    NEW AND ADDITIONAL

CONFERENCES (STAFF, VOLUNTEERS, PARTNERS)

    ACCOMMODATIONS

    MEALS

    TRANSPORTATION

    REGISTRATION FEES

    SUPPLIES (FOR PRESENTERS)

    MISCELLANEOUS

HOSPITALITY (MEALS, SITE USAGE, ETC.)

TELEPHONE

GENERAL BUSINESS EXPENSES

RECOGNITION (AWARDS, CERTIFICATES, ETC.)

MISCELLANEOUS (ENTRANCE FEES, ETC.)

SCHOOL SITE COORDINATORS

    ADMINISTRATORS

    TEACHERS

POSTAGE

IN-SERVICE PAYMENTS

INDIRECT COSTS

Budget Preparation

Living with Available Funding. Your business office knows *never* to count on promises of additional funding. Therefore, business staff will help you

    a. plan activities within the limits of existing funding

    b. project program expenses for the school year

    c. develop a cushion of funding for contingencies

Note: In-kind services (human resources, equipment, and materials) should be given a value to help determine what is the *real* cost of operating your partnership. If such in-kind support is decreased or terminated, early determination of the value attached to these services will help prepare you to identify and plan for the full costs associated both with maintaining current levels of operations and future program expansion.

Timing of Budget Preparation. Good budget planning also dictates that budget formats be developed with some financial advice *before* any disbursement of funding for program activities. Such consultation helps the partnership's director

a. set up budget categories that meet the needs of the project.

b. allocate available funding to specified accounts.

c. obtain information regarding business office procedures for reporting and submitting purchase orders and other forms allied to budget requests. Particular attention should be paid to procedures relative to (1) consultants, (2) part-time personnel, (3) evaluation, (4) conference registration and out-of-district travel, and (5) required support documentation (bids, agendas, lists of participants) supporting expenditures.

d. "read" financial printouts (balance sheets, encumbrances, and so forth)

e. learn procedures related to waivers, board resolutions, and fiscal reporting

Submitting Your Budget for Approval

Certain forms must be submitted, duly signed by authorized representatives of the organization, submitted to the organization's board or council, and approved at a public session. To obtain timely approval of the program's budget, the partnership director obtains accurate information about these forms and the process described above and *meticulously* follows the prescribed procedures. The organization's business office and the office of the superintendent can assist you through this process.

One special reminder: Make certain that sufficient time is allowed for the process. You must meet the schedules of regular board meetings; boards have different schedules and usually do not meet more often than bimonthly or monthly.

Ongoing Monitoring of the Budget

Once you have submitted your budget and it has been approved, you will receive regular printouts of budget expenditures and deposits. Even the most carefully prepared budgets require changes. Business experts can assist you in long-range planning to alleviate particular problems and expedite any changes. Once again, your responsibility is to complete forms correctly, obtain necessary approvals, and submit all required materials in a timely manner.

Please remember that shifting monies from one account to another (an ordinary task in these programs) might take more time than you anticipated and your business office may not have *that* transfer as a priority. Allow two weeks to one month for any change procedures before you draw upon accounts to which you have transferred funds, especially in large school districts.

Preparing Financial Reports

Depending on the size of the project and the financial guidelines of the organization that controls the funding, financial reports are requested and usually submitted at least yearly, or, more usually, on a quarterly basis. Sometimes short monthly reports are required, and a final report is submitted at the end of the school year (in July).

Format of Financial Reports. In some school districts, the partnership's yearly expenditures are submitted as an integral part of an all-district programs' report. A short financial statement then becomes an addendum to this final evaluation. With other partnerships, the initial budget is submitted side by side with the yearly financial statement, illustrating the differences between proposed and final budget allocations and expenditures.

Financial reports may be presented in global terms with specific items listed but only totals given, as is shown in the financial statement from the Peninsula Academies, CA (see Figure 11-1). A fiscal statement, in a more detailed form, can be seen in the Corporate Action Committee's report, CA (see Figure 11-2).

Purposes of Financial Reports

These financial reports

- inform district supervisors, boards of education, and governing councils of program income, expenses, and allocations of resources to specific project areas, over specified periods of time.
- provide opportunities to observe project growth and to chart actual and potential fiscal problems.
- provide a fiscal record related to funding and human and material resources. Such in-kind resources can be translated into income and printed as part of a project's income statement (see Figure 11-3, from the PIPE Program, Seattle, WA).
- become the basis for partnership program planning for the coming school year.

FUND RAISING

Most partnerships, like any other supplemental program, require a measure of financial support to enable them to concentrate on current operations in addition to program expansion. Therefore, attracting and generating consistent funding for program management and activities assumes a priority status. Specific fund-raising tasks must be carefully organized to achieve maximum financial benefits for each partnership and avoid detracting from program effectiveness by spending inordinate amounts of time on maintaining fiscal solvency.

Fund raising is no easy task. There are usually obstacles—especially because you are asking for funds in support of *public* education. The community at large already pays taxes that support public schools; people will question why they should provide additional revenues. Recent negative perceptions of achievement by public education provide additional obstacles to a climate of giving.

Short- and Long-Range Planning

The obstacles mentioned above can be overcome; the emphasis once again is on planning. Consideration is given to the scope of your partnership, remembering that scope is determined by *both* needs and available resources. To ensure that expectations are appropriate in relation to resources, you should be able to answer the following questions:

• What is the community climate regarding contributions to local projects? Have recent efforts to secure funding by the school district or other nonprofit groups been successful? If so, why? If not, why not?

• Has your school district been the recent recipient of monies or large in-kind donations? Have donors been satisfied with the way these donations were used?

• What are the potential sources of funding? Who (school district personnel or friends of the school district) has access to these funding sources?

• How much additional funding is required to maintain or extend the program efficiently and effectively?

If you can respond positively to these questions, and if additional funds are needed, the next step is to design a fund-raising plan that ensures achievement of financial goals.

The Organization of Fund Raising

The process of planning, targeting, developing, and implementing financial support may be packaged through

- funding proposals
- a series of fund-raising events
- submission to partners of a yearly operating budget with an accompanying cover report
- telephone campaign solicitations
- written campaign solicitations
- hiring an outside consultant to conduct a fund-raising campaign
- a combination of the above

Close, concentrated coordination and supervision of fund-raising efforts ensures that potential donors are neither missed nor bombarded by multiple requests.

Depending on the magnitude of the task, part- or full-time volunteers or paid staff are solicited or assigned to assist the fund-raising chairperson. Sometimes, business advisory or fund-raising committees—staffed by both paid and volunteer workers—are formed to both identify and recruit funding sources.

What if your program's staff is too small in number or too busy to assume additional yearly fund-raising responsibilities? Some survey respondents use volunteer governing council members or other key people from the business and civic community to support or completely run fund-raising efforts. Leaders said their volunteers, plus other members from the community at large, assisted in fund raising as follows:

- They gave money.
- They wrote proposals.
- They prepared and facilitated bulk mailings.
- They made solicitation phone calls.
- They wrote solicitation and follow-up letters.
- They added potential donor names to mailing lists.
- They spoke at or hosted functions eliciting support.
- They contributed mailing lists.
- They met and solicited large donor prospects.
- They developed and facilitated the implementation of strategies and events.
- They lobbied for the program at all government levels.

Fund-Raising Schedules

Fund raising may be a scheduled component that functions on an ongoing basis or as a yearly event. Such events as bake sales, car washes, fairs, and magazine or food concessions are common forms of fund raising, particularly at the school level. These fund-raising activities can be broadened to the district or community level to include auctions; holiday and recognition lunches or dinners; social activities (for example, receptions); or performances by students, parents, staff and community (or of partners). Advertising in school newspapers or calendars (both prepared by students) often provides additional monies for partnership projects. One example of a carefully designed fund-raising schedule comes from the San Francisco Education Fund, CA (see Figure 11-4).

Large-scale fund raising usually depends on more formal action plans. To solicit sizable amounts of money, partnership staffs schedule particular times during the school year. If fund raising occurs early in the program's fiscal year, the partnership can take advantage (before major planned expenditures are made) of the interest received from invested contributions. Such interest can be used to pay for future expenditures.

Fund-Raising Sources

Any local business or community agency, organization, or group is a potential source of funds. To connect with viable local sources, there are a few key steps to take that will save time and avoid problems associated with "reinventing the wheel":

1. Assess the community at large for people who will serve on a fund-raising advisory committee, write letters of support, make personal phone calls, or become early donors. If they can't give their time or expertise, ask them to lend their names to a letterhead that will be sent to solicit potential donors.

2. Identify potential individual and group contributors through personal contacts; lists from local organizations (chamber of commerce, private industry councils, Rotary); community agencies; foundations; and such aids as business or nonprofit directories, the Foundation Center, and the public library.

3. Divide these contributors into categories based on financial or in-kind contributions.

4. Review sources of contributions periodically to determine the increase of donations over time.

The San Francisco Education Fund, CA, has developed a computer database through which partnership staff can easily input and access information regarding donors; through the entry screens (see Figure 11-5 for two examples), new donors are entered and information regarding current donors is updated.

Fund-Raising Aids

Most partnerships develop action plans based on their own available resources and use a variety of aids that support efficient and effective implementation of fund-raising strategies. Some examples of successful fund-raising aids include a solicitation for funds from Denver, CO (see Figure 11-6), and letters to lapsed donors (see Figure 11-7) and to prospective donors (see Figure 11-8) from the San Francisco Education Fund, CA.

PENINSULA ACADEMIES

START-UP INCOME AND EXPENDITURES
(1980–1984)

INCOME

Foundation grants	$600,000	
Corporate contributions	90,000	
State/federal grants to school district, directed to Academies	150,000	
	TOTAL:	$840,000

EXPENDITURES

Cash expenditures:
Salaries, fringe benefits, and overhead
for Director, Coordinator, support
staff, and lab instructors; textbooks,
instructional equipment, and materials;
remodeling; evaluation; postage, telephone, insurance, and miscellaneous

	TOTAL:	$840,000

ADDITIONAL IN-KIND DONATIONS

Equipment	$100,000	
Services		
School district personnel	135,000	
Industry:		
Personnel	390,000	
Student jobs	420,000	
	TOTAL:	$1,045,000

Reprinted by permission of
The American Institutes for Research in the Behavioral Sciences, CA.

Figure 11–1

CORPORATE ACTION COMMITTEE
- Schools, Business and the Community Working Together -

BUDGET
July 1, 1984 to June 30, 1985

I   PERSONNEL

1.	Project Director – fulltime ($1908/mo. × 12 months)	$ 22,896
2.	Coordinator – ½ time ($810/mo. × 5 months)	4,050
3.	Office Assistant – 40% time ($315/mo. × 10 months)	3,150
4.	Fringe @ 15%	
	—Project Director	3,435
	—Coordinator	608
	—Office Assistant	473
	TOTAL PERSONNEL	**34,612**

II   OPERATING

1.	Mileage	150
2.	Supplies	550
3.	Reproduction	500
4.	Accounting	405
5.	Recognition	150
6.	Equipment	550
7.	Hospitality	150
8.	Conferences	300
9.	Business Expenses	200
	TOTAL OPERATING	**2,955**

III   OTHER

1.	Teacher Planning Time	
	—Balboa Coordinator (12 hours @ $13.95)	168
	—Balboa Teacher (12 hours @ $13.95)	168
	TOTAL OTHER	**336**
	TOTAL	**$ 37,903**

Reprinted by permission of the Corporate Action Committee, San Francisco, CA.

Figure 11–2

INCOME STATEMENT

September 1, 1983 – August 31, 1984

INCOME;

Partners	$ 33,750
Contributors	11,750
Seattle School District	10,000
Prior Year's Carryover	12,997
Total Income	$ 68,497

EXPENSES:

Personnel	$ 57,906
Operating	8,903
Total Expenses	$ 66,809
Net Income Over Expenses	$ 1,688

IN-KIND INCOME:

Greater Seattle Chamber of Commerce	
Office Space	$ 9,000
Support Services	$ 3,660
Seattle School District	
PIPE Consultant	$ 14,000
Seattle school coordinators' stipends	$ 22,484
Audit Fee performed by	
Arthur Andersen	$ 3,500
Printing performed by	
Rainier Bank	$ 300
Murray Publishing Co.	$ 300
Computer Prize donated by	
Swan Computers	$ 1,300
Airfare and tuition to Education Conference at Tarrytown, NY from SAFECO	$ 1,200
Volunteers: 1,553 gave 7,009 hours at $15/hr.	$105,135
Total In-Kind Income	$160,579

Graphic Design donated by
John Cherkas

Figure 11–3

Timeline for the 1984 Year-End Individual Donor Campaign

December 12, 1984
San Francisco Education Fund Development Department

DATE	TASKS	RESPONSIBLE PERSON	STATUS
Tuesday December 11:	Identify the people we need to write and call.	GST & AB	DONE!
	Plan the letters to be written: one for each of five different groups: Year-End Donors, Patrons, Board, Large HL Donors, General Donors	GST & AB & Jackie	DONE!
Wednesday December 12:	Set timeline	AB & GST	
Thursday December 13:	Divide between staff and volunteers all tasks we plan to accomplish	GST & AB	
	Plan for getting the help we need to do these	GST & AB	
	Recruit helpers to do remaining jobs	GST & AB	
	Draft the most pressing texts: letters to Year-End Donors and Patrons	AB	
	Begin preparation for large General Donor mailing: mailing labels production, printing of the approved General Donor text, purchase stamps, order or begin producing 1,000 return envelopes	AB & Production Team	

138

Friday December 14:	Send out first batch of Year-end and Patron letters	AB & Production Team, GST Signatures
	Draft the Board, Large Holiday Lunch, and General Donor texts	AB
Monday December 17:	Send out second batch year-end and Patron letters	AB & Production Team
	Send out first batch of Board, Large Holiday lunch givers	AB & Production Team
Tuesday December 18:	Send any remaining Year-End and Patron letters	AB & Production Team
	Send remaining Board, Large Holiday Lunch Giver letters	AB & Production Team
Wednesday December 19:	Begin General Donor Mailing: addressing the envelopes	Production Team and Volunteers?
	Tie up loose ends, check to be sure all planned contacts were made, etc.	AB
Thursday December 20:	Conclude the General Donor Mailing: stuffing, stamping, sealing, and mailing	Production Team and Volunteers
	Follow-up, final tasks	AB

Reprinted by permission of the San Francisco Education Fund, CA.

Figure 11–4

139

```
DATE:  1/17/85         FUNDRAISING & GRANT TRACKING SYSTEM      SCREEN NO: 01
                            MAIL LIST MAINTENANCE

      IDENTIFYING CODE *          SORT NAME *_____      PRIM/ALT _  (P/A)

              NAME  ------------------------------------------
    TITLE/ATTN NAME  ------------------------------------------
         ADDRESS 1  ------------------------------------------  CONTACT   ___
         ADDRESS 2  ------------------------------------------  SEND MAIL _  (Y/N)
   CITY, STATE, ZIP  ---------------------- --------           ALT ADDR  _  (Y/N)
       ENTITY TYPE  ___  ----------------------------           STATUS   _  (A/I)
         INTERESTS  ___  ___  ___  ___              WORK PHONE (___) ___-____
                    ___  ___  ___  ___              HOME PHONE (___) ___-____

  AFFILIATED ID CODE  _____  ------------------------    STRT DATE  _____
   AFFILIATION CODE  ___  ------------------------     END DATE  _____

                                                            H INITS SEQ#
      NEW COMMENTS  ------------------------------------------  - ___  ____
                    ------------------------------------------  - ___  ____
                    ------------------------------------------  - ___  ____
                    ------------------------------------------  - ___  ____
                    _____  ADDED--DATE--CHANGED  _____
```

```
DATE:  1/17/85         FUNDRAISING & GRANT TRACKING SYSTEM      SCREEN NO: 22
                            DONATION ENTRY

        DONOR ID CODE *              DONATION NUMBER *____
          DONOR NAME  ------------------------------------------

       DONATION TYPE  ___  ----------------------------  STATUS  _  (P/D)
        DONATED ITEM  ___  ----------------------------  ACCT #  _____
     ASSOCIATED EVENT  ___  ----------------------------
     SOLICITOR ID CODE  _____  ----------------------------------
      PLEDGE PAY DATE  _____         PLEDGE AMOUNT  _____
       DONATION DATE  _____         DONATION AMOUNT  _____

     ACKNOWLEDGE DATE  _____     FISCAL PERIOD  ___  _____
     ACKNOWLEDGED BY  _____  ----------------------------------
     RELATED PROGRAM  _____  ----------------------------------
      RELATED SCHOOL  _____  ----------------------------------------
  SPECL GROUP SERVED  ___  ----------------------------          H INITS SEQ#
        NEW COMMENTS  ------------------------------------------  - ___  ____
                      ------------------------------------------  - ___  ____
                      ------------------------------------------  - ___  ____
                      _____  ADDED--DATE--CHANGED  _____
```

Reprinted by permission of the San Francisco Education Fund, CA.

Figure 11–5

Adopt-A-School
Update
Fall, 1984

Here's a letter from my Mom.

Dear Adopt-A-School,

Earlier this fall, my daughter came home bubbling about a special program she attended on how to resolve arguments. When she shared her papers with me, I discovered that business volunteers from their adopting company had put on this Adopt-A-School activity. Last year, she was able to compete in an attendance contest, and when her picture was displayed in the front hall for good citizenship, she felt ten feet tall.

She was so thrilled when you selected her letter to be part of your fund-raising efforts, and we have sent copies to all of our relatives out-of-town.

As a former teacher, I greatly appreciate the positive reinforcement and educational enrichment your organization provides. I want to take this opportunity to thank you and all of the businesses that share their resources with our children. I was delighted to hear about the nice contribution you received from the Coors Foundation, because I understand how critical that support is for nonprofit organizations.

Enclosed is my check. I'm sorry that it can't be more. Best of luck in reaching your goal. I know other parents feel the way I do, and I'm sure you will be successful.

Keep up the good work,

Mindy Jo's Mom

ADOPT-A-SCHOOL IS PLEASED TO ANNOUNCE THE RECEIPT OF FOUR VERY GENEROUS GRANTS AWARDED BY THE CHEVRON FUND OF THE DENVER FOUNDATION, McGRAW-HILL, ADOLPH COORS, AND THE HELEN K. AND ARTHUR E. JOHNSON FOUNDATIONS. THIS SUPPORT ALONG WITH CORPORATE CONTRIBUTIONS PROVIDES THE FINANCIAL BASE FOR THE WORK OF OUR ORGANIZATION.

WE WOULD LIKE TO TAKE THIS OPPORTUNITY TO PUBLICLY EXPRESS OUR DEEPEST APPRECIATION TO THE FOUNDATION DIRECTORS FOR THEIR GENEROSITY AND VOTE OF CONFIDENCE. BOTH THE COORS AND JOHNSON GRANTS PROVIDED AN INITIAL GIFT, ALONG WITH A CHALLENGE GRANT, ESTABLISHING CONDITIONS WHICH MUST BE MET PRIOR TO DECEMBER 15, 1984. AT THE TIME OF PUBLICATION, APPROXIMATELY 66% OF THE MONIES FOR THE CHALLENGE GRANTS HAVE BEEN RAISED.

To each of you who have already sent your check, our deepest gratitude. To the rest of you, the time is growing short. WE NEED YOUR HELP TODAY! Please take a moment to send your tax-deductible contribution to the Adopt-A-School office. No contribution is too small.

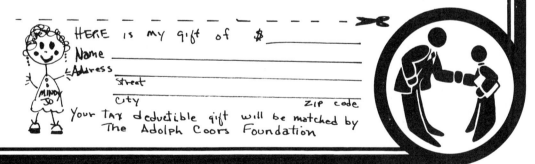

HERE is my gift of $ _____
Name _____
Address _____
Street
City _____ Zip code _____
Your tax deductible gift will be matched by The Adolph Coors Foundation

Reprinted by permission of Adopt-A-School in Denver, CO.

Figure 11–6

San Francisco Education Fund
1095 Market Street, Suite 719   San Francisco, CA 94103   Telephone (415) 621-4878

December 23, 1984

Dear Friend of the Public Schools,

Thank you. Your generosity has made a
difference! By supporting the San Francisco
Education Fund, you have enabled many students,
teachers, and principals to reach new levels of
skill and achievement.

On behalf of those your gift has supported,
I am sending you the FUND's 1983-84 Annual
Grants Report. I hope you will find time to
enjoy a few minutes looking over the range and
quality of the programs you have helped to
create.

With thanks for your commitment and concern,
and best wishes for the New Year,

Sincerely,

Glady

Gladys S. Thacher
Executive Director

enclosure

*P.S. I do hope you know how much
your contribution means to the
FUND and the Schools! Best, Glady*

Reprinted by permission of the San Francisco Education Fund, CA.
Figure 11–7

San Francisco Education Fund

1095 Market Street, Room 719   San Francisco, CA 94103   Telephone (415) 621-4878

May 14, 1984

Mrs. Prospective Donor
1000 Bountiful Way
San Francisco, Ca 94118

Dear (first name or other appropriate salutation),

I'd like to take a moment to share with you my enthusiasm for the work of the San Francisco Education Fund. In my years of service on the Board, I have been repeatedly amazed at how much of a difference the FUND can make with its well-placed grants to teachers in the Public Schools. Over the past five years, the FUND has become an indispensable part of the community's growing involvement in the schools. I am writing because I think this work deserves your support, and I want to ask your help.

In the next few months, the FUND has an opportunity to match a $25,000 challenge grant, if we can raise that amount of money from individuals. I would like to ask you to make a gift to the FUND in support of its work towards excellence in public education.

As you know, public education is in trouble. Everywhere attention is drawn to the failure of the schools to address the needs of our society's children adequately. In San Francisco, where we are privileged to enjoy one of the most ethnically and culturally diverse urban communities in the nation, we face an enormous set of challenges to meet the educational and social needs of our city's youth.

And yet, the picture is not entirely bleak. Throughout the country, and especially here in California, people are recognizing that they have a stake in public education, and that their ideas and commitment can make a difference in the quality of our schools.

Figure 11–8

Mrs. Prospective Donor
May 14, 1984
Page two

At the FUND, we think that of the many things citizens can do to ensure their society's future, none is more essential than the revitalization of our public education system.

As the enclosed Facts on the FUND explains, the FUND is a community organization making grants in the public schools for projects which otherwise would not happen. Teachers and principals initiate programs for students in all areas of curriculum, and projects are closely evaluated by the FUND staff. Often, a new project which works well in one classroom or school will spread to others as its effectiveness becomes known. In this way, San Franciscans are able to participate actively in the development of excellence in public education.

Those of us who work with the FUND, as Board members, volunteers and staff, are especially fortunate because we can observe the projects in action. Again and again, in classrooms and in our meetings with teachers and administrators, I am encouraged and deeply affected by the positive and enthusiastic attitudes of teachers, students, administrators and parents, and by the effectiveness of their projects.

The grants made by the FUND are enabling us to discover what works! Over time, we have come to support the very best of the work that is being done to improve the schools.

Gifts made to the FUND are used to support these grants to the schools. Your gift could accomplish a great many things. Here are some samples; there are countless other possibilities:

$250   would fund a classroom mini-grant in arts, music, or science
$500   would pay for materials to mount a school-wide reading program
$1,000   would develop a full year's project in computer application
          for use in building math and English skills
$2,500   would support a model project in improving study habits
          for middle school students
$5,000   would support up to a six mini-grants in any of a dozen
          curriculum areas, or one special school-wide
          project with potential for replication at other
          schools

Figure 11–8 (continued)

Mrs. Prospective Donor
May 14, 1984
Page three

        We know that the strongest natural constituency for youth are
individual citizens who stand for excellence in education and commitment
to children. With your support, this growing body of individuals who feel
they have such a stake in the schools can further the changes in education
that are so urgently needed.

        I would very much like to meet with you to discuss the Fund's work
and your contribution to it. I will call you next week to arrange a time
when we can meet.

Thank you for your interest.

With very best wishes,

Cordially,

Board Member Extraordinaire

P.S. Our $25,000 challenge must be met by the end of our fiscal year,
June 30, 1984.   Your gift will be doubled in value if you give to the
FUND soon!

Reprinted by permission of the San Francisco Education Fund, CA.

Figure 11–8 (continued)

Recordkeeping as a Tool for Administration, Program Development, and Monitoring

Regular, accurate maintenance of records will support the effective and efficient operations of a partnership program. Recordkeeping procedures and forms should be in place before partnership activities begin. In this way, records become tools for planning, implementation, and monitoring of goals, objectives, tasks, and activities.

Most partnership leaders use some standard forms (purchase orders, fiscal forms, time sheets, transportation records) of their supervising organizations. However, these leaders have also developed specialized forms to meet their particular recordkeeping needs in the areas of

- general program administration
- planning and program development
- monitoring of program tasks and activities

This section's discussion will be enriched with examples of sample forms sent by partnership leaders from around the country. It is interesting to note that many of these forms were developed for a particular program format; that is, for a foundation, for an adopt-a-school project, or for a volunteer program. Nevertheless, the forms are sufficiently generic to be revised and/or adapted to meet the recordkeeping needs of a variety of different partnership formats.

GENERAL PROGRAM ADMINISTRATION RECORDKEEPING

General administrative recordkeeping for partnerships falls into specific areas, namely records related to employee and general office management and to arrangements between partners. During the partnership's initiation phase, decisions about forms and procedures to be used must often meet the requirements of the partnership's supervising agency. Depending on the guidelines for the program,

- forms may be identical to those employed by the program's school district or governing agency
- forms of the program's supervising organization may be adapted and revised
- entirely new forms may be designed

Employee and General Office Management Procedures and Records

In terms of general office management procedures, partnerships usually find it easier and more efficient to use the same standard recordkeeping forms as their supervising organization in such areas as transportation, payroll, purchase orders, and time sheets. These special programs might print the partnership's name at the top of these forms; this helps those processing the forms to distinguish partnership recordkeeping from that of other programs. Some examples of simple, but effective general administrative forms that are "to the point," include

- a mileage report form (see Figure 12-1) from the Charlotte-Mecklenburg Schools, NC
- a memorandum regarding payment procedures for grants funds (see Figure 12-2) from the San Francisco Education Fund

Partnership Arrangements

Procedures developed to facilitate partnership arrangements provide a good balance between partners' expectations and actual performance and accomplishment of objectives. Effective administrative forms help

- clarify procedures
- provide guidelines to all arrangements
- transmit a consistent message
- encourage positive perceptions regarding program management and program capacity to accomplish stated goals and objectives

The following forms are examples of recordkeeping tools—*related to partnership arrangements*—that meet the criteria discussed above:

- a partnership agreement form from Columbia, MO (see Figure 12-3)
- a partner recruitment form from PG and E through the Corporate Action in Public Schools (CAPS), CA (see Figure 12-4)
- Resource request forms from the National Bureau of Standards, US Dept of Commerce, CO (see Figure 12-5); Charlotte-Mecklenburg, NC (see Figure 12-6, 7, 8); and the PIPE Program, Seattle, WA (see Figure 12-9)

RECORDKEEPING FOR PLANNING AND PROGRAM DEVELOPMENT

Some of the most useful procedures and forms submitted by partnership leaders were in the areas of planning and program development. Formats and formality of forms differed; however, *all* forms clearly defined short- and long-range planning that included the following components (as appropriate): objectives, needs, available resources, activities (tasks), designated responsible staff, timeline for accomplishment of tasks, and criteria for evaluation. Partnership leaders stated that these carefully designed action plans are used

- to provide guidelines within which leaders plan, determine priorities, and make decisions that are directly related to program goals
- for public dissemination as *the* written planning statement of partnership program development and implementation
- as base documents and guides for program monitoring and evaluation

One example of a planning form that incorporates the components discussed above comes from Wichita, KA (see Figure 12-10).

Other organizational forms that leaders found helpful in program planning and development included

- an application for volunteer service (see Figure 12-11) and a volunteer service form (see Figure 12-12) from Tulsa, OK
- the following forms available from the Partners in Education Program, Columbia, MO: form for scheduled activities (see Figure 12-13); business-community contact sheet (see Figure 12-14); school contact sheet (see Figure 12-15); business-community checklist (see Figure 12-16); form for facilitating partnership meetings (see Figure 12-17); and a program checklist for the principal (see Figure 12-18)

MONITORING PROGRAM TASKS AND ACTIVITIES

A full discussion of the process of formative and summative program evaluation will be found in Section 15 of this guide. Outlined at this time are recordkeeping procedures and forms to assist program leaders with the daily, weekly, and monthly monitoring of their programs. This monitoring involves scheduled checkups on the achievement of program activities and objectives and assigned staff tasks. Recordkeeping tools such as short reports, check sheets, and charts complement and facilitate this process.

Reports

Brief written reports can be effective monitoring tools, as seen in the form used by the TwinWest Business-Education Partnership, MN (see Figure 12-19).

Check Sheets

Checklist-short-answer reporting forms are useful for charting program progress over brief periods of time as seen in the example from Houston, TX (see Figure 12-20).

Charts

Charting the quantity and kind of partnership activities—and resources supporting them—over varying periods of time is a third effective recordkeeping procedure used in monitoring partnerships. A good example of this format comes from the Corporate Action Committee, CA (see Figure 12-21).

COMMUNITY RESOURCE PROGRAM

AUTOMOBILE MILEAGE REPORT

Prepared by the Charlotte-Mecklenburg Schools for your record of visits to the schools as a Community Resource Volunteer, this report is not to be returned to us; it is for your own records for income tax deductions. If you need additional sheets, call the Community Resource representative in the Teaching/Learning Center, 376-0122, ext. 61.

Date	From (Location)	To (School)	Odometer Reading Start	End	# Miles	Purpose of Trip

Reprinted by permission of Community Resource Program, Charlotte, NC.

Figure 12–1

SAN FRANCISCO EDUCATION FUND

March 2, 1982

MEMO: To All SAN FRANCISCO EDUCATION FUND Project Directors

FROM: Bonnie Engel, Program Administrator

RE: Payment Procedures for Grant Funds

The SAN FRANCISCO EDUCATION FUND acts as fiscal agent for all monies supporting Regular and Mini-Grant Programs approved by the Board of Directors. The following instructions explain how to claim payment for your project expenses. You do not need to go through the San Francisco Unified School District for your purchases. However, large items should have the principal's sign-off before sending the claim to the FUND.

1. All claims for payment should be made in writing to the FUND Program Administrator, Ms. Bonnie Engel.

2. Use your account number on all claims for payment. This number was assigned to your project as indicated in the Letter of Grant. The number begins 200.___ ___ ___.

3. Reimbursement:

    a. For small purchases, you may pay for the items and send the receipts to the FUND for reimbursement.

    b. Specify which items purchased are for your project.

    c. Please wait until you have collected receipts totalling $25.00 before claiming reimbursement.

    d. Claims for reimbursement should be accompanied by a letter or written statement clearly indicating to whom checks should be made out and where they should be sent. If there are no instructions, the checks will go to the Project Director at school.

4. Charge Accounts:

    a. The FUND authorizes Project Directors to open charge accounts with vendors for large purchases or multiple orders. Your Letter of Grant should be sufficient to establish credit. Please have vendors call Bonnie at the FUND if there is any problem.

    b. All charge account invoices should be sent to the Project Director first so that amounts can be noted and shipments can be checked for completeness and suitability. The Project Director may then submit them to the FUND for payment.

    c. If the vendor insists, the bills may be sent directly to the FUND for payment.

    d. Please be sure your program account number is reflected on all charge invoices. It also helps to provide the name of the school.

Figure 12–2

5. Payment in Advance:

Occasionally vendors will not allow charges. In these cases, the FUND will advance you the money. Be sure to get the correct amount of the purchase and send a claim in writing. Afterward, please follow up the purchase by sending the FUND a copy of the receipt.

6. Personnel Payments:

In the event that your project pays stipends or honoraria to consultants, students, paraprofessionals, etc., please send a record of the hours worked along with the claim in writing. Specific instructions about who receives the check and where it should be sent must accompany all claims for payment. Again, please include the account number.

7. Credit Memos:

On occasion, merchandise that has already been paid for is returned or is not available. Please send credit memos to the FUND. Bonnie will then write for the reimbursement and add that amount back into the Project's budget.

8. Budget Changes:

The total amount of the budget cannot be changed without additional approval by the Board of Directors of the FUND. Line items changes may be made within the budget by notifying the Executive Director, Ms. Gladys Thacher, in writing.

9. Timeline

All claims for payment should be sent in by June 1 because the FUND closes its books on June 30. If you wish an extension on your project, please let us know by June 1.

10. Problems

If you have any questions or problems, please call Bonnie at the office, 541-0575.

Please remember that you, as Project Director, are responsible for accounting for your expenditures and that the FUND expects a financial report at the conclusion of your program.

Congratulations and good luck with your program!

Reprinted by permission of the San Francisco Education Fund, CA.
Figure 12–2 (continued)

DECLARATION OF PARTNERSHIP
COLUMBIA, MISSOURI

_____
Business/Community Organization

and

_____
School

hereby declares their partnership.

This cooperative venture joins the hands of said business/community organizations and public school in a uniquely designed partnership. Both may pursue a mutually enriching relationship with each other with full benefits accruing to both partners.

In witness, thereof, all parties execute this Partnership on this _____ day of _____, 19____

_____   _____
School Principal   Partnership Representative

Reprinted by permission of Partners in Education, Columbia Public Schools, MO.

Figure 12–3

153

PG and E WEEK.

Volunteer tutors sought

SEPTEMBER 30 is the deadline for San Francisco Division and General Office employees to volunteer as tutors in the San Francisco School District.

Tutors are particularly needed in reading and math. A foreign language skill is especially helpful in some cases.

PG&E tutors spend from one to three hours a week working with individuals and groups of students during regular school sessions. Time required away from work must be approved and arranged by the employee's supervisor prior to consideration of the employee's qualifications for tutoring.

Interested employees should complete the form below and return it to George L. Livingston, Room 3000, 77 Beale Street, San Francisco (Phone: 4202).

Please select the subject and grade level of interest.

Age Level:
___ Elementary
___ Junior High

Individual Help:
___ Reading
___ English
___ Math
___ Social Science
___ Foreign Lang.
___ Other

Enrichment:
___ Art
___ Arts & Crafts
___ Library
___ Music
___ Science
___ Other

Name _____

Department _____

Location _____

Co. extension _____ Date _____

Supervisor's name _____

Approval signature _____

Location _____

Co. extension _____ Date _____

Figure 12–4

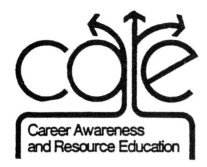

Career Awareness and Resource Education

UNITED STATES DEPARTMENT OF COMMERCE
National Bureau of Standards

325 Broadway
Boulder, Colorado 80303

ROOM 1-4019
497-5525

REQUEST DATE:_____

<u>TYPE OF RESOURCE REQUESTED:</u>

CARE PROGRAM #_____   TITLE/TOPIC _____

REQUEST SOURCE_____

ADDRESS_____

CONTACT PERSON_____   TELEPHONE_____

_____

GRADE LEVEL(S)_____   #PRESENTATIONS_____   TOTAL IMPACTED_____

PRESENTATION LOCATION_____   ROOM #_____

PRESENTER(S)_____   _____

_____   _____

_____   _____

PREFERRED DATE_____   DAY_____   TIME_____TO_____

PREFERRED DATE_____   DAY_____   TIME_____TO_____

CONFIRMED W/SCHOOL_____   CONFIRMED W/PRESENTER_____

REMINDER TO PRESENTER_____   GSA CAR NEEDED_____

COMMENTS:_____

_____

_____

Contribution of the National Bureau of Standards, not subject to copyright.

Figure 12–5

CHARLOTTE-MECKLENBURG SCHOOLS
COMMUNITY RESOURCE REQUEST

1250.2
1/84

(Please print in ink)

RESOURCE TOPIC_____

SUBJECT & GRADE OF CLASS_____

DATES & TIMES REQUESTED:
(If more than one date is necessary to meet your needs, please fill out both # 1 and # 2 and the respective alternate choices.)

1. Date:_____   Time:_____ to _____   _____ Number of presentations per day
Alternate:_____   Time:_____ to _____   _____ Number of students per class
Alternate:_____   Time:_____ to _____

2. Date:_____   Time:_____ to _____   _____ Number of presentations per day
Alternate:_____   Time:_____ to _____   _____ Number of students per class
Alternate:_____   Time:_____ to _____

WHAT CURRICULUM CONCEPT SHOULD BE THE FOCUS OF THE PRESENTATION?_____

_____

REQUESTING TEACHER_____   APL_____

SCHOOL_____   TELEPHONE_____

ADDRESS_____   COURIER CODE_____

Please be sure all blanks are completed (unless # 2 is not necessary) and allow at least ten school days for processing.

OFFICE USE ONLY   DATE RECEIVED_____ DATE CONFIRMATIONS SENT_____

Reprinted by permission of Community Resource Program, Charlotte, NC.

Figure 12–6

CHARLOTTE-MECKLENBURG SCHOOLS
COMMUNITY RESOURCE DATA SHEET

1250.1
1/84

PLEASE RETURN TO: Community Resource Program
Teaching/Learning Center
428 West Blvd.
Charlotte, N.C. 28203

(Please print)

NAME: Ms. _____   DATE _____
Mr.   (last)   (first)   (middle initial)

ADDRESS: Home_____   PHONE _____
                                                    (zip)

             Business_____   PHONE _____
                                                    (zip)

EMPLOYER: _____

WHEN CAN YOU SERVE?
(Complete one or more)

☐ Mondays   from _____ to _____
☐ Tuesdays   from _____ to _____
☐ Wednesdays   from _____ to _____
☐ Thursdays   from _____ to _____
☐ Fridays   from _____ to _____

_____ Maximum number of times per year.
_____ How far in advance should we contact you?

WHERE CAN YOU SERVE?

Do you have travel limitations?
☐ yes   ☐ no
If yes, what are they?_____

_____

_____

_____

PRESENTATION INFORMATION

TOPIC TITLE _____

Will you be making this presentation as a corporation or agency representative?   ☐ yes   ☐ no

BACKGROUND or EXPERIENCE related to presentation: (school, job, technical training, hobby, travel experience, etc.)_____

_____

_____

TYPE(S) OF INFORMATION IN PRESENTATION:
☐ Job skill
☐ Travel
☐ Hobby
☐ Cultural Background
☐ Other _____

STUDENT GRADE LEVEL(S) APPROPRIATE FOR PRESENTATION:
☐ K-3 (ages 5-9)
☐ 4-6 (ages 9-12)
☐ 7-9 (ages 12-15)
☐ 10-12 (ages 15-18)

METHOD(S) OF PRESENTATION:
☐ Hands-on display
☐ Student participation/craft
☐ Lecture
☐ Audio-visual
☐ Field trip
☐ Kit of materials
☐ Brochure/hand-outs
☐ Other _____

OTHER SPECIFICS:

_____ Amount of time needed to make presentation

_____ Optimum number in student group

Special equipment and/or arrangements needed:

_____

Please specify equipment you can provide.

_____

_____

GENERAL DESCRIPTION OF YOUR PRESENTATION:

_____

_____

_____

Reprinted by permission of Community Resource Program, Charlotte, NC.

Figure 12-7

157

CHARLOTTE-MECKLENBURG SCHOOLS

1250.3
1/84

COMMUNITY RESOURCE CONFIRMATION

WHO IS PRESENTING? _____

WHAT IS THE SUBJECT? _____

Resource person

Topic Title

Address

Method of presentation
Special equipment needed: _____

Telephone

To be provided by _____ school _____ resource

WHEN? _____

M   T   W   TH   F

WHERE? _____

School name

FOR WHOM? _____

Requesting teacher

Date

Address

Grade/Subject

Time(s)

Telephone   Room #   # Students   # Presentation

Please complete the enclosed evaluation sheet after the visit.

If you have any questions, please call the Community Resource representative in the Teaching/Learning Center at 376-0122, ext. 61.

Notification of postponement/cancellation is necessary 24 hours prior to scheduled visit.

Confirmation sent _____ by _____

Copies to teacher, resource person, API, resource bank.

Reprinted by permission of Community Resource Program, Charlotte, NC.

Figure 12–8

P.I.P.E.
Private Initiatives in Public Education
Greater Seattle Chamber of Commerce 447-7244
Seattle Public Schools 587-6353

Private Initiatives in Public Education

. . . In support of Seattle's public schools

Submit this Skills Bank Reference Sheet to participate in preparing Seattle
students for their roles as citizens, workers, parents, and problem solvers.

You could assist young learners as:

A classroom speaker

A panelist

A workplace tour guide

A mentor

A donator of surplus equipment

A consultant to students completing research papers

A career consultant engaging in 1/2 hour telephone interviews

A host to summer or student interns

A tutor

A developer of supplementary teaching materials

Return form to:

Louise Wasson   or   Cynthia Shelton
Career Education Coordinator   Private Initiatives in Public Education
Seattle School District   Greater Seattle Chamber of Commerce
Broadview-Thompson School   1200 One Union Square
13052 Greenwood N.   Sixth and University Street
Seattle, WA 98117   Seattle, WA 98101

Figure 12–9

SEATTLE PUBLIC SCHOOLS/PRIVATE INITIATIVES IN PUBLIC EDUCATION

COMMUNITY RESOURCE BANK

Date:_____   File Number:_____

CONTACT PERSON   Please Print or Type
_____

Name:_____   Work Address:_____

(Last) _____

(First) _____   City   State   Zip   County

Work Phone:_____   Employer:_____

Occupation:_____ | CODE |

Background Information: | CODE | Firm's/Agency's Major Activity/Service: | CODE |

( ) Male   ( ) Female

Ethnicity:_____

The School District is particularly interested in identifying community resources relevant to the following subjects. Please check to indicate related activities at your firm.

		CODE			CODE
Accounting____	Drama____		Government____	Natural Resources____	
Applied Mathematics____	Economics____		Health Careers____	Physics____	
Biology____	Electronics____		History____	Radio/TV____	
Chemistry____	Engineering____		International Trade____	Retailing____	
Commercial Art____	Fashion____		Leadership Development____	Speaking____	
Computer Applications____	Food Service Management____		Mechanics____	Writing____	
Drafting____	Foreign Language____		Multicultural____	Music____	

Other Skills/Activities? Please describe:

My firm could on occasion provide the following resources for Seattle Public School students:

____Workplace tours . . . . | CODE | ____Judge school contests, projects related to our business . . . . | CODE |

____Classroom speakers on products or processes at our business . . . .   ____Tutor students, volunteering two-three hours per week, day or evening . . . .

____Instructional materials, perhaps from your in-house training program . . . .   ____Panelist for in-school presentations related to our business . . . .

____Sponsor high school intern interested in our business . . . .   ____Meeting space for teacher workshops . . . . (15-30)

____Provide sample piece work projects for handicapped students   ____Consult with students on special projects related to our business . . . .

____Surplus equipment, donated office or technical equipment for classroom use . . . .   ____Host teachers interested in learning about our business . . . .

____Speak with students on the phone regarding planning for careers in our field . . . .   ____Provide part-time employment for students . . . . .

Please note special circumstances related to your availability/interest (or that of your company) in participating.

- -
FOR OFFICE USE:

Source:_____   Training:_____

Figure 12-9 (continued)

ADOPT-A-SCHOOL PROGRAM
IMPLEMENTATION FORM

Date: _____

School: _____

Adopter: _____

Adoptee Representative: _____

Adopter Representative: _____

AREAS OF IDENTIFIED NEEDS	PROJECTS TO BE IMPLEMENTED	EXPECTED DATE OF IMPLEMENTATION	SCHOOL PERSONNEL INVOLVED	BUSINESS PERSONNEL INVOLVED	PROGRESS OF PROJECT

Reprinted by permission of the Wichita Public Schools, KS.

Figure 12–10

161

Mail to:
Nancy McDonald
School Volunteers
P.O. Box 45208
Tulsa, OK 74145

SCHOOL VOLUNTEERS
TULSA PUBLIC SCHOOLS
APPLICATION FOR VOLUNTEER SERVICE

School Assigned

Date _____ 19 _____

Name (Miss, Mrs., Mr.) _____ Phone _____

Address _____ Zip _____
                    Street   City

Age: Under 20 _____   21–40 _____   41–60 _____   Over 60 _____

Children Attending Public Schools   Yes _____   No _____   School _____

Education: _____ High School   _____ College   _____ Degree

Special Training: _____

Foreign Language _____ Speak _____   Write _____

Health (Any Physical Limitation) _____

Car: Yes _____   No _____   Teaching Experience   Yes _____   No _____

YOUR VOLUNTEER EXPERIENCE

Type of Service _____ Organization _____

_____

Interests, Hobbies _____

_____

_____

Figure 12–11

PREFERENCES

Please express your preference, checking as many items as you wish:

(1) Do you prefer working with individual children (1 to 1) _____   or groups _____

(2) Choice of assignment: Elementary School _____   Kindergarten _____

Grades 1–3 _____   4–6 _____

Middle School _____   Junior High _____   Senior High _____

(3) Types of Work Preferred: (Check one or several)

_____ General Classroom Assistance _____ Kindergarten _____ Storytelling

_____ Math Tutor _____ Reading Tutor _____ Library/Media Center

_____ Special Education _____ Skills Program _____ Music _____ Art

_____ Bilingual Program _____ Gifted Program _____ Great Books

_____ Physical Education _____ School Clinic _____ Clerical _____ Type

SCHOOL PREFERRED _____

How often will you serve and how many hours: Available Time: (Example: 9:00–11:00 a.m.)

_____ Once a week   _____ Twice a week

_____ Daily   _____ Other

	A.M.	P.M.
Mon.		
Tues.		
Wed.		
Thurs.		
Fri.		

Approved: Dr. Jack Griffin

Associate Superintendent
for Instruction   Signed _____
                                    Name of Volunteer

Reprinted by permission of the Tulsa Public Schools Volunteer Program, OK.

Figure 12–11 (continued)

PLEASE RETURN TIME SHEETS
TO Nancy McDonald AT THE END
OF EACH CALENDAR MONTH.   **TULSA PUBLIC SCHOOLS
SCHOOL VOLUNTEERS**

Registration and Record of Volunteers and Hours Served:

SCHOOL _____

MONTH OF _____ MONTHLY TOTAL HOURS _____

Date	Name	Type of Volunteer Job	Arrived	Left	Number of Hours Served

Approved: Dr. Jack Griffin

Reprinted by permission of the Tulsa Public Schools Volunteer Program, OK.
Figure 12–12

FORM FOR SCHEDULED ACTIVITIES WITH PARTNERS IN EDUCATION

Business/Partner _____

School Partner _____

Activity _____

_____

How Partner is involved _____

_____

Date _____

Time _____

Location _____

Address _____

Contact Person _____

Telephone Number _____

This form should be filled in and mailed to: Jolene Schultz, Partners In Education Coordinator, 310 North Providence Road, Columbia, Missouri 65201, in time to perhaps schedule publicity to cover the event—Thank You.

Reprinted by permission of Partners in Education, Columbia Public Schools, MO.

Figure 12–13

PARTNERS IN EDUCATION
Business-Community Contact Sheet

Business: _____   President: _____

Address: _____   Phone: _____

_____   Contact Person(s): _____

1st contact date: _____   Phone: _____

Place: _____

Attended by: _____

_____

_____

Comments: _____

_____

_____

_____

_____

_____

_____

Ideas and suggestions: _____

_____

_____

_____

_____

_____

Contact again: _____

Reprinted by permission of Partners in Education, Columbia Public Schools, MO.
Figure 12–14

PARTNERS IN EDUCATION SCHOOL CONTACT SHEET

SCHOOL _____ PRINCIPAL _____

*1st Meeting Date: _____ PHONE _____

Attended By: _____

_____

Comments: _____

_____

_____

_____

Contact Again: _____

- -

**2nd Meeting Date: _____

Attended By: _____

_____

Comments: _____

_____

_____

_____

Contact Again: _____

- -

***3rd Meeting Date: _____

Attended By: _____

_____

Comments: _____

_____

_____

_____

Contact Again: _____

Reprinted by permission of Partners in Education, Columbia Public Schools, MO.

Figure 12–15

PARTNERS IN EDUCATION
CHECKLIST FOR
BUSINESS-COMMUNITY

_____ 1. Designate a coordinator for the program.

_____ 2. Conduct a needs assessment and resource assessment.

_____ 3. Familiarize yourself with possible projects.

_____ 4. Have ideas for a get-acquainted activity with your school before initial meeting with the building principal.

_____ 5. Share a profile of your organization with your school and publicize the school's profile in your newsletter.

_____ 6. Meet with school coordinator and building principal to determine initial project, to discuss other possible services and to plan the get-acquainted activity.

_____ 7. Inform employees/members of projects determined thus far and the roles they will have in them.

_____ 8. Promote the Partners-In-Education Program in your organization with requests for input, letters in paychecks, personal letters sent to homes, posters, enthusiasm.

_____ 9. Set up employee volunteer release time where necessary.

_____ 10. Arrange recognition for your participants in newsletters, bulletins, etc.

Reprinted by permission of Partners in Education, Columbia Public Schools, MO.

Figure 12–16

FIRST BUSINESS/COMMUNITY AND SCHOOL PARTNERS MEETING

SCHOOL DATA	BUSINESS DATA
Special Activities: _____	Special Activities: _____
_____	_____
_____	_____
_____	_____
_____	_____
_____	_____
_____	_____
_____	_____
Additional Information: _____	Additional Information: _____
_____	_____
_____	_____
_____	_____
_____	_____
_____	_____
_____	_____
_____	_____
Remarks: _____	_____
_____	_____
_____	_____
_____	_____
_____	_____
Contact again: _____	Contact again: _____

Figure 12–17

School: _____   Business: _____

Contact Person(s): _____   Contact Person(s): _____

_____   _____

_____   _____

Address: _____   Address: _____

_____   _____

Telephone: _____   Telephone: _____

First on-site contact: _____ Date: _____

Attended by: _____

_____

SCHOOL DATA	BUSINESS DATA

SCHOOL DATA

Needs assess. completed: ____   ____
                           yes   no

Resource assess. completed: ____   ____
                            yes   no

Additional help needed: ____   ____
                           yes   no

No. of faculty: _____

No. of students: _____

Special programs: _____

_____

_____

_____

_____

_____

_____

_____

BUSINESS DATA

Needs assess. completed: ____   ____
                           yes   no

Resource assess. completed: ____   ____
                            yes   no

Additional help needed: ____   ____
                           yes   no

No. of employees: _____

Special programs: _____

_____

_____

_____

_____

_____

_____

_____

Reprinted by permission of Partners in Education, Columbia Public Schools, MO.

Figure 12–17 (continued)

PARTNERS IN EDUCATION PROGRAM
1984–1985 CHECKLIST

_____ 1. Name a coordinator (or two, if you wish).

_____ 2. Return the enclosed registration form for the first Partner Sharing and Learning Session scheduled for _____, just as quickly as possible.

_____ 3. Consider inviting representatives from your partner group to participate in your In-service Days prior to school opening, if only to meet the faculty.

_____ 4. Remind faculty of the purpose of the Partnership program. It was designed to gain community support for schools by changing the negative attitudes towards public education. This is a "people" program, not a "money" program. All partners are not equal in terms of size, number of volunteers, time given to the school, and possibility of monetary assistance.

_____ 5. Ask faculty for their input in establishing your school needs assessment. Prepare them, however, for the fact that everyone's wish will not necessarily be satisfied. Please focus on requests for human resources; and, if monetary assistance is available, it will come naturally.

_____ 6. Remind faculty that <u>only you</u> and <u>your coordinator</u> should make contact with your Partner to make requests. Everyone else should submit their requests to you.

_____ 7. Establish a Partner-In-Education committee to assist in developing ideas and carrying out activites.

_____ 8. <u>Invite your Partner to an early kick-off assembly program and re-welcome them to your school</u>.

_____ 9. Invite your Liaison to this same assembly and to other Partnership activities at your school.

_____ 10. Invite your Partner to school to develop plans for activities for the year.

_____ 11. Send a copy of your plans to Partners-In-Education Office, Missouri Facilitator Center, 310 North Providence Road (Room 311).

_____ 12. Mark your calendar for the following dates:

Reprinted by permission of Partners in Education, Columbia Public Schools, MO.

Figure 12–18

TwinWest Business–Education Partnership
Standing Committee Leader's Report

Date Of Meeting:
Members Present:
Project Working On:
Discussion Items:
Decisions Made:
Next Meeting Scheduled For:

Reprinted by permission of TwinWest Business-Education Partnership, MN.
Figure 12–19

COORDINATORS REPORT

_____   _____
(School)   (Period Covered)

_____   _____
(Coordinator's Name)   (Area)

PLEASE INDICATE BELOW THE NUMBER OF VOLUNTEERS ACTIVE IN EACH AREA AT YOUR SCHOOL THIS PERIOD, AND THE TOTAL NUMBER HOURS WORKED IN EACH AREA. Please list any new volunteers on the back of this sheet. Send this report by school mail to VIPS, Route 10.

ACTIVITIES	NO. OF VOL.	HOURS WORKED	COMPANY
Classroom Teacher Assts.	_____	_____	
Speakers	_____	_____	
Field Trips	_____	_____	
Tutors: Bilingual	_____	_____	
Math	_____	_____	
Reading	_____	_____	
Other (please list)			
_____	_____	_____	
_____	_____	_____	
_____	_____	_____	
Total No. of classes involved	_____		

Any noteworthy volunteer news items, achievements, or human interest stories to report from your school?

Any suggestions, requests, or comments?

Figure 12–20

NEW VOLUNTEERS

NAME	PHONE	BUSINESS

<u>Donations</u>

Funds (Amount)   Purpose

_____   _____

_____   _____

In-Kind (Item)   Purpose

_____   _____

_____   _____

Reprinted by permission of the Houston Independent School District, TX.

Figure 12–20 (continued)

ELEMENTARY SCHOOL SERVICES

SERVICE Company/Agency	Curriculum/ Materials/ Units	Films	Field Trips	Speakers/ Presenta- tions	Volunteer Services	Other
●						
●						
●						
●						
●						
●						
●						
●						
●						

Reprinted by permission of the Corporate Action Committee, San Francisco, CA.

Figure 12–21

Communications: Quality, Quantity, and Control

Partnerships are enhanced by strong, ongoing communications. With attention paid not only to *form* and *content*, but also to the *quality* and *quantity* of communications, program staff can expect a positive return for their efforts. A discussion of this process is developed within the following context:

- Quality versus quantity; need there be a controversy?
- Who should facilitate, monitor, and control the communications process?
- What are necessary staff communications skills?
- What is the communications process?
- What content should be communicated?
- How do staff adjust their communications strategies to reach a variety of audiences effectively?
- What vehicles should be used for communicating partnership ideas, events, and activities?

THE DEBATE: QUALITY VERSUS QUANTITY

As you know, *more* is not necessarily *better*. When partnership staff design and develop their communications plan, there is always the tendency to try to disseminate every scrap of information related to the program. An information blitz (with such associated problems as poor timing, miscalculations in judgment, and errors in copy and speeches) can result in negative reactions to the program. The alternative is to build in procedures that will establish priorities and control the flow of information, thereby ensuring that communications process *and* products are both of the highest quality.

WHO SHOULD FACILITATE, MONITOR, AND CONTROL THE COMMUNICATIONS PROCESS?

Designated partnership staff or partners' associates, hired consultants, or a school district's office of communications can be assigned responsibility for facilitating communications procedures and the preparation of materials. *However, communications is one area in which* no *materials or procedure should be implemented without written (memo or initials) approval from the partnership's office.* Careful attention to established and clearly defined procedures will prevent or at least restrict problems that occur when information

- lacks content accuracy
- requires corrections (typos, misspellings)
- requires substitutions
- requires additions or deletions
- requires other changes (for example, changes regarding to whom, when, and how information will be disseminated)

Sometimes, these communications are also reviewed by a senior administrator of the school district, the board of education, or the partnership's governing council (as appropriate).

WHAT ARE NECESSARY STAFF COMMUNICATIONS SKILLS?

Necessary communications skills include writing skills, editing skills, layout preparation, verbal communication skills (particularly as regards phone skills and meeting and conference presentations), and interrelationship skills—with groups and individuals. In addition, sensitivity to the needs and concerns of a variety of supervisors and colleagues, the media, and ethnic and socioeconomic groups is definitely helpful.

It is an asset to a program if staff already possess some—if not all— of these skills. Ongoing staff development for the partnership staff as a team—with training related to oral and written communication—will improve and solidify both communications skills and positive public perceptions of the partnership as a coordinated and effective program. This training can be carried out by the partnership's director together with appropriate professionals (public-/or community-relations staff) from the school district. Directors might also seek assistance from consultants on loan from business-community partners who have expertise in the area of communications. There are special books written to support communications efforts. One outstanding example, *Going Public: A Public Relations Guide for the Public Schools* (1985), was developed under the auspices of a partnership, the New York Alliance for the Public Schools, NYC. Another excellent resource is *A Guide for Improving School Communication*, from the Allegheny Conference Education Fund, PA (Pittsburgh, PA, Public Schools, 1979).

WHAT IS THE COMMUNICATIONS PROCESS?

How can communications support the achievement of program objectives? You will need to develop a communications plan that considers

- program goals and specific project objectives.
- the audience that must be reached in relation to each objective. (*Note:* partnership audiences include students, school staff, partners' staff, the general public, parents, and the media.)
- who will be responsible for each set of communications tasks.
- schedules for the planning, development, preparation, and dissemination of communications materials.
- criteria for evaluation of each task in relation to determined objectives.

An action plan work sheet at the end of this section (see Figure 13-1) can assist you in developing your partnership's communications process.

WHAT CONTENT SHOULD BE COMMUNICATED?

Once communications objectives have been determined (use your planning sheet), and decisions made regarding the audience to be targeted for each objective, the director and staff then focus on *what* information they wish to communicate and the *form* that communication will take. Let's talk first about the content of a partnership's communications. This content usually falls into a number of areas:

1. program administration and management (memorandum, recordkeeping forms, purchase orders, meeting and workshop arrangements) in relation to standard operating procedures
2. program planning, development, and implementation for activities involving students, staff, and partners
3. program monitoring and evaluation
4. recognition of students, staff, and partners for their achievements and contributions (human, material, and financial) to public education
5. general public relations (good will)

VEHICLES USED FOR PARTNERSHIP COMMUNICATION

General Forms Reviewed

As discussed in Section 12, most partnerships use the communication format of their supervising organization when it comes to standard operating procedures. General administrative forms are thus used as they are, or are minimally adapted to meet partnership needs, so as not to confuse staff who are required to process the partnership's forms for the supervising organization.

Range of Communication Strategies

We will be discussing the form and content of communication vehicles that are *other than general management forms*. Communication takes many forms—written, oral, and audiovisual. Through the survey, program leaders shared samples of their instruments—many of which will be used as examples throughout the remainder of this section. The following listing introduces the range of communications tools currently being used:

STRATEGIES USED TO DISSEMINATE PARTNERSHIP INFORMATION TO SCHOOL STAFF, STUDENTS, PARTNERS, AND THE COMMUNITY AT LARGE

presentations	letters
mailings (bulk/select)	bulletin boards
information packets	meetings/conferences/seminars
posters	assemblies
newsletters	news releases/feature stories
by school district	in newspapers
by partners	in magazines
annual/periodic reports	trade
corporate	general
partnership	handbooks
community	announcements
school district	telephone calls
pamphlets	School ETV
slide shows	house organs/employee pubs.
notices	PTA communications
receptions	bulletins/memos/notices
advertisements	luncheons/dinners/breakfasts
billboards	interviews (print/TV/radio)
grants reports	local TV/radio "spots" and
"thank-you" notes	public service announcements
booths at trade fairs	special events

Newsletters

Newsletters appear to be the primary messengers of activities from approximately 50 percent of the partnership programs to their communities at large. Newsletters are usually sent by the program, although community-business partners often include partnership news in their own house organs. In some cases, newsletters are published with funding support and/or technical assistance from partners. Newsletters print:

- districtwide schedules related to partnership activities (events, workshops, school holidays, vacation days)
- information regarding general student and staff achievement
- administrative information about how to contact the partnership staff/office
- articles focused on recognition of partners' efforts and highlighting partnership activities
- information of partnership activities on regional, state, and national levels
- open solicitation (through articles, coupons, and tearsheets) to the community to provide resources (human and material/in-kind) to schools, students, and staff
- photographs and graphics that lighten the newsletter's format

Partnership leaders state that they make an effort to disseminate their newsletters on a regular schedule—at least twice during the school year (quarterly is better!). The format of the newsletter has added appeal when a partnership's logo and title are printed prominently on the newsletter's front page (see more about logos under "Other Written Communications" in this section). Examples of attractive, successful, partnership newsletters come from the Cleveland Scholarship Programs, Inc., OH (see Figure 13-2); the Los Angeles Unified School District, CA (see Figure 13-3); St. Louis, MO (see Figure 13-4); and Erie, PA (see Figure 13-5).

Handbooks

The value of handbooks for partners in connection with staff development has been discussed. As a major communications tool, handbooks perform other functions, including

- defining program development, goals, and objectives
- describing partnership format, activities, and management structure
- outlining program procedures related to: (a) soliciting new partners, (b) staff/volunteer training, (c) contractual arrangements between partners, (d) recognition activities, (e) use of volunteers (as appropriate to program), (f) communications and public relations "hints," and (g) Program "do's and don'ts"

In addition to those partnership handbooks mentioned previously, in Section 10, the following programs have developed effective, comprehensive handbooks: Dade County, FL; Houston, TX; and San Francisco, CA (CAPS). (*Note:* See the resource section at the end of this handbook for contact information on all listed sources.)

Resource Guides

Many school districts have developed resource guides that are used by school staff to access community-business resources in support of school improvement efforts. These guides will be discussed fully within the context of partnership activities in Section 14.

Brochures and Fliers

Nearly all partnerships use two-color brochures and fliers that focus on disseminating partnership information and recruiting new partners; the materials perform the following functions:

- They provide basic information about the school district and partnership program; that is, goals, objectives, needs, activity areas.
- They invite participation in the program and tell the reader how to become involved.
- They outline advantages to be gained by students *and* by partners.
- If the program is already established, they recognize both program achievements and partners' supportive efforts.
- Contact information is clearly defined, including name of program, address, and phone number.

Some pamphlets, which include the functions described above, were devised by school districts' partners, for example, Mountain Bell's brochure (see Figure 13-6) for the Salt Lake City, UT program. Examples of effective brochures prepared directly by the partnership's staff come from Salem, OR (see Figure 13-7); the West Shore School District, PA (see Figure 13-8); and the Emeritus Teachers Project, Washington, DC (See Figure 13-9).

Material Directed to the Media (Print, TV, Radio)

Working with the media. The media are newspapers, television, radio, wire services, and cable television. The media work through private advertisers and public sponsorship (for example, educational television and radio). According to the survey, media coverage is handled through different structures, for example:

- the office of the Superintendent
- the district's public information-press office
- the partnership office
- a hired public relations firm, advertising agency, or consultant
- an in-kind, part-time loan of media expertise from a program partner
- a subcommittee of a governing council

- a school principal
- a partner's public-/or community-relations office

Whatever the format, media relations are an integral part of a partnership's communications component. One of the first tasks of partnership staff, assigned the responsibility of working with the media, is to research local media sources—both to gain a general understanding of available resources and to develop individual media contacts.

Most media people have little patience with ignorance or inexperience. Understanding, and knowing how to respond to, media deadlines and requirements establishes a firm base for productive relationships that benefit the partnership program as well as all participating partners. One good example of a useful and efficient tool that supports this process is the mailing list form, for disseminating information to local, national, and regional media (see Figure 13-10), that was developed by the St. Louis, MO, partnership program.

Learning Special Media Skills. If staff lack experience in working with or writing for their local press or TV, *they should seek technical assistance regarding material, format, and content* before *they contact or send material to the media.* Expertise can be sought from colleagues within the school district or from partners' staffs on loan for short periods of time for specific projects.

When such expertise is supplied, *all* partnership staff should participate in the training process. Topics for this staff development—addressing both print and nonprint media—could include

- developing short- and long-range media action plans
- where and when to give your media presentations
- format and content of media presentations
- differentiating between feature stories (in-depth, background, human interest) and hard news (immediate events, ceremonies, conferences)
- selecting activity priorities for media presentation (programs, services, events, awards, recognition)
- deadlines—the importance of timing
- contacting the media (form and style)
- follow-up (form and style)
- networking—building relationships between the partnership program and the media and between partners and the media
- press conferences and briefings

Press Releases as a Specialty. Partnership programs hold activities and events to spark the interest of the media. Press releases that tell about a partnership activity or invite the press to an event are the most common form of communicating with local media.

How often should these press releases be given and contacts made to publicize the program? Is overkill a possibility? The survey showed that partnerships, in general, did not bombard their local press with program information. According to partnership leaders, the frequency of issuing *and* of printing releases to the press varied widely—depending on the size of the program, the activities involved, relations with the press . . . and sometimes local politics!

When writing a press release, keep in mind the objectives of this communication. The dissemination of the release should cause the following to happen: (1) program information reaches as large an audience as possible; and (2) media who receive the communications read it, want to disseminate it to their audiences, interpret your information accurately and in a favorable light, and contact the partnership office for clarification or additional information regarding the program.

To accomplish these objectives, your press releases should

- be clearly and succinctly written (no more than two pages long, double-spaced)
- have short paragraphs with descriptive lead sentences
- contain no grammatical, typographical, or spelling errors (watch those names!)
- be written on partnership letterhead with contact information defined and available

When you become an expert in writing press releases, you often find that the media report your stories almost exactly as written in your releases, or reporters will use your material and then call the partnership office for additional background information to amplify the basic facts. When you've received positive news coverage, good manners suggest a thank-you note or call. Following are some good examples of press releases that received wide-range news coverage: from the St. Louis Public Schools, MO (see Figure 13-11); and the Los Angeles Dodgers, a partner of the Los Angeles Unified School District, CA (see Figure 13-12).

Other Written Communications

General Overview. In this area fall general correspondence, memorandums, testimonial letters, reports, thank-you notes, announcements, recognition or award materials and invitations. All written communication should be straightforward and to the point. The reader then knows the sender's intent after reading the first line or, at most, the first paragraph. Otherwise, the communication becomes wastebasket fodder!

The format of the material should be attractive and uncluttered. Most partnerships have developed a logo—a symbol of the partnership—that is usually displayed on all printed material. One eye-catching example is the logo from Lancaster, PA (see Figure 13-13).

Report Writing. Report writing is another essential area of communications for a partnership program. Reports are prepared for supervisors, governing councils, colleagues, partners, and the board of education. Because of its special importance, report writing will be discussed fully in Section 15.

Recognition Materials. Recognition of partnership achievements—student and staff activities, donation of materials, sponsoring of events, volunteer services, and so forth—disseminates program accomplishments to the larger community and expresses public appreciation for partners' efforts. Recognition activities can come in many forms: through speeches, ceremonies, presentations, and written communication. Examples of written communication related to a variety of appreciation activities come from Richmond, VA (see Figure 13-14), and Charlotte-Mecklenburg, NC (see Figure 13-15). *The ABC's of Adopt-A-School Handbook* from Memphis, TN, contains numerous examples of news releases focused on recognition of adopters' efforts in support of the city's schools. A complete packet of materials, which clearly defines how to initiate a "Partner Exemplary Awards Process," is available through Dade Partners, FL.

Verbal Communication

Overview. Partnerships are a "people" business. Oral expression, like written communication, encourages positive responses from a variety of audiences. Public perceptions about the program are built by all staff members, whether they answer the telephone or conduct partnership business over the phone or at meetings, conferences, and other events.

Like written communications, *all* oral communications concerning program activities and staff should be reviewed and approved by the director. Content and format of activities that involve oral communication are carefully planned and implemented. Recommendations for written communication, presented earlier in this section, apply equally to oral communication; in addition, there are some suggestions particular to interviews and speeches that will be reviewed at this time.

Interviews. Whenever there is a choice, interviews should be conducted face to face with the interviewer; the person interviewed can then gauge the interviewer's body language and more clearly define both the focus and direction of the interview. The partnership's director screens and approves the interview and guides staff in developing the following effective interview process and skills:

a. A mutually convenient time and place are set for the interview.

b. Partnership staff or partners who will be interviewed coordinate information on the subject and procedures of the interview.

c. Questions are issued sufficiently in advance so that those being interviewed can adequately prepare their responses.

d. If the interview is "live" or pretaped, there is opportunity to rehearse beforehand.

e. If there is a phone interview, the person interviewed does not speak "off the record." For the interviewer or reporter all news is "for the record." Therefore, if there is uncertainty about a particular question, the interviewer is told that answers will be forthcoming after being checked. Return calls are *always* made when questions are left unanswered.

Speeches and Presentations. Speeches and presentations are made during special events (recognition ceremonies, "adoptions"), workshops, meetings and conferences, and at news briefings. Preparation, orientation, training for, and supervision of these presentations are emphasized; an event can fall flat on the basis of the oral presentation. Following are some guidelines that program leaders should provide for their staff:

a. Guidelines regarding the length of the oral presentation are set *and* kept.

b. The subject matter of the presentation complements the objective of the partnership activity.

c. The presentation is clearly focused. It has a beginning, a middle, and an end.

d. If the presentation is for a workshop, a meeting or a news briefing, an outline or summary is available to the audience and participants.

Audiovisual Presentations

Audiovisual presentations are slide presentations, tapes, videotapes, photographs, and overlays (used with overhead projectors). Try to avoid the homemade look when using audiovisuals. It is better to have a direct, well-executed oral presentation *without* audiovisuals than to use aids that detract from, rather than enhance, a presentation.

Most school districts have professionals with audiovisual expertise and experience. These experts or others on loan from business and community organizations can help the partnership develop a quality library of audiovisual materials that can be updated or refined each year. In the long run, it is more effective and efficient and, probably, less costly to use and work with audiovisual experts, than to train yourself or your staff to do the job. A comprehensive handbook from the Genigraphics Corporation of Liverpool, NY, is *The Art of Making a Successful Slide Presentation*. Although this handbook is directed to the making of slide presentations, it also provides the following guidance to partnership leaders as they plan the development of *all* audiovisual materials:

a. Make certain that the type on all audiovisual materials can be read by everyone in the room; using phrases and words, rather than complete sentences, will help.

b. Your speaking level should complement the site you are using. If you require additional amplification, arrange for microphones during the presentation.

c. The content of your presentation should suit your audience. Mistakes are often made when the same audiovisual presentation is used over and over again for different audiences for whom the material may not be appropriate. People "tune out" at such presentations. Leaders are advised to consider

- what response they wish to provoke from their audiences: conveying information or stimulating action.

- what format would make the content most interesting. Simple is better; for example, highlighting one idea per slide and presenting statistics in graph form.
- what and how much information must be conveyed to ensure that the message of the audiovisual is clearly and succinctly stated. The length of the audiovisual presentation becomes an important consideration—so key points require emphasis.
- ensuring that slides and the visual part of videotape presentations match the oral script.
- their own role in an audiovisual presentation. Therefore, they should remember

1. not to stand in front of the screen.
2. *always* to rehearse a presentation with its audiovisual aids well ahead of time.
3. to check their slides and audiovisual equipment themselves before the presentation.
4. to keep their presentation focused, thereby avoiding irrelevant or un-related remarks that detract from a presentation's objective.
5. to speak in a conversational tone.

ACTION PLAN WORK SHEET
COMMUNICATIONS

I. Communications Goal _____

II. Communications Objective _____

SCHEDULE/TIMELINE (date due/completed) _____

Task A	Audience to Be Reached	Responsib Agent(s)	Planning Steps	Preparation Steps	Dissemination Steps	Criteria for Evaluation
1.			1.	1.	1.	
2.			2.	2.	2.	
3.			3.	3.	3.	
4.			4.	4.	4.	
5.			5.	5.	5.	

_____
Signature of staff member

_____
Signature of director

Figure 13–1

187

CLEVELAND SCHOLARSHIP PROGRAMS, INC.
CSP NEWSLETTER

Fall 1984

CSP Alumnus is White House Fellow

Throughout the years CSP has had many occasions to be proud of our alumni. From time to time, however, there comes a person whose contributions and accomplishments warrant special recognition. Jose C. Feliciano is such an individual.

Feliciano is part of CSP's early history. He was selected as a finalist as a senior in high school and earned a B.A. in Psychology at John Carroll University, graduating cum laude in 1972. In 1975 he received his J.D. from Cleveland Marshall College of Law. Feliciano worked as staff attorney for the Cleveland Legal Aid Society until 1978 when he was appointed Assistant Public Defender for Cuyahoga County. He was appointed to his present position as Chief Prosecuting Attorney for the City of Cleveland in 1980. During his four years as chief prosecutor, he "constantly demonstrated dilligence, sensitivity, and compassion for the interests of all citizens of our community," Cleveland Mayor George Voinivich said in a recent news release.

Feliciano's civic affiliations further demonstrate his contributions to the community. He has served on the Board of Trustees of the Cleveland Bar Association,

United Way, Federation for Community Planning, Greater Cleveland Round Table, Red Cross, Cuyahoga County Catholic Social Service, Legal Aid Society, Cuyahoga Community College Advisory Board, Center for Human Services, United Negro College Advisory Board, Hough Area Development Corporation/Cleveland Midtown Development Corporation, Hispanic Community Project, Hispanic Community Forum, Neighborhood Housing Services, and Spanish- American Committee and General Counsel. He somehow found time to earn an Executive M.B.A. from Cleveland State in June of this year. He is a member of the Visiting Committee at Case Western Reserve Law School and is an adjunct professor at John Carroll University.

In 1982, the Cleveland Jaycees named Feliciano Outstanding Citizen and also selected him for their Distinguished Service Award. In 1983, he received the Ernest J. Bohn Public Administrator of the Year Award and was selected by the Ohio Jaycees as one of the five outstanding young men in the state.

(Continued on page 6.)

Choices Still Available for CSP Students

CSP has been able to retain open student choice in college enrollment as a feature of the program. Last year our students attended one hundred twenty-nine four year colleges/universities nationwide and thirty-five two year colleges or vocational programs.

The distribution of CSP students enrolled in the various types of colleges and schools reflects the fact that most CSP students choose to remain within Ohio. The availability of the Ohio Instructional Grant (OIG) for public and private in-state institutions is an influential factor for most students, and a smaller percentage of freshman than usual chose to begin their studies out of the state in the 83-84 academic year.

Beginning with the initial contact, CSP high school Advisors stress that students, while applying to a wide variety of schools, should always include a local or Ohio

institution so that they will have options for enrollment if financial aid becomes a problem. As college costs increase, more families are qualifying for aid. At the same time, the level of Federal student aid funding has declined in real dollars. Funds available to colleges for financial aid awards do not meet financial need for an increasing number of students. Such students must assume a disproportionate burden of Student Loan or term-time work as financial aid awards become increasingly "unequal". CSP urges all students to give themselves a range of acceptable institutions from which to choose.

Every year a certain number of students return to the Cleveland area to attend school while living at home.

(Continued on page 2.)

Figure 13–2

adopt-a-school news

February 1985   Published by the Adopt-A-School Council   Issue No. 10

Chevron "adopts" Cowan School

Cowan Avenue Schools' recent affiliation with Chevron U.S.A., Inc. through the Los Angeles School District's Adopt-A-School program is increasingly evident on the school's campus.

Chevron announced its adoption plans in June, amid summer vacation planning, and then it went to work structuring a program for the 330 students enrolled in kindergarten through fifth grades at Cowan.

When classes began in September, the foundation had been laid for a math/science center, a six-plot garden and student participation in Chevron's Adopt-A-Ship program.

Chevron employees, led by coordinator Mardena Fehling, have designed and will provide volunteer instruction on the prehistoric life of our planet and its modern applications throughout the year, following the curriculum guidelines of the Los Angeles Unified School District.

The program will involve many employees of the adoptive corporation in a person-to-person commitment to compliment and enhance elementary-level instruction provided in the classroom.

The science center features weekly topics presented by Chevron employees to fourth and fifth graders.

Highlights during the year will include docents from the Page Museum who will present fossils, skeletons and "dig" samples for examination; a study of the human body inlcuding the five senses; hygiene, nutrition and yoga; and learning about the Earth including volcanoes, earthquakes, underwater life, rocks and minerals, animals, plants and people.

All fifth graders have participated in one-day excursions to Chevron's research facility in La Habra where they toured the Ice Room, the Heliochronometer and the Core Sample room and viewed rock samples and insects through the scanning electron microscope.

A highlight of the trip was a chance to dig for and keep 4- to 5-million-year-old fossilized shells.

In the spring the students will be taken on a tour of the Chevron refinery in El Segundo.

(Continued on back page)

Aragon Avenue School and Southern Pacific Transportation Company joined forces with (front row) student council members, Miguel Lopez, Sandra Rivas, Hein Le Cong and Michael Amador; (rear row) Patricia Moran, Adopt-A-School coordinator; Lorena Hornby, principal; Thomas C. Buckley, vice president of Southern Transportation Company; Annette Held, Adopt-A-School coordinator; and Sami Kushida, school program coordinator in attendance.

Aragon Avenue and So. Pacific unite

The new Adopt-A-School partnership of Aragon Avenue School and Southern Pacific Transportation Company was formalized on Oct. 25, 1984 at the school plant.

An outdoor assembly of the total student body served to welcome Thomas C. Buckley, vice president of Southern Pacific Transportation.

The children performed for Buckley with a musical program of railroad songs and presented him with a poster of the Southern Pacific logo. A reception was held after school to introduce Buckley to the staff and the parents of the pupils.

On Nov. 2, 1984, 14 Aragon pupils were invited to the Southern Pacific Railroad yards to participate in the filming of a railroad safety segment of the Channel 28 Children's Workshop series on safety, to be aired this month. The pupils had a tour of the yards and the official Southern Pacific Olympic engine. Participants were given souvenir T-shirts and hats by the Southern Pacific Transportation Corp.

Reprinted by permission of Adopt-A-School Program, Los Angeles Unified School District, CA.

Figure 13–3

CONNECTIONS

School
Partnership
Program

SOUTHWESTERN BELL BEGINS
PARTNERSHIP WITH SUMNER HIGH SCHOOL

ST. LOUIS PUBLIC SCHOOLS
VOL. 2, ISSUE 1 NOV. 1984

Two classes are already benefiting from the Sumner High School/Southwestern Bell School Partnership, which began early this fall with programs in computer programming and communication. Three additional programs will begin soon in accounting, marketing and the Junior Toastmaster's Club.

Southwestern Bell's Partnership involvement with Sumner High School expands upon the company's past and existing programs with the St. Louis Public Schools. Leroy Grant, Staff Manager – Public Relations, responded to Partnership's requests to share their expertise in the classroom because of Southwestern Bell's firm belief in and support of the public school system.

Sandra Gerber, Sumner computer programming teacher, is emphatic in her appreciation of Partnership Programs and the ways in which outside business resources strengthen her classroom instruction.

"Mr. Hogan will cover areas in which I am not as well-versed, like Hollerith coding, and arrange a tour where students can actually follow their phone bills through the entire computer

Keith Hogan from Southwestern Bell explains computer card to Sumner student.

Leroy Grant of Southwestern Bell

system. Exposure to someone like Mr. Hogan who has 20 years of computer experience is invaluable!"

Hogan's response was equally enthusiastic, "It's a darn good program." He intends to provide a step-by-step, easy-to-follow program that will give students the same basic instruction he gives in his first year college computer course.

"My goal is to reduce their apprehension about college . . . to help them build confidence in themselves." Hogan asserts.

Carter Dunkin from Southwestern Bell's Public Information Office is drawing upon his experiences as a newspaper editor and college instructor in implementing a seven-session Partnership Program at Summer. A public relations plan for the school is part of the program.

Teacher, Linda Fowler, and Southwestern Bell volunteer, Carter Dunkin, plan their Partnership in communications

BUSINESS HIGHLIGHT

Reprinted by permission of the St. Louis Public Schools, MO.

Figure 13–4

Breakfast anyone. . . see page 4

ERIE SCHOOL DISTRICT

newsletter

Volume 4	January 29, 1982	Number 8

Hammermill "Adopts" Burton Students

Hammermill Paper Company has adopted all the Burton Elementary School students. Figuretively, speaking, of course.

Burton principal Greg Myers this past week announced he and Hammermill officials and Burton PTA members just completed arrangements for final adoption papers for Burton School Students.

Myers, who considers community involvement in the public schools a priority goal for Burton, was instrumental in arranging the unique program. He contacted several local industries and

The program certainly has promising implications for both the schools and local industry and business."

— Myers

businesses before Hammermill accepted the challenge.

According to Myers, the program will increase community understanding of the schools, while providing students with some important benefits, including a better understanding of the work world.

"This kind of cooperative program, I think, offers some real opportunities for career awareness."

— Stephany

The program, a first for Erie and the state of Pennsylvania, is being handled by Mike Stephany, Hammermill Manager of Corporate Affirmative Action; Ken Manno, Hammermill Public Relations Officer in change of tours; Greg Myers and the Burton PTA

"We cannot continue to ask teachers to do a better job without supporting them."

— Manno

The program offers many positive possibilities for students and Hammermill alike, including occupational information, educational incentives, classroom assistance, special interest sponsors, communications, fund raising school environment improvement and teacher education.

Myers, Manno, Stephany and PTA members already met in an organizational session to discuss the direction and future of the program. A second meeting will be held at Burton School in the very near future. □

Reprinted by permission of the Erie School District, PA.

Figure 13–5

Adopt a School Program

"It's obvious, from the student, they have a real thirst for one-on-one teaching. It is tremendously satisfying to me to help fulfill that desire."

—Dale Wallace
Tutor, Whittier Elem.

"I get as much out of tutoring as the students. It's a special treat for me to become acquainted with teens and help them prepare for an exciting future!"

—Martha Knowlton
Tutor, South High School

To: Linda Debs
Adopt A School Program
Room 416
250 Bell Plaza
Salt Lake City, Utah 84111

I would like to learn more about the Mountain Bell Adopt A School Program.

Name _____

Address _____

Phone _____

Figure 13–6

192

EXPAND YOUR WORLD — TUTOR!

HAVE YOU EVER THOUGHT ABOUT TUTORING?

You've been around. You've seen lots of things. You've dealt with lots of people. You could be sharing that knowledge and experience with young people through tutoring.

WHO IS WELCOME?

Everyone (and their spouses). Age does not matter. You don't need a college degree. You don't need to be able to speak a foreign language or do math equations on the Einstein level.

WHAT DO YOU NEED?

Patience and the desire to work with young children and teenagers who need special help with all sorts of subjects.

If you have good basic skills in English, Math or even personal computers, you can contribute a great deal.

WHERE WOULD YOU TUTOR?

Mountain Bell has "adopted" both South High School and Whittier Elementary.

WHEN WOULD YOU TUTOR?

From September to June, during regular school hours. You can volunteer as much as you wish—usually an hour a week is given.

And there's no problem if you go out of town for a few weeks during the school year. Just inform the teacher and he or she will be waiting with open arms when you return.

WHY SHOULD YOU TUTOR?

For the thrill of it! Most of the work is done one-on-one. That's the kind of attention that gets results. And the more you work with the students, the more their victories become yours.

— You may be helping a teen, new to our country, who is learning English and the "how-to's" of living in America. What a thrill when understanding dawns and the concept you've helped instill is grasped.

— You may work with an elementary child. What a joy you'll feel when that student's face lights up and happy arms are wrapped around you. Satisfaction? You bet!

HOW DO YOU VOLUNTEER?

For more information and to sign up call Linda Debs on 237-6384.

She'll be glad to answer your questions.

REMEMBER————

You have a lot to offer.

When you tutor — you're needed,
— you're helping,
— you're growing.

And when the students smile at you and say "Thank you", then you know it's worth it.

JOIN US TODAY!!!

Reprinted by permission of Utah Mountain Bell.

Figure 13–6 (continued)

193

Business Partnership In Education

SALEM PUBLIC SCHOOLS

TO GET INVOLVED

The Business Partnership program is co-ordinated by the Salem Public Schools Office of Federal, State and Community Relations. It is co-sponsored by the Salem Area Chamber of Commerce, which assists with publicity, business recruitment and evaluation of program activities.

For more information contact:

Office of Federal, State
and Community Relations
Salem Public Schools
1309 Ferry Street SE
Salem, Oregon 97301
(503) 399-3038

Salem Area Chamber of Commerce
220 Cottage Street NE
Salem, Oregon 97301
(503) 581-1466

Printing Courtesy of
Sylvan Learning Center
and
Salem School District 24J

Figure 13–7

WHAT OTHERS SAY

Not only businesses and schools, but all Salem residents benefit when public schools use community resources to enhance the education of our young.

Sue Harris
Mayor of Salem

The Business Partnership program is an outstanding example of what is possible when a local school district and an active Chamber of Commerce decide they need to be partners in the education of the community's youth. Our students are growing up understanding the important role that business plays in the overall community.

William Kendrick
Superintendent
Salem Public Schools

The Business Partnership program provides an essential step in creating stronger partners in education with the business community. The closer ties between business and education have positive long-term results.

Jay Hoyer
Executive Vice-President
Salem Area Chamber of Commerce

Tight budgets and high expectations of the schools necessitate cooperation with other public and private institutions . . . . Business and community organizations are essential in achieving district goals.

**The Citizens' Task Force
on Excellence in Education**

The Business Partnership program provides a unique opportunity for our students to be exposed to the benefits of a free enterprise system.

Joseph Loe
Vice-chairperson
Salem School Board

194

THE BUSINESS PARTNERSHIP PROGRAM

links a local business or association with an elementary school. Its primary purpose is to form an alliance so the school may use the business's resources to enhance its learning environment.

The expertise of personnel and the use of facilities, materials and equipment benefit and enrich the curriculum without spending additional tax dollars.

It allows businesses to give students first hand knowledge of our competitive, free enterprise system, to give visible public service, and to encourage volunteerism by its employees.

THE BUSINESS PARTNERSHIP CONCEPT

is gaining in importance and popularity nationwide. At a national conference at the White House for business leaders and educators who are at the forefront of this movement, President Reagan said, "I am convinced that collaborative efforts between the public and private sectors will succeed because they reflect the spirit of volunteerism and community self-help which has served America so well throughout our history. The adopt-a-school program is a commendable model for others to follow."

GOALS OF THE PROGRAM

1. To bring business people into a school to work with students, teachers and administrators on projects which the school believes will be helpful and which business people are qualified to accomplish.

2. To give students and teachers a realistic picture of the business world.

3. To supplement classroom studies with relevant learning experiences in business and industry.

4. To give business people an understanding of the educational system; how it works, its strengths and its problems..

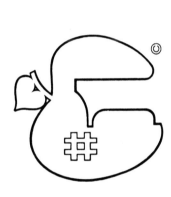

Your public schools...
There's no better place to learn.

SOME SUGGESTED ACTIVITIES

- Assist with programs to motivate students.

- Present a class or a mini-course on computers, science, photography, grooming, citizenship or other appropriate areas.

- Sponsor a writing or art contest.

- Conduct tours of the business place. Invite students to "shadow" employees at work.

- Display student work at the business.

- Lend company films, displays, equipment.

- Tutor individual students.

- Sponsor a career exploration day.

- Show students how classroom learning is used in the world of work.

- Use school facilities for company meetings or athletic events.

- Set up first aid or wellness classes for employees.

- Provide help with publications and public relations.

- Work on joint community project during the holidays.

Reprinted by permission of the Salem-Keizer Public Schools, OR.

Figure 13–7 (continued)

West Shore School District

ADOPT-A-SCHOOL
PROGRAM

KEY IN . . .

TO EDUCATION

1984-1985

WEST SHORE
SCHOOL BOARD MEMBERS

Robert C. Baker, Jr., President
Donald E. Schell, Jr.,Vice President
Charles J. Bender, Sr.
Lana M. Forconi
David W. Hunter
Pamela L. Iams
William J. Jordan
Harry L. Messick
Marsha A.Stetler

Dr. Larry A. Sayre, Superintendent

ADOPT-A-SCHOOL PROGRAM
TASK FORCE
West Shore School District

Brenda Young, ACES
James Honafius, Appleton Papers Inc.
Gretchen Haertsch, CCNB, N.A.
Russell E. Clouser, Hardee's
Robert Kessler, Sr., Kessler's, Inc.
William Lunsford, Jr., Patriot-News
Dale L. Baker, Chairman

West Shore School District
1000 Hummel Avenue
Lemoyne, Pennsylvania 17043
(717) 763-7101

Figure 13-8

1984-85
ADOPT-A-SCHOOL
PARTNERSHIPS

Walter Witmer, CEDAR CLIFF
James Honafius, Appleton Papers, Inc.

Gary Smith, RED LAND
Barry Paxton, Berg Electronics

Jeffrey Breighner, ALLEN
Timothy Miller, Iceland Seafood Corp.

Joseph Marcin, LEMOYNE
Robert Kessler, Sr., Kessler's, Inc.

James Starr, NEW CUMBERLAND
William Lunsford, Jr., Patriot-News

Dreher Richards, FAIRVIEW/MT. ZION
Glenn Schlosser, Whiteco Metrocom, Inc.

Jayne Coover, FISHING CREEK
A. W. Heinz, IBM Corporation

J. Richard Henry, HERMAN AVENUE/
WASHINGTON HEIGHTS
Russell Clouser, Hardee's Family
Restaurant

Ronald Shuey, HIGHLAND
Gretchen Haertsch, CCNB, N.A.

Richard Shepps, HILLSIDE
James Dudley, American Can Co.

H. Charles Ryder, LOWER ALLEN/ROSSMOYNE
Carolyn Fisher, Davenport's

Deloris McElroy, NEWBERRY
David and Barbara Forgas
Forgas Lawn & Garden Center

WHAT IS THE ADOPT-A-SCHOOL PROGRAM?

The Adopt-A-School program is a co-operative program between the schools of the West Shore School District community—business and industry, civic organizations, churches and other interested groups.

The program is designed to enrich educational programs for students while offering community groups the chance for direct interaction and rewarding involvement. Each partnership is uniquely designed to benefit both parties.

WHAT WILL THE ADOPT-A-SCHOOL PROGRAM DO?

The purpose of Adopt-A-School is to strengthen and improve school programs through the involvement of the community. Adopt-A-School fosters a better understanding of the public school system within the West Shore community. By creating a climate of involvement and interaction between community and schools, the community will prepare for its own economic future.

ADOPT-A-SCHOOL PROGRAMS 1984-85

Cedar Cliff High School
APPLETON PAPERS, INC.
To provide expertise and technical assistance to students; to help develop a better understanding of the free enterprise system among the students and professional staff.

197

Red Land High School
BERG ELECTRONICS
To work with the school to develop a good educational system; to provide opportunities for student interaction with the industry.

Allen Middle School
ICELAND SEAFOOD CORPORATION
To reinforce social studies, economics and nutrition programs with students as it relates to the Iceland Seafood Corporation operations.

Lemoyne Middle School
KESSLER'S, INC.
To give the middle school students experiences relating to the manufacturing process through field trips, resource speakers and audio-visual presentations.

New Cumberland Middle School
PATRIOT-NEWS
To provide technical assistance to help the school upgrade and improve the school newsletter; to work with the Newspaper in the Classroom project.

Fairview/Mt. Zion Elementary Schools
WHITECO METROCOM, INC.
To provide students with an understanding of the part outdoor advertising plays in marketing products; to give students an understanding of job availability and educational requirements for positions in the advertising field.

Fishing Creek Elementary School
IBM CORPORATION
To provide experiences for staff in computer technology and applications in society.

Herman Avenue/Washington Heights Elementary Schools
HARDEE'S of CAMP HILL
To provide the children with an awareness of business contributions, especially within the community.

Highland Elementary School
CCNB BANK, N.A.
To increase the knowledge of students in the general area of banking and personal finance through tours, speakers and other activities.

Hillside Elementary
AMERICAN CAN COMPANY
To provide resources such as films and speakers to explain the manufacturing process to the students.

Lower Allen/Rossmoyne Elementary Schools
DAVENPORT'S
To work in the area of advertising through student developed ads on display at the restaurants; to provide resources for the 4th grade nutrition program.

Newberry Elementary School
FORGAS LAWN & GARDEN CENTER
To provide expertise and planning necessary for a long range plan to beautify the exterior of the school.

FOR FURTHER INFORMATION CONTACT:

Dr. Dale L. Baker, Asst. Superintendent
West Shore School District
(717) 763-7101

Reprinted by permission of the Adopt-A-School Program, West Shore School District, PA.

Figure 13–8 (continued)

THE EMERITUS TEACHERS PROJECT

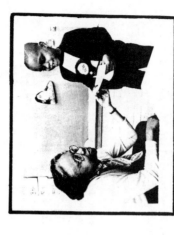

A Project of

ASSOCIATES FOR RENEWAL IN EDUCATION, INC.

The Edmonds School Building
9th and D Streets, N.E.
Washington, D.C. 20002
(202) 547-8030

ADVISORY COUNCIL

LeGrand Baldwin
Dr. William H. Brown
Edward Buckson
Elizabeth Canter
Emanuel Carr
Idella M. Costner
Joyce Green
Dr. James T. Guines
Mary L. Harris
Dr. Mary Johnson
James R. Lindsay
Lawrence H. Mirel
William H. Simon
Gloria F. Smith
C. Vanessa Spinner
Dr. Helen Turner
Dr. James Van Dien

Mattie W. Carey, Director
Hortense M. Fitzgerald, Coordinator

Funded by:

**The Eugene and Agnes E. Meyer
Foundation**

and the

District of Columbia Public Schools

WHAT THE CLASSROOM TEACHERS SAY:

"The children bring their work back to the classroom to be displayed."

"I do not have to stop to tell the retired teachers how to teach or tutor. Their experience is what I like."

"My students seem more confident and are starting to respond more in class."

WHAT THE EMERITUS TEACHERS SAY:

"I want to keep busy, and working with young people keeps me on my toes."

"I can keep in touch with the profession I love."

"I like the enthusiastic manner in which we are received in the schools by the students and the teachers."

WHAT THE CHILDREN SAY:

"I like it when my tutor reads to us."

"She's nice. She puts math problems on the board and then she lets us do them."

"We write stories about the pictures she shows us and I like that."

"I always have work to show my classroom teacher."

Figure 13–9

THE EMERITUS TEACHERS PROJECT IS . . . .

An exemplary tutorial program focusing on retired teacher volunteers who share their life-long experience, knowledge, and expertise with elementary students in the Capitol Hill area of the District of Columbia Public Schools. Operational since 1980, the project's merit has been adequately demonstrated by the improved academic performance of its participating students on each grade level. Evaluation is based on extensive documentation by Emeritus Teachers, informal teacher assessment, and standardized test results.

GOALS:

● To provide an avenue for retired educators to make use of their life-long experiences, knowledge, and skills in a satisfying and meaningful manner.

● To assist in upgrading the academic achievement of participating students.

● To help determine the effectiveness of retired teacher volunteers on student achievement.

GOALS ARE ACCOMPLISHED:

● Through tutoring sessions
   Individual
   Small group

● Through workshops for Emeritus Teachers focusing on volunteerism and current method of tutoring

● Through training workshops conducted by Emeritus Teachers for
   Classroom Teachers
   Educational Aides
   Community Volunteers
   Conference Participants

● Through classroom teacher assessment and standardized test scores of participating students

BENEFITS DERIVED:

For Retirees

● community involvement
● contact with peers
● association with young people
● feeling of usefulness

For the Students

● individual attention
● improved performance
● increased self-esteem
● non-threatening environment
● positive role models
● a link with the cultural past

For the Classroom Teachers

● in-depth assistance for students
● more effective teaching time
● an additional source

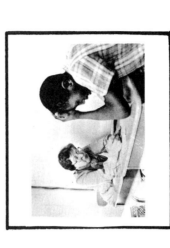

Reprinted by permission of the Emeritus Teachers Project, Washington, DC.

Figure 13–9 (continued)

199

RELEASE TOPIC _____

MEDIA MAILING LIST

DAILY NEWSPAPERS

St. Louis Post-Dispatch

_____

_____

_____

_____

St. Louis Globe-Democrat

_____

_____

_____

_____

WEEKLY NEWSPAPERS

Citizen Newspapers
Florissant Valley Reporter
Journal Newspapers
Ladue News
Naborhood Link News
Northside Community News
St. Louis County Star
The Riverfront Times
Suburban Newspapers
  Southside Journal
  South County Journal
  West County Journal
  Lafayette Press Journal
  Neighborhood News
South St. Louis County News
Webster Kirkwood Times
West End Word

SPECIAL INTEREST NEWSPAPERS

St. Louis Business Journal
St. Louis American
St. Louis Sentinel
St. Louis Argus
The Crusade

_____

_____

MAGAZINES

St. Louis Commerce
St. Louis Magazine
St. Louis Living
Proud

NATIONAL NEWSPAPERS

New York Times Correspondent
Associated Press
United Press

TELEVISION

KSDK-TV (5)	KDNL-TV (30)
KTVI-TV (2)	KMOX-TV (4)
KETC-TV (9)	KPLR-TV (11)

RADIO

KADI-FM	KWUR-FM
KATZ-AM	KWK-AM-FM
KFUO-AM/FM	KXOK-AM
KHTR-FM	KYKY-FM
KMOX-AM	WGNU-AM
KUSA	WIL AM-FM
KS94	WRTH-AM
KSHE-FM	KCFM-FM
KWMU-FM	KHTR-FM
KSTL-AM	

CABLE

Continental Cablevision
Group W Cable
Storer Cable Communications
Horizon Cable TV
United Video Cablevision
Warner Amex

OTHERS

_____

_____

_____

Reprinted by permission of the St. Louis Public Schools, MO.
Figure 13–10

St. Louis Public School

news

FOR IMMEDIATE RELEASE   October 8, 1984

PARTNERSHIP PROGRAM INVOLVES CITY AND COUNTY STUDENTS
IN RIVER FACES FESTIVAL

Over 250 St. Louis city and county students will don masks they have been creating since the beginning of the school year at the River Faces Parade and Show Day to be held Saturday, October 13 at 10 a.m. on the grounds of the Gateway Arch. The students' active participation in this creative festival is part of a St. Louis School Partnership Program.

The River Faces Festival, under the direction of In the Heart of the Beast Puppet and Mask Theatre from Minneapolis, will feature huge puppets, stiltwalkers and papier-mache creatures of earth, sky and water. A variety of community bands will perform during the parade and pageant which are open to the public.

The River Faces partnership program involved students in grades four through twelve from seven St. Louis Public Schools and three county schools. In eight separate workshops, they learned about the River Faces theme, masking movement for parades and mask construction. Area artists skilled in mask making visited the schools and worked with students in papier-mache, clay and cardboard mediums.

Teachers had attended a workshop incorporating the same concepts last spring so they, too, could help the children design their own masks.

The city schools involved are: Humboldt Visual & Performing Arts Middle School, Marquette Visual & Performing Arts Middle School, Shaw Visual & Performing Arts Elementary School, Marshall Elementary School, Academy of Math & Science High School, Mark Twain Elementary School and Walbridge Elementary School.

MORE

Public Affairs Division, 911 Locust, St. Louis, MO 63101   Contact: Glenda Partlow

Figure 13-11

PARTNERSHIP PROGRAM INVOLVES CITY AND COUNTY STUDENTS
IN RIVER FACES FESTIVAL Add - 1

The county schools are Maplewood-Richmond Heights High School,
Delmar-Harvard Elementary School and Ivland Elementary School.

The River Faces Festival is a project of the St. Louis Arts and Humanities
Commission with assistance from the St. Louis Ambassadors and Home Box Office,
Inc.

Sharon Blockage, a member of the Arts and Humanities Commission, said
the River Faces partnership program has allowed students to be creatively
involved in the festival. "It gives them the opportunity to contribute to
the celebration instead of simply viewing it," she said.

For more information on the River Faces partnership program, contact
Mary Ferguson or Glenda Partlow at 361-5588.

Reprinted by permission of the St. Louis Public Schools, MO.

Figure 13–11 (continued)

NEWS RELEASE

AUTOMATIC RADIO-TV — AUDIO NEWS RELEASES

DODGERS AT HOME
FOR AM RELEASES: (213) 221-5163 or 221-5164
FOR PM RELEASES: (213) 476-2277 or 476-2278

DODGERS ON ROAD
AM AND PM RELEASES: (213) 476-2277 or 476-2278

LOS ANGELES DODGERS, INC.
1000 ELYSIAN PARK AVENUE • LOS ANGELES, CALIFORNIA 90012
TELEPHONE: 224-1301 • STEVE BRENER, Publicity Director

1983
Western Division
Champions

LOS ANGELES 1984
JULY 28 – AUGUST 12

FOR IMMEDIATE RELEASE

SOLANO STUDENT TO CARRY OLYMPIC TORCH FOR DODGERS

Larry Lien, a sixth grade student at Solano Avenue School, will represent the Los Angeles Dodgers in the Olympic Torch Relay to benefit the Boys Club of America.

Lien, 12, will carry the torch for one kilometer through a yet undetermined route in Los Angeles as the Olympic Torch makes its way from Athens, Greece, to the Los Angeles Memorial Coliseum for Opening Ceremonies of the 1984 Summer Olympics on Saturday, July 28th.

Lien, who was born in Saigon, South Vietnam, has attended Solano Avenue School for six years. He was selected by the Solano faculty because of his well-rounded academic and athletic skills.

"Larry typifies the ideal Solano student," says Principal James Messrah. "He has come here from a foreign country, learned a new language, and has begun a new life in a different society. His courage and determination are traits we hope every Solano student will develop during their years of elementary school."

The Dodgers and Solano have been partners in the Los Angeles Unified School District's Adopt-A-School program since 1980. Dodger employees take time away from their Dodger Stadium duties to teach the students the skills needed to work in a major league sports organization.

Along with the educational portion of the program, there are also a number of special events, including: a Solano Night at Dodger Stadium, a character-building assembly featuring Dodger players, sixth grade commencement exercises in the Stadium Club, and a student-employee-for-the-day contest for sixth graders.

Reprinted by permission of the Adopt-A-School Program, Los Angeles Unified School District, CA.
Figure 13–12

Reprinted by permission of Partners in Education, Lancaster, PA.
Figure 13–13

RICHMOND PUBLIC SCHOOLS

CERTIFICATE OF APPRECIATION

Awarded to

_____

for

"Capturing the Spirit" of volunteerism
by rendering distinguished service
in the 1983-84 Volunteer Program.

_____
Superintendent

_____
School Board Chairman

_____
Principal/Supervisor/Department Head

_____
Volunteer Coordinator

_____
Date

Reprinted by permission of the Adopt-A-School Program, Richmond Public Schools, VA.

Figure 13–14

COMMUNITY RESOURCE PROGRAM
(suggested Thank You Note)

_____ Date

Dear _____,

Our class enjoyed your interesting presentation on _____

_____.

Many thanks for your time, interest, and energy. You made a big dif-

ference in our day and in our studies.

Sincerely,

_____ Teacher

_____ School

Reprinted by permission of Community Resource Program, Charlotte, NC.
Figure 13–15

Partnership Activities: Development and Implementation

In the partnerships survey, leaders were asked to reply to the question, "What are your partnership's activities?" A listing of these activities gives the readers some idea of the range of partnership activities currently being implemented throughout the country.

field trips*

lobbying

executive-on-loan

adopt-a-school

clubs

staff development*

award ceremonies*

work-study

staff internships
  (paid/unpaid)

clearinghouse-brokering

resource centers

summer youth employment

mentors*

aides

career exploration*

minigrants

fellowships

skills training classes

consultation services*

resource banks

technology programs

research studies

management training

workshops-conferences*

on-the-job training

student internships
  (paid/unpaid)

speakers bureau*

fairs

summer teacher employment

"shadowing"

economic education experiences

"exploration" days

maxigrants

scholarships

---

*Implemented most often by partnerships.

underwriting program costs for curriculum-staff development

volunteerism*: tutoring; building maintenance and repair; and supplemental-enrichment activities

disseminating information to support local schools*

educator, scientist, artist in-residence

donation and distribution of materials and equipment*

Program leaders added the following activities to the list:

- competitions at local, state, and national levels
- teaching courses
- raising funds
- colloquia and symposia
- development and distribution of demonstration materials
- creating broadcasting programming with students
- assistance with athletic and cultural programs

As program leaders develop partnership activities to meet educational needs within the context of available resources, careful thought is given to

- the size of the program
- activity planning, development, and implementation
- activities—kind and quality
- the potential impact of activity on project participants and the larger community

PARTNERSHIP SIZE: GUIDELINES FOR PROGRAM ACTIVITIES

Partnership programs come in all shapes and sizes. Often difficult problems face the fledgling program. For example,

1. Needs may greatly outweigh resources (especially in newly developed programs) and the same priority need may be critical to different staff, students, or schools.

2. There may be political pressures on the partnership to give available resources to one group at the expense of another.

3. Uneven depth and breadth of commitment by school staff may provoke uncertainty on the part of new business and community partners.

4. Financial recordkeeping and budget procedures, although developed and submitted to the district business office, may not be officially in place (in large districts this might take weeks); standard operating procedures dictate that expenditures cannot be made if accounts are not encumbered.

---

*Implemented most often by partnerships.

5. Initial communication networks are developed, but program links may not be solidified between partners and the school district and between staff within the school district.

6. Necessary approvals for program activity must wend their way through all administrative levels. All partners become frustrated as the approval process causes delays in beginning program activities.

7. Staff may require more training than the leader anticipated in order to respond proactively and positively to the problems stated above.

ACTIVITY PLANNING, DEVELOPMENT, AND IMPLEMENTATION

Given the concerns just discussed, the partnership leader might do well to start with a modest set of activities—activities that can be successfully implemented without straining the resources of *any* partners (partnership office, school district, community and business partners). Following are general guidelines that can be set to complement this point of view.

1. Examine your needs (determined through your assessment[s]).
2. Meet and talk with representatives of all partners' groups.
3. Place needs in priority order.
4. Assess available human, material, financial, and in-kind resources.
5. Select an advisory committee that will work with partnership staff to develop program activities.
6. Identify and select school site coordinators and parent representatives as appropriate to activities.
7. Identify and select coordinators from business-community organization partners as appropriate. The coordinators of *all* partners (whether school, business, or community) have the following responsibilities:
   - help to determine school needs and available resources.
   - help to design and develop partnership activities.
   - prepare materials to recruit other participants from their organizations.
   - recruit participants.
   - obtain required support and authorizations from management to release partnership participants.
   - facilitate solutions to participants' problems (released time, substitutes, transportation).
   - arrange for participants to attend orientation and training sessions (if appropriate).
   - facilitate implementation of partnership activities.
   - facilitate communication between organization and school district partners.

- contribute to appreciation and recognition of participants' achievements.
- be available—as needed— to organization's program participants.

8. School staff and partners determine activity goals and objectives. After goals and objectives are developed jointly by representatives of all partners, commitments to participation are transferred to contractual forms.

9. Consider alternative activities that both meet needs and use—but do not strain—resources. (*Always keep part of your resources in reserve*).

10. Choose your partnership activities; for example, comprehensive activities lists come from; Los Angeles, CA (see Figure 14-1); and Private Initiatives in Public Education (PIPE), WA (see Figure 14-2).

11. Match needs to resources, giving priority to greatest needs.

12. Partnership staff tailor accompanying recordkeeping forms and procedures to facilitate the implementation of activities. At this time, resources are assigned to activities.

13. Organize your orientations.
    - Introduce program to school staff, students and parents.
    - Introduce program to partners' organizations.

14. Facilitate training activities as appropriate for all partners.

15. Obtain necessary and appropriate approvals for activities from all partners.

16. Implement the activity (ies).
    - Organize arrangements for activities.
    - Confirm arrangements regarding: (a) activity procedures; (b) participants (including background, size, and age level of groups; (c) hosts, speakers, presenters; and (d) general logistical arrangements (date, time, place, meals, transportation).

17. Monitor activities. Adjust, refine and change activities as necessary.

18. Consistently disseminate information about activity development and adjustments to site coordinators, staff, partners, supervisors, and—as appropriate—to the board of education, the partnership's governing council, and the media.

19. Subscribe to national publications, for example, *ProEducation* and NSVP's newsletter, *The Volunteer in Education*, for additional program ideas and guidance in the development, implementation, and extension of partnership activities (more about the use of national, state, and regional resources in Part Four of this handbook).

ACTIVITIES: KIND AND QUALITY

After a review of available materials and discussion with program leaders, it seemed clear that a general review of the myriad activities being implemented currently in partnerships around the country, would be, at best, a superficial exercise. Program leaders had developed strategies and procedures to successfully implement activities that were unique to their individual partnerships. Therefore, to assist the reader to sort out and readily access available resources and assistance related to activity development, the handbook

- divides the activities into four general areas: (1) "people" activities; (2) distribution of materials and equipment; (3) financial assistance; and (4) in-kind apportionment of resources
- researches and analyzes the four areas in relation to the quality and quantity of particular activities
- extracts selected resources that appear to be most relevant and useful to professionals who are developing program activities
- shares this information with readers of this handbook

Note: This information is clarified in chart form at the end of this chapter. Additional contact information is available in the appendixes of this handbook.

"People" Activities

Community Resource Guides. Community resource guides can be packaged as formal handbooks or mimeographed lists. In any form, these guides provide information regarding available supplemental resources to enrich instructional programs. A good guide, like those listed below, provides complete contact information for each source.

a. *An Educator's Guide to Cleveland's Resources: Business, Labor and Higher Education* (OH)

b. *Cleveland Scholarship Program's Resource Directory* (sources for financial assistance for post–high school education) (OH)

c. *Teachers' and Administrators' Guide to Educational Programs at Cultural Institutions Throughout Greater St. Louis* (MO)

d. *The Nashua Community and Business Resource Manual* (NH)

e. *Linking Schools to the Workplace: A Teacher's Guide to Career-Related Business and Agency Resources in San Francisco* (through the Corporate Action Committee) (CA)

Staff Development. Partnerships are ideal programs for supporting school district staff development efforts. Professional self-development activities for teachers and administrators through these programs include

- internships for teachers at partners' sites
- training and retraining in new technologies
- institutes, workshops, seminars, colloquia in many curriculum and management areas
- newsletters to staff on curriculum development

- coursework related to updating and extending certification
- opportunities for curriculum development
- work-course experiences related to the area of career education for students
- teachers' centers

Programs with extensive experience and success in staff development are listed in Figures 14-3, 14-4, and 14-5 at the end of this section.

Management (General, Program, Instruction). Many partnerships have concentrated their activities in the areas of (a) general management (operations and finance), (b) program management, and (c) management of instruction. Currently, they are also using (on request) loaned executives and other consultants to support these activities. Businesses, nonprofit organizations, and civic agencies have shown their willingness to share their experience and expertise with school districts through part- or full-time loan of executives and workers for specified periods of time. The services of these partners are wide-ranging, for example: legal, accounting, advertising, public relations, and program management, as well as support in curriculum development and team teaching activities. (See Figures 14-4 and 14-5 for resource listings for management activities.)

Field Trips and Tours. Through field trips and tours, students and staff have experiences in visiting programs, departments, and facilities of their business–community agency–civic organization partners. Partnerships indicated that concerted efforts had been made to use trips and tours in close coordination with instruction in basic curriculum areas. (See Figure 14-4 for resource listings for field trips and tours.)

Recognition Ceremonies and Awards. Recognition of partners' support *and* students' or staff's achievements is an integral component of partnership programs. These ceremonies are held at a variety of sites, such as schools, businesses, public auditoriums, and hotels. Recognition takes such forms as certificates of merit and appreciation, awards (financial and other), entertainment, and luncheons, breakfasts, or dinners honoring recipients. Recognition-awards activities can be reciprocal activities—thanks for a job well done! (See Figure 14-4 for resource listings for recognition ceremonies and awards.)

Contests and Fairs. Contests and fairs are festive events that gather a community of partners in support of activities ranging from career education to spelling! Partners often act as contest judges and donate prizes (certificates, tickets to events, equipment, scholarships, and sometimes money). Partnership fairs are primarily thematic, focused on students' achievements *and* career opportunities in the arts, technology, careers, business, and professions. (See Figure 14-4 for resource listings for contests and fairs.)

Events. In this category fall the many cultural performances, assemblies, workshops, meetings, seminars, and trip days for both large and small groups of students. Activities include archaeological digs, artists-in-residence, ensemble work with practicing artists, free performances (or specially priced tickets) in the following areas: puppetry, storytelling, vocal coaching, choreography, mime, geography and archaeology, creative writing—and one could go on and on. (See Figure 14-4 for resource listing for events.)

Public Information. As "people" programs, all partnerships are involved in the dissemination of information to a variety of audiences. Public campaigns in support of public education and professional production of videotapes showcase the partnership and teach ways to facilitate partnership activities. (See Figures 14-4 and 14-5 for resources listings for public information activities.)

Demonstrations/Presentations. Demonstrations and presentations through partnership programs address the complete range of curriculum areas. Subjects include communications, leadership, job interview skills, publishing, all areas of technology, careers, accounting, law, actuarial sciences, banking, science experiments, and puppet-making. The presentations are made either at schools, at special events, or at partners' sites or offices. (See Figure 14-4 for resource listings for demonstrations and presentations.)

Basic Curriculum and Instruction. By stretching the definition of "basic curriculum," we could probably say that all partnership activities touch curriculum and instruction in some way. More recently, many partnerships are working on developing activities that *directly* address both curriculum and instruction; in many cases, these activities are coordinated with districtwide instructional and achievement objectives. (See Figure 14-4 for resource listings for programs that concentrate on activities directly related to basic curriculum and instruction.)

Career Education and Work Preparation for Students. Programs in career education are sources of numerous partnership activities, such as shadowing, apprenticeships, on-the-job training, workshops, and summer employment. The Memphis, TN, Adopt-A-School Program, for example, has an excellent handbook devoted entirely to assisting adopters in implementing these career education activities.

The majority of career education-work preparation activities for students fall into the following categories:

a. Summer employment for pay.

b. Internships and work-education experiences at partners' sites. Here, students learn to use specialized, updated equipment, hone their basic skills, and receive on-the-job training in such diverse areas as accounting, general business, marketing, word processing, bricklaying, carpentry, electricity, food services, floral arrangements, interior design, landscaping, plumbing, printing, public relations, advertising, and selling.

c. Shadowing, Apprenticeships, and Mentorships are work experiences offered through partnership programs for gifted, handicapped, general, and vocational students. Sites in use range from regular business offices and factories to professional offices, hotels, restaurants, and nonprofit and civic organizations.

d. Career Workshops, Conferences, and Seminars provide support to students experiencing a variety of on-the-job exposure and training through the activities listed above. Within these workshops and clinics, students learn and practice skills related to job seeking, interviewing for jobs, leadership, speaking, attitudes, and prevocational and vocational skills (such as drafting, banking, insurance, general business, design, data processing, office work, retailing, reading, writing, and computing). In other work sessions, students gain awareness of such topics as economics, money and banking, consumerism, and career opportunities. Montgomery County's (MD) comprehensive districtwide career education–work preparation program for students includes such components as

- an Executive High School Internship Program
- a Summer Internship Program (Specialized, Science, and Exploratory)
- a Students' Construction Trades Foundation, Inc.
- a Students' Automotive Trades Foundation, Inc.
- Project Business

(See Figures 14-4 and 14-5 for additional resource listings in career education and work preparation for students.)

Community Speakers Bureau. Partnerships organize their speakers within both formal and informal structures. Organization ranges from word-of-mouth personal contacts to a formally established speakers bureau. Partners pool their sources of community experience and expertise into one central information bank so that district staff can efficiently access needed resources. Partnership staff then organizes and periodically updates this information; these bureaus can also be used by partners for "bartering" purposes. (See Figure 14-4 for additional resource listings for community speakers bureaus.)

Teaching Minicourses and Team Teaching. Partners have been careful not to become involved (they have neither the time nor legal right) in regular teaching of courses. However, community and business partners have successfully taught with regular staff in minicourses, in seminar sessions, and in course units. They lend their experience and special expertise to bring life and enrichment to all curriculum areas. (See Figures 14-4 and 14-5 for resource listings of programs in which minicourses and team teaching activities have been particularly successful.)

Extracurricular Activities. Extracurricular activities (teams, clubs, workshops, etc.) in all curriculum areas are another successful way for partnerships to enrich and extend educational opportunities for students. The variety of programs sponsored by partnerships can be seen through the following *selected* list of teams, clubs, and projects:

art	science
future teachers	debating
photography	dramatics
dancing	computers

BS9 1618$$$21   05-27-86 15-52-56

engineering	school newspaper
gardening	stamp/coin collecting
knitting and sewing	woodworking
sports	Explorer Post
yearbooks	school store

career clubs (banking, job skills, allied medical professions)

(See Figure 14-4 for resource listings of extracurricular activities.)

Bartering. One activity that is peculiar to partnership programs is bartering. In different programs it can mean different things; basically there is an exchange of resources in a variety of activity formats: programs for products, products for services, services for programs, services for services, programs for programs, and products for products. A wide range of surplus materials, supplies, hobbies, services (for example, transportation and tutoring), and equipment can be bartered. (See Figure 14-4 for resource listings for bartering activities.)

Developing Magnet Programs. Probably the most ambitious partnership program involves developing new school programs—either within an existing school *or* as a new school. Developing or extending magnet programs takes a great deal of resources, effort, and continuing support from partnerships to get them started and keep them going until they have established themselves in their own right. That is why it appears that most of these programs are located in larger urban areas where a wealth of resources is available to support both new schools and other partnership activities. (See Figure 14-4 for resource listings for developing magnet programs.)

Post–High School Education and Training. Many partnerships are dedicated—in part or totally—to assisting young adults to continue their education or training following graduation from high school. Program services include: career counseling; assisting students to seek out and obtain resources for financial aid; guiding students through the application process; awarding scholarships; providing special counseling to college freshmen; helping to secure part-time and summer employment during college; help in obtaining continuing financial aid for college; internships for college students; assisting students to get jobs after college; and extending services to adults, already out of high school, who want to attend college. For example, the Cleveland, Ohio, Scholarship Programs, Inc. offers a wide range of support, including (1) the Cleveland Scholarship Program; (2) a Resource Directory; (3) a Professorial Internship Program; (4) an Adult Career Education Fair; (5) a National College Fair; and (6) a National Scholarship Service and Fund for Negro Students. Richmond, VA, has also developed effective activities through its Richmond Area Program for Minorities in Engineering. (See Figures 14-4 and 14-5 for resource listings for post–high school education and training.)

Adopt-A-School. By far the most common partnership format *and* partnership activity is "adopt-a-school." As an activity, adopt-a-school means that one school is joined with one or more partners (business, civic, nonprofit) to support and supplement instruction, management, and staff development for the individual school. There is always an exchange of resources as schools' partners are provided with products and activities, including: help with day care, art work, assistance with conferences and landscaping, musicales, facilities, and technological training. This simple pairing of partners is effectively employed both in large and small school districts. In larger districts, the adopt-a-school activity (along with other activities) is usually coordinated at the central partnership office; in smaller districts the pairing of schools and partner(s) may be organized and implemented directly at the school level. (See Figures 14-4 and 14-5 for listing for adopt-a-school activities.)

Volunteers. Volunteer services to assist school staff and students have been formalized through partnership programs. Volunteers come in all shapes, ages, and sizes and—according to the survey—are considered invaluable human resources. Like adopt-a-school, volunteerism is well developed and organized around the country. Volunteers tutor; provide clerical assistance; mimeograph materials; speak; present; demonstrate; teach; conduct tours; act as chaperones and mentors; coach; perform duties as aides; give homework assistance; conduct safety clinics; organize celebrity auctions and other fundraising activities; sponsor day camps and after-school activities; and paint, plaster, renovate, and build additions for schools. (See Figures 14-4 and 14-5 for resource listings for volunteer programs.)

Note: Three excellent sources of information on volunteer activities are available through: (1) Susan Taranto's book, *Coordinating Your School Volunteer Program*, VORT Corporation, Palo Alto, CA 94306, 1983; (2) the National School Volunteer Program (NSVP), Alexandria, VA (please contact NSVP for a complete listing of their materials, training institutes and other technical assistance); and (3) Energize Associates, PA (a consulting firm specializing in volunteerism).

Activities for Parents. Parent activities in partnerships appear focused on strengthening parent organizations, thereby making these organizations more effective supports to the educational process. Partnership activities center on assistance in fund raising, membership drives, legal rights of students, organizational management, and parent education (in a wide range of areas, for example, drug abuse prevention, homework support, parenting). (See Figure 14-4 for resource listings in the area of parents activities.)

Distribution of Materials and Equipment

Partnership arrangements are ideal vehicles to help schools obtain additional new or used equipment as well as surplus materials for educational activities. Partners often donate such equipment, supply equipment at a reduced cost, and prepare audiovisual aids and other needs for schools. The range of materials and equipment is wide and includes such articles as computers, typewriters, furniture, paper and cardboard, art supplies, playground equipment, lumber, films, videotapes, books, slides, sample kits, models, posters, charts, and tools, as well as necessary (and expensive) repair services. (See Figure 14-4 for resource listings in activities related to the distribution of materials and equipment.)

Financial Assistance

Activities involving financial assistance are development of grants programs, support for budgets, scholarships, financial awards, and general fund raising for specific projects and for minigrants or maxigrants.

A Special Note on Grants. Grants are usually given to teachers, principals, or individual schools. When you have obtained sufficient funding to allocate monies for even a small grants program, you will need assistance in developing the format and procedures related to (a) guidelines for proposals; (b) the grants process (receipt, review, and approval of proposals); and (c) on-site supervision and monitoring of grants activities. Assistance in developing the structure of grants programs and foundations can be obtained, for example, through a nationally known organization in the foundation field, the Public Education Fund. (See Figures 14-4 and 14-5 for local and regional resource listings for assistance in the areas of grants, scholarships, support for budgets and donations, awards and fund raising.)

In-Kind Resources

Activities related to the use of in-kind resources can include

- borrowing or donating facilities and equipment (at no cost)
- staff-volunteered time and services
- tours
- preparation and printing of materials
- donations of general and specialized supplies
- preparation of audiovisual materials
- repairs and renovations
- receptions, meals, and transportation

Bartering (as discussed earlier) ties in successfully with the range of potential or actual in-kind resources. (See Figures 14-4 and 14-5 for resource listings for activities in the area of in-kind resources.)

LOS ANGELES UNIFIED SCHOOL DISTRICT

Adopt-A-School Program

Selected Activities

In the Los Angeles Unified School District's publication, <u>Basic Activities</u>, Superintendent Harry Handler identified District priorities in terms of five goals. These goals are stated below and examples of correlating Adopt-A-School activities are listed.

Goal 1: <u>IMPROVE STUDENT ACHIEVEMENT</u>

Company volunteers tutor in all areas of the curriculum and at all levels including the learning disabled.

Students receive instruction and access to computers and word processors provided by companies.

Companies sponsor reading programs.

Companies participate in assembly programs stressing good health, safety and character building.

Schools and companies initiate attendance incentive programs.

Companies provide bus transportation for educational field trips.

Educational materials and equipment are donated to schools.

Companies provide speakers, displays and handouts for career days.

Companies provide scholarships.

Companies donate math, science and language materials and help schools set up laboratories.

Companies provide training on computers for school staffs.

Company films are made available for loan to schools.

Companies provide incentives for academic achievement.

Companies donate class sets of daily newspapers for instructional purposes.

Goal 2: <u>IMPROVE THE ENVIRONMENT IN WHICH TEACHING AND LEARNING OCCUR</u>

Company volunteers assist with mural projects and paint-outs to reduce graffiti on campus and in the community.

Companies donate curtains, used furniture and plants.

Volunteers refurbish and paint school rooms and hallways.

Companies donate lumber and labor for school beautification.

Companies assist with school and neighborhood beautification projects.

Company volunteers, school staff, parents and students work together to landscape school grounds.

Companies assist schools in neighborhood watch programs.

Companies provide assembly speakers to promote safety on the campus and in the community.

Figure 14–1

Goal 3: <u>STRENGTHEN THE SUPPORT FROM PARENTS AND THE COMMUNITY AT LARGE AND</u>
<u>ITS LEADERS FOR OUR PROGRAM</u>

Schools and companies generate positive press.

Company representatives participate in school advisory councils.

To encourage involvement in the total school, companies are invited to attend athletic events and other campus activities.

Company personnel speak to parent groups about careers, health, safety and financial issues.

Schools include companies on mailing lists to receive school newsletters, bulletins, etc.

Companies assist in schools' fund raising activities.

Companies provide printing for school newspapers, graduation annuals, parent handbooks and programs for special events.

Student artwork and decorations are provided for display in company offices and lobbies.

Schools host recognition breakfasts and luncheons for company volunteers.

Company volunteers and students assist with community mural projects.

Company volunteers help judge special activities; i.e., Academic Decathlon, essay contests, spelling bees, etc.

Goal 4: <u>IMPROVE STAFF MORALE</u>

Companies host end-of-the year recognition/appreciation events for school staffs.

Companies provide time management, computer technology and space exploration inservice training for school staffs.

Off-site locations are made available for faculty meetings and staff development.

Adopters provide internships for teachers during summer months.

Companies provide resources which augment and enrich the curriculum and cooperate with teachers in making new learning experiences possible for students.

Goal 5: <u>IMPROVE RELATIONSHIPS AND OUR CREDIBILITY WITH STATE AND FEDERAL</u>
<u>LEGISLATORS</u>

The California Roundtable endorses relationships between education, legislation and business. Many of the 88 member companies on the California Roundtable support LAUSD schools via Adopt-A-School.

Broadcasting companies who participate in Adopt-A-School have generated public service announcement time to promote public education.

Adopters assist the District as a result of a better understanding of education's goals and needs.

Los Angeles Unified School District's Adopt-A-School Program has received national recognition and has been selected as a model by the White House Office of Private Sector Initiatives, Washington, D.C.

The relationships with state and federal legislators are improved as a result of Adopt-A-School partnerships.

Reprinted by permission of the Adopt-A-School Program, Los Angeles Unified School District, CA.

Figure 14–1 (continued)

PIPE PARTNERSHIP REQUEST FORM

Mail to: PIPE
215 Columbia
Seattle, WA 98104

Today's Date _____

PLEASE COMPLETE A SEPARATE REQUEST FORM FOR EACH ACTIVITY OR CLASS PERIOD. In order that the Individual Partner or Partner-at-Large filling the request may have sufficient time to process your request, please allow THIRTY (30) DAYS OF ADVANCE NOTICE for each request.

PLEASE PRINT OR TYPE

SCHOOL _____ STREET _____

PHONE _____ ZIP _____

PIPE COORDINATOR _____

TEACHER _____

GRADE _____ COURSE _____ NUMBER PARTICIPATING _____

BEST TIME TO CALL _____

I. Check Type of Resource Requested:

____Individual Student Interview

____Student Shadowing Experience

____One-to-One Student Internship

____Student Work Experience

____Occupational Field Trip

Indicate Occupation Area for Above Request: _____ _____ Code # _____

II. Indicate Special Requests for Sharing of Employee Personal Talents or Interest

Areas: _____

III. Classroom Discussion on Current Topics

Title: _____ Code Number _____

Indicate Desired Topic Coverage:

____Overview of Occupation/Current Topic

____Specific Element or Elements of Occupation/Current Topic to be Addressed

IV. Preferred Date _____ Time _____ am/pm to _____ am/pm

Alternate _____ Time _____ am/pm to _____ am/pm

See other side for definitions of above terms.

Figure 14–2

For Office Use Only

Confirmed Date_____ Time_____ am/pm to_____ am/pm

Resource or Contact Person_____ Phone_____

Firm_____ Street_____

City_____ State_____ ZIP_____

Additional Information_____

Date_____ By_____

DEFINITIONS

1. Individual Student Interview
   Student talks with adult; asks questions, usually following a structured format; may be in person or by telephone; normally lasts less than an hour.

2. Student Shadowing Experience
   Student follows adult through regualr daily routine; may last from a couple of hours through a full day; main activity is observation with some questions and answers; usually follows a structured format.

3. One-to-One Student Internship
   Student and adult develop close working relationship; adult teaches, "counsels", and provides hands-on experiences; activity may become independent of constant supervision; may involve frequent contact over a period of several days, or less frequent contact over a period of several weeks or months.

4. Student Work Experience
   Student becomes a paid employee; on-the-job training and other learning experiences may lead to high school credit.

Figure 14–2 (continued)

OCCUPATIONS

Accounting/Bookkeeping 45.

Account Clerk	1
Accountant	2
Accounts Supervisor	3
Appraiser & Underwriters	4
Auditor	5
Bookkeeper	6
Controller	7
Credit Analysis	8
Credit Coordinator	9
Office Equipment Maint. & Repair	10
Teller	11

Agriculture 46.

Agronomist	1
Buyer	2
County Agent	3
Ecologist	4
Entomologist	5
Farm Equipment Mechanic	6
Farm Manager	7
Fisherman	8
Floral Designer	9
Food Processing Plant Manager	10
Forester	11
Game Management	12
Gardener	13
Greenskeeper	14
Horticulturist	15
Microbiologist	16
Nursery Worker	17
Rancher	18
Soil Scientist	19.
Tractor Operator	20

Arts/Entertainment/Communications 47.

Actor (Teacher)	1
Art Director	2
Choreographer	3
Copy Writer	4
Dancer (Teacher)	5
Decorator	6
Managing Editor	7
Music Instrument Teacher	8
Music Voice Teacher	9
Music Director	10
Painter	11
Photographer	12
Photographer's Apprentice	13
Radio & Television Announcer	14
Radio/TV Program Director	15
Reporter	16
Sculptor (Teacher)	17
Students of the Arts (Music/Writing/Painting)	18
Writers - Radio/TV	19

Construction 48.

Apprentice	1
Architect	2
Bricklayer	3
Carpenter	4
Concrete Finisher	5
Construction Foreperson	6
Construction Superintendant	7
Construction Worker	8
Contractor	9
Drafter	10
Floor Layer	11
Operating Engineer	12
Painter	13
Plasterer	14
Plumber	15
Roofer	16
Safety Operations	17

Electrical/Electronics 49.

Assembly Line Worker	1
District Manager	2
Electrician	3
Helper	4
Installer Repairperson/Phone	5
Lineperson Utility/Telephone	6
Meter Reader	7
Production Machine Operator	8
Production Supervisor	9
Radio & Television Repairperson	10

Engineering 50.

Advanced Graphite Composite Op.	1
Aeronautical Engineer	2
Astronautical Engineer	3
Chemist	4
Civil Engineer	5
Computing Analyst	6
Design Engineer	7
Drafter	8
Electrical Engineer	9
Electronics Engineer	10
General Engineer	11
Industrial Engineer	12
Lab Technician	13
Manufacturing Engineer	14
Marine Systems Diver	15
Mechanical Engineer	16
Numberical-Controlled Machine Op.	17
Physicist	18
Pilot	19
Technical Illustrator	20
Technical Writer	21
Tool Engineer	22

Food Service 51.

Baker	1
Bartender	2
Catering Manager	3
Chef	4
Dinner Cook	5
Food Service Supervisor	6
Meat Cutter	7
Restaurant Owner/Manager	8
Short Order Cook	9
Waiter/Waitress	10

Graphic Arts 52.

Advertising Manager	1
Bookbinder	2
Commercial Artist	3
Commercial Photographer	4
Compositor	5
Line Machine Operator	6
Offset Press Operator	7
Paste-Up Person	8
Printing Salesperson	9
Printmaker	10
Printshop Helper	11
Production Supervisor	12

Health Services 53.

Biologist	1
Chemist	2
Chiropractor	3
Dental Assistant	4
Dental Hygienist	5
Dentist	6
Dietician	7
Hearing & Speech Specialist	8
Hospital Administrator	9
Laboratory Assistant	10
Laboratory Supervisor	11
Medical Director	12
Nurse Aides & Orderlies	13
Nurse, L.P.N.	14
Nurse, R.N.	15
Optician	16
Optometrist	17
Pharmacist	18
Physical Therapist	19
Physician	20
Psychologist	21
Radiologic Technician	22
Sanitarian	23
Veterinarian	24
Ward Clerk	25

Industrial Mechanics 54.

Aircraft & Engine Mechanic	1
Appliance Repairperson	2
Auto Mechanic	3
Heating Engineer	4
Heavy Equipment Mechanic	5
Instrument Repairperson	6
Marine Engineer	7
Mechanic's Helper	8
Millwright	9
Office Machine Repairperson	10
Parts Manager	11
Refrigeration Repairperson	12
Service Manager	13
Service Station Attendant	14
Shop Foreperson	15
Small Engine Mechanic	16

Marketing/Financial 55.

Advertising Account Executive	1
Advertising Manager	2
Automotive Salesperson	3
Bank Manager	4
Bank Officer	5
Business Service Salesperson	6
Car Loader	7
Cashier/Checker	8
Commodity Salesperson	9
Community Relations	10
Government Relations	11
Industrial Relations Manager	12
Insurance Salesperson	13
International Relations	14
Investments	15
Mail Carrier	16
Market Analyst	17
Model	18
Packaging Engineer	19
Personnel Manager	20
Public Relations Manager	21
Purchasing Agent	22
Real Estate Salesperson	23
Retail Salesperson	24
Routeperson	25
Sales Manager	26
Salesperson General	27
Security Salesperson	28
Service Manager	29
Shipping & Recieving Clerk	30
Sign Maker	31
Stock Clerk	32
Store/Business Manager	33
Tellers	34

Figure 14–2 (continued)

Metals   56.

Blacksmith & Forge Worker	1
Body & Fender Repairperson	2
Boilermaker	3
Die Designer	4
Foreperson	5
Foundry Worker	6
Industrial Engineer	7
Machine Operator	8
Machinist	9
Manufacturing Engineer	10
Metal Finisher	11
Metal Refinishing Occupations	12
Molder	13
Oiling Machine Operator	14
Pattern Maker	15
Production Machine Operator	16
Production Manager	17
Sheet Metal Worker	18
Shop Superintendant	19
Tool Crib Attendant	20
Tool & Die Maker	21
Welder	22
Welder Helper	23

Secretarial/Clerical   57.

Chief Clerk	1
Computer Center Manager	2
Computer Operator	3
Computer Programmer	4
Executive Secretary	5
General Office Clerical	6
Keypunch Operator	7
Office Manager	8
Postal Clerk	9
Receptionist	10
Stenographer	11
Systems Analyst	12
Telephone/Telegraph Operator	13
Word Processor	14

Service   58.

Barber	1
Case Worker	2
Case Worker Supervisor	3
Child Care Attendant	4
Classroom Teacher	5
Clergyman	6
Cosmetologist	7
Counselor	8
Education Administrator	9
Fire Fighter	10
Governmental Agency Admin.	11
Guard	12
Hotel Clerk	13
Hotel Manager	14
Law Enforcement Officer	15
Lawyer	16
Librarian	17
Life Guard	18
Lobbyist	19
Military	20
Mortician	21
Recreation Facility Attendant	22
Recreation Leader	23
Recreation Supervisor	24
Social Service Specialists	25
Teaching Assistants	26

Textile/Apparel   59.

Clothing Designer	1
Laundry Operator	2
Pattern Maker	3
Plant Manager	4
Sewing Machine Operator	5
Shop Repair	6
Tailor	7
Upholsterer	8

Transportation   60.

Air Traffic Controller	1
Airplane Pilot	2
Airport Serviceperson	3
Brakeperson	4
Bus & Taxi Driver	5
Railroad Engineer	6
Ships' Officer	7
Traffic/Rateperson	8
Transportation Manager	9
Truck Driver	10
Yard Laborer	11

Reprinted by permission of Private Initiatives in Public Education (PIPE), WA.

Figure 14–2 (continued)

RESOURCES FOR PARTNERSHIP ACTIVITIES IN STAFF DEVELOPMENT

ACTIVITY: / PROGRAMS:	CARE, Nat'l Bureau of Standards Denver, CO	Project Science Stamford, CT	Atlanta Principals Institute, GA	Educators-In-Industry Montgomery Co., MD	School Partnership Program St. Louis, MO	Upper Midwest Small Schools Project Grand Forks, ND	Principal as Curriculum Leader, NYC	Teacher Internship Program Cleveland, OH	Partners in Education Cincinnati, OH	PATHS, Philadelphia, PA	Adopt-A-School, Lemoyne, PA	Adopt-A-School, Dallas, TX	Business-School Partnership Program Houston, TX	PIPE, Seattle, WA
1. Internships for teachers at partners' sites				•				•						•
2. Training and retraining in technologies	•	•			•		•				•			•
3. Institutes/workshops/seminars/colloquia in curricula and management areas	•	•	•	•	•	•	•		•	•		•		•

4. Newsletters to staff on curriculum development

5. Coursework related to updating and extending certification

6. Opportunities for curriculum development

7. Work-course experience related to career education for students

8. Teachers' centers

Figure 14–3

RESOURCES FOR PARTNERSHIP ACTIVITIES
LOCAL SCHOOL DISTRICTS

ACTIVITY / DISTRICT	Little Rock, AR	San Francisco, CA	Stanford, CA	Irvine, CA	Los Angeles, CA	San Diego, CA	Denver, CO	Stamford, CT	Washington, DC	Dade County, FL	Atlanta, GA	Chicago, IL	Montgomery Co., MD	St. Louis Park, MN	St. Louis, MO	New York, NY	Cincinnati, OH	Tulsa, OK	Philadelphia, PA	Erie, PA	Lemoyne, PA	Memphis, TN	Dallas, TX	Houston, TX	Salt Lake City, UT	Arlington, VA	Richmond, VA	Seattle, WA	Milwaukee, WI
1. Staff Development			•			•	•	•	•		•		•	•	•	•	•		•		•		•	•	•			•	
2. Management		•	•										•		•	•								•				•	
3. Field Trips/Tours		•	•			•	•		•	•		•			•			•		•	•	•			•			•	
4. Recognition Ceremonies	•	•			•	•	•		•	•	•	•		•			•			•		•	•	•	•		•	•	
5. Contests/Fairs					•		•		•	•		•								•	•			•	•			•	
6. Events		•		•	•		•		•			•		•	•	•				•					•				
7. Public Information																						•							
8. Demonstrations/Presentations		•	•						•											•				•					
9. Basic Curriculum and Instruction					•	•	•			•		•		•	•		•		•	•			•	•	•				
10. Career Ed./Work Preparation		•	•		•	•	•		•	•		•		•	•	•		•		•	•	•	•	•		•	•	•	•
11. Community Speakers Bureau		•	•				•			•		•						•						•		•		•	
12. Teaching Minicourses						•	•							•	•		•							•					

226

Figure 14-4

DISTRICT	13. Extracurricular Activities	14. Bartering	15. Magnet Programs	16. Post-High School Ed./Training	17. Adopt-A-School	18. Volunteer Programs	19. Parent Activities	20. Distribution of Materials/Equipment	21a. grants	21b. scholarships	21c. support for budgets	21d. donations/awards/fund raising	22. In-Kind Resources
Little Rock, AR													
San Francisco, CA					•								
Stanford, CA			•										
Irvine, CA					•								
Los Angeles, CA		•			•	•							•
San Diego, CA	•	•										•	•
Denver, CO	•				•	•		•					
Stamford, CT													
Washington, DC	•		•		•	•							
Dade County, FL		•			•				•	•			
Atlanta, GA			•		•	•		•				•	
Chicago, IL	•				•	•							
Montgomery Co., MD					•	•							
St. Louis Park, MN		•				•							
St. Louis, MO			•			•			•	•			•
New York, NY			•		•								
Cincinnati, OH	•	•			•	•				•	•		•
Tulsa, OK						•							
Philadelphia, PA									•				
Erie, PA					•								
Lemoyne, PA					•								
Memphis, TN	•	•			•	•		•		•		•	•
Dallas, TX					•								•
Houston, TX	•				•	•		•		•		•	
Salt Lake City, UT						•							
Arlington, VA					•								
Richmond, VA				•	•						•		
Seattle, WA		•			•			•				•	•
Milwaukee, WI					•								

227

RESOURCES FOR PARTNERSHIP ACTIVITIES
REGIONAL PROGRAMS

ACTIVITY:	The California Roundtable CA	San Francisco Education Fund CA	National Association for the Exchange of Industrial Resources IL	Upper Midwest Small Schools Coalition ND	Senior Volunteers in the Schools NY	NYC Partnership NY	NY Alliance NY	Cleveland Teachers Institute OH	Cleveland Scholarship Programs OH	National School Volunteer Program VA	National Community Education Association VA
1. Staff Development				•			•	•		•	•
2. Management							•			•	
3. Public Information	•					•	•		•		•
4. Career Ed./Work Preparation						•	•		•		
5. Teaching Minicourses											
6. Post-High School Ed./Training									•		
7. Adopt-A-School						•					
8. Volunteer Programs		•			•					•	•
9. In-Kind Resources			•								
10. Financial Assistance											
a. grants		•							•		
b. scholarships									•		
c. support for budgets	•	•							•		
d. donations/awards/fund raising		•							•		

Figure 14–5

Evaluation and Reports:
The Basis for Change

Even the most seasoned leader can shudder at the mere mention of the word "evaluation," since evaluation is underdeveloped in most partnership programs. Fewer than 50 percent of the partnerships surveyed implemented formative (monthly, or quarterly) evaluation reports. Nearly 60 percent of the same group stated they prepared summative evaluation reports (on a yearly basis or at the end of a project activity). Tentativeness about evaluation is normal and appropriate in relation to such young programs. Deterrents to active, aggressive evaluation usually stem from

- lack of experience in conducting evaluations of special programs
- program activities that are difficult to evaluate with the usual instrumentation
- supervisors who regard partnerships as "frill" programs requiring little or no evaluation

Some program leaders have defined for themselves the characteristics of effective and efficient partnership programs (for example, see Figure 15-1 from the Los Angeles Unified School District, CA). With such criteria for evaluation firmly in place, program leaders will value a well-planned and implemented evaluation process

- that provides scheduled feedback about program strengths and weaknesses. Evaluation then forms the basis for activity and project change and extension.
- that is perceived positively by partners, many of whom are used to some form of public accountability in their business and organizational lives. Evaluation then encourages continued and new participation in partnership activities.

GENERAL EVALUATION GUIDELINES

When the partnership is initiated, representatives of all partner groups should meet to determine (1) the procedures and instruments for evaluating both individual activities and the overall partnership program and (2) the particular roles of students, staff, partners, and the community at large in the evaluation process. Evaluation may address such partnership activities as

- school, district, and instructional management
- staff development (coursework, workshops, conferences, on-the-job mentorships)
- curriculum
- student career opportunities
- cultural events
- speakers
- demonstrations
- tutoring
- other volunteer activities
- scholarships
- use of materials and equipment
- site usage

There are two strands to the evaluation process that function simultaneously and often overlap. There is *formative* evaluation, in which you gather data and monitor the ongoing program and *summative* evaluation, a yearly program assessment. Both evaluation strands develop from program goals and objectives and focus on such questions as the following:

- Should the evaluation be conducted independently or in house?
- What activities, procedures, and communications took place?
- Were these activities, procedures, and communications efficiently and effectively facilitated and implemented? If not, why not?
- Were program activities clearly related to the school district's instructional and/or staff development goals? If not, why not?
- To what degree did partnership-developed materials maximally support program activities?
- What was the short- and long-range impact of the program on students, school district, staff, and partner participants?
- What opportunities are available to replicate particularly successful program activities and procedures?
- Should some program activities be curtailed or eliminated?
- How can the program be improved to better meet participants' needs?
- Within a specified time, has the program solidified and/or extended commitment to the idea *and* fact of a partnership?

EVALUATION PLANNING, PREPARATION, AND IMPLEMENTATION

Evaluation, like any other program component, requires careful planning *before* data assessment, collection, and analysis tasks are implemented. Evaluation activities can be formal or informal, depending on the breadth and depth of the partnership program *and* program goals and objectives. Partnership leaders submitted samples of evaluation instruments and plans to share with readers of this handbook. A review and discussion of these tools helps to put the evaluation component in perspective in relation to an individual program.

Evaluation Planning and Design

General procedures for effective program evaluation are easily applied to partnerships. However, because partnerships entail broader and more diverse adult participation than most school programs, and involve the collaboration of both the public and private sectors, it may be appropriate at this time to outline evaluation procedures that should be given particular attention.

1. An evaluation plan can become the basis for productive change.

2. A variety of methods are used when conducting the evaluation, for example: interviewing, surveys, questionnaires, and direct observation. This variety encourages a close and direct understanding of how the overall program and specific activities operate.

3. Evaluation data is successfully collected by partnership staff, school site coordinators, business partners, classroom teachers, research and evaluation departments of school districts, and consultants—with administrative assistance (from central office or school site). The data is usually analyzed, organized, and prepared in a report format under the supervision of the partnership's director, a senior administrator (for example, an assistant superintendent), a subcommittee of the program's governing council, a consultant, or the school district's office of research and evaluation.

4. Formative and summative evaluations are designed to complement each other, one being an extension of the other. Information elicited from these evaluations provides a complete quantitative and qualitative picture of the program.

5. Evaluation results and recommendations for future program planning are disseminated to all partners and the community at large. This information is communicated in format and language appropriate to the audience receiving the reports. Also included in the report are vehicles through which various audiences can respond and react to the information. Often the evaluation acts as material that will solicit future partners.

6. The survey indicated that most evaluations are prepared in-house and paid for through the regular school district budget or out of the partnership's

budget. However, *if financially feasible*, evaluations should be designed and conducted by independent evaluators, assisted by partnership staff who can help guide the evaluation process. Many partners, particularly those from the business community, will feel more comfortable renewing or extending their commitment to the partnership on the basis of such independent evaluation.

Specifics on Formative Evaluation

Formative evaluation is a form of continuing evaluation that takes place (1) upon the completion of an individual task or activity *or* (2) following natural monthly or quarterly program breaks. This program monitoring

- provides management guidelines to the overall program as well as particular activities
- guides adjustment and refinements related to ongoing program planning and implementation
- develops a data base and/or descriptive record of the partnership program
- forms the basis for comprehensive program summative evaluation and yearly reports

Partnership programs have developed a variety of informal and formal forms and procedures for ongoing evaluation and monitoring. From a review of these materials, it is clear that purpose dictates form. Therefore, maximum amounts of useful information will be elicited if forms (1) clearly delineate their objectives; (2) are easy to use; (3) are completed; and (4) contain information that can be efficiently coordinated and analyzed. The following effective tools are being used, at the present time, to assist in the improvement of program management and activities:

1. The TwinWest Business-Education Partnership, MN, uses report forms to monitor proceedings and decision making related to meetings (Figure 15-2).
2. Private Initiatives in Public Education (PIPE) Program, WA, uses a simple, yet effective monthly program reporting form (Figure 15-3).
3. Columbia, MO, uses a progress report to monitor ongoing Partners-in-Education activities (Figure 15-4).
4. An evaluation form from St. Louis, MO (Figure 15-5), is filled out by the classroom teacher and students following a particular partnership activity.
5. To elicit information from presenters regarding their partnership activities at school or off-site, Charlotte-Mecklenburg, NC, has developed a short evaluation card (Figure 15-6).
6. The San Francisco School Volunteers Program, CA, sends a questionnaire (Figure 15-7) to teachers to obtain information related to the success of a released-time tutoring program.

7. A school-based coordinator's report summary, from the Business-School Partnership Program in Houston, TX (Figure 15-8), solicits periodic basic information, quantitative data, and news items and recommendations for program improvement.

8. The Adopt-A-School Program in Jackson, MS, uses Monthly Projects Report Forms in its ongoing monitoring (Figure 15-9).

Specifics on Summative Evaluation

Introduction. In smaller school districts and in projects where evaluation is focused on the individual school, year-end evaluations usually consist of short summary reports based on data gathered throughout the school year; information from the school's newsletter, observations, summative surveys, and interviews is integrated into this final report. Materials are also reviewed that indicate some degree of relationship between instructional objectives, test scores (as appropriate), and partnership activities.

This is not to say that large partnership projects don't also make good use of these same evaluation procedures and tools. However, since larger programs have numerous activities operating at multiple sites, final evaluations use the same tools and procedures to gather data at *all* project sites; information is then summarized and blended into a larger, more generic final report.

Useful Tools for Summative Evaluation. Most of the tools used for year-end evaluations are used for evaluations in general. However, partnership leaders did submit samples of forms that proved to be particularly useful and appropriate to their particular supplemental program format.

a. *Teachers* participating in the San Francisco School Volunteers program, CA, use a summary program information form (see Figure 15-10).

b. Evaluation tools, directed to *community and business partners* who have volunteered their time and expertise throughout the school year, were submitted by the Irvine Partnership in Education, CA (see Figure 15-11), and the Saturday Scholars Program, Chicago, IL (see Figure 15-12). A complementary student evaluation form is also used in the Chicago program (see Figure 15-13).

c. Many of the useful summative evaluation tools are disseminated directly by the school site coordinator *or* the partnership's central office, seeking information from a *varied audience.* Information solicited deals with the total program—either at the individual school or districtwide. Some examples are included from the Los Angeles Unified School District (Figure 15-14); the West Shore School District, PA (Figure 15-15); and the Tri-Lateral Council for Quality Education, Inc., now merged with the Boston Private Industry Council (see Figure 15-16.) Adopt-A-School evaluation forms for (1) the school coordinator and principal (See Figure 15-17) and (2) the adopter coordinator and CEO (See Figure 15-18) come from Jackson, MS. A questionnaire, prepared in the form of a report card pamphlet, can be secured from the National School Volunteer Program (NSVP), VA.

Reports and Report Writing

Overview. All partnership programs must write reports both during and at the end of a school year. Reports, particularly those that are focused on evaluation, are often considered burdens—best disposed of as quickly as possible. However, there are other ways to look at reports; they can be seen as opportunities

- to maintain and extend current partnership support and participation
- to solicit new partners
- to "showcase" program achievements
- to recognize partners' efforts
- to document the relationship between partnership and school district goals and objectives
- to disseminate information about program plans for improvement, refinement, and change

Reports are written for different audiences. The survey indicated that reports were most often sent to schools and school staff, to boards of education, to the partnership's advisory council, to partners, and to school district administrators. Sometimes, reports were also sent to state departments of education, to the community at large, and to parents.

The breadth and depth of the project will determine both the form and content of a report. Therefore, those who are writing, preparing and disseminating reports should take the following suggestions into consideration *before* they begin the process:

- Determine (1) your audiences; (2) the guidelines for quantity, form, and content of your reports; and (3) which audience will receive which report. These decisions will affect the length of required preparation time. The survey showed that partnership leaders (depending on the size and kind of report) spent from two hours to three years preparing these reports! Most reports, however, appeared to take between one week and three months to design, write, and prepare in final form.
- If possible, solicit resources to support the preparation and dissemination of the report. Such resources could include funding for or loan of an outside evaluation consultant as well as expertise and monies to design, print, and mail the report.
- Schedules and arrangements for planning, preparation, and dissemination of all reports should be done before the school year begins (late summer or

early fall). Most reports are issued quarterly, biannually or annually. Whether a full- or part-time staff person is assigned to facilitate and monitor the report process will depend on how often reports are to be disseminated and the extent of the product.

- Forms and other materials and procedures scheduled to access program data are prepared ahead of time, ready for dissemination and collection. Partnership leaders agreed that the program director or coordinator is responsible to guide and monitor this process. That leader assigns staff to ensure

  1. that data is collected in a timely manner
  2. that interviews and observations are scheduled and completed
  3. that contractual arrangements are made and fulfilled (either within or outside the school district) to input, process, access, analyze, and summarize available information

- Use guidelines for evaluation prepared by your own school district (research and development offices), state departments of education, or other partnerships as appropriate; these guidelines can be adapted to assist you in this process. (Note that the San Francisco Education Fund, CA, and Partnerships in Education, IN, have prepared special guidelines for evaluation of partnership projects.)

Forms of Reports. Reports come in many sizes and shapes. They come in different forms: formal or informal, short or long, filled with quantitative data or simple summaries and analyses. Reports may be presented as three-page summaries (see Figure 15-19 from the Governor's Human Resources Committee of the Cabinet, PA), as packets of duplicated sheets, as newsletters; they may be spiral-bound, casebound, paperbound, printed in black-and-white, two-color and four-color.

Partnership leaders said their reports were primarily written as newsletters in the usual report format (introduction, body, conclusion, appendixes). Photographs or graphics were ordinarily facilitated by district media specialists or contracted out to a photographer. Occasionally, this work was donated as an in-kind activity from a business or community partner.

Everyone knows that an attractive report invites readers to review its contents beyond the cover page. However, some partnership leaders maintain that readers of their reports are interested only in content, not form. Some contend that "simple is better" and that a fancy report (unless prepared through contributions of partners) signals waste to the partnership's audiences. You will have to consider how much funding has been budgeted for this task. As stated earlier, partnership reports are usually paid for through school district or program budgets, while mailing costs are donated, in many cases, by a business or community partner.

Content of Reports. Since a report's content is largely determined by (a) partnership goals and objectives as well as (b) projected audiences, content does differ from report to report. Nevertheless, scanning of reports submitted from programs throughout the country, reveals common themes:

- Some background and history of the partnership are discussed in order to place current program activities within a particular context or perspective.
- The partnership's organization structure and hierarchy are outlined. Key leaders (governing council or committee) and staff members are identified, along with their roles and responsibilities. Often this discussion is accompanied by an organizational chart.
- Data related to funding, resource support, and quantity and quality of partnership activities is summarized. Accompanying indexes (charts, graphs) expand this discussion and assist the reader to understand more fully the impact of the program upon instruction and educational opportunities for students.
- Recognition is given to partners and program staff. Outstanding program achievements are highlighted.
- Future directions (short- and long-range) related to program refinement, extension, limitations, and maintenance are presented. If there are particular concerns or problems with the program—that can be solved through partners' collaboration—requests for support in areas of both decision making and additional resources are outlined.
- Credits for report preparation are listed (as appropriate). Contact information, related to the partnership, is printed usually at the beginning or end of the report.

Space does not permit the reproduction of report materials from partnership programs, but listed below are some of the reports of partnership programs that were reviewed for this handbook; those listed were selected as examples of reports that show experience and expertise in their reporting to a variety of community audiences. You can obtain copies of these materials (refer to the resource lists in the appendixes at the end of this handbook) for review and guidance in your own report preparation:

St. Louis Public Schools, MO: (1) *Annual Report of School Partnership Program* and (2) *Executive Summary: Evaluation of the Partnership Program.*

San Francisco Education Fund, CA: (1) *Year-End Report to the Patrons of Public Education*, (2) *Cluster Reports* (individual reports relating the impact of the partnership on special project areas, and (3) *The Continuation and Long-Term Impact of Programs Granted by the San Francisco Education Fund.*

The Cleveland Scholarship Programs, Inc., OH: *Newsletter.*

Liberty Mutual, Boston, MA: *Life with Liberty*, a report of their company's partnership with Charlestown High School.

Dallas Independent School District, TX: (1) *Celebrating 15 Years* and the (2) *Annual Report* (both about the district's Volunteer/Adopt-A-School Program).

Pittsburgh, PA: *Report on Minigrants for Teachers*, prepared by the Allegheny Conference on Community Development.

John Hancock, Boston, MA: *Annual Report on the John Hancock/English High School Partnership Program.*

National Bureau of Standards, CO: *Final Summary, CARE Program.*

Memphis City Schools, TN: *Adopt-A-School Annual Report.*

Houston Independent School District, TX: (1) *VIPS Business School Partnership Report* and (2) *Some Partnerships that Succeeded.*

Nashua, NH: *Program Evaluation* of the project's Community and Business Resource Manual.

Greater Cincinnati Chamber of Commerce, OH: *Partners in Education Annual Report.*

Los Angeles Unified School District, CA: (1) *Adopt-A-School News* (newsletter) and (2) *Correlating Adopt-A-School Activities to a Shared Responsibility* (report).

Chattanooga Public Schools, TN: *Adopt-A-School Annual Report.*

Jackson Public Schools, MS: *Semiannual Report: Adopt-A-School Activities.*

LOS ANGELES UNIFIED SCHOOL DISTRICT

Adopt-A-School Program

CHARACTERISTICS OF A QUALITY ADOPT-A-SCHOOL PROGRAM

1. The company and school have worked together to establish attainable goals and reasonable expectations.

2. The company and school have cooperatively planned activities to enrich the educational program.

3. Each partner has established an Adopt-A-School committee which assures continuity of the program regardless of personnel assignment.

4. There is open communication and on-going articulation between the company and school which includes an annual review of the program and the development of strategies to renew and nurture the relationship.

5. As a result of shared experiences, the company and school better understand each other.

NOTE: These characteristics of a quality Adopt-A-School Program are the result of group consensus during the meeting of region/division Adopt-A-School teams September 6, 1984, at the Los Angeles Dodgers Stadium Club.

Reprinted by permission of the Adopt-A-School Program, Los Angeles Unified School District, CA.

Figure 15–1

TwinWest Business–Education Partnership
Standing Committee Leader's Report

Date Of Meeting:	
Members Present:	
Project Working On:	
Discussion Items:	
Decisions Made:	
Next Meeting Scheduled For:	

Reprinted by Permission of the TwinWest Business-Education Partnership, MN.
Figure 15–2

PIPE **PRIVATE INITIATIVES IN PUBLIC EDUCATION**
215 Columbia   Seattle, Washington 98104   (206) 447-7244

PARTNERSHIP REPORT FORM

MONTH: _____   SCHOOL: _____

SCHOOL CONTACT: _____
                          (Name)

BUSINESS CONTACT: _____
                           (Name)

ACTIVITIES REPORT: (Accomplished, ongoing, and upcoming)

Be specific. Describe who, when, and where was involved in the activity.

TYPE OF MEETING HELD: DATE:

_____ SCHOOL ADVISORY MEETING   _____

_____ BUSINESS ADVISORY MEETING   _____

_____ BUSINESS COORDINATOR MEETING   _____

Reprinted by permission of Private Initiatives in Public Education (PIPE), WA.

Figure 15–3

**COLUMBIA MISSOURI
PARTNERS-IN-EDUCATION
PROGRESS REPORT**

NAME OF SCHOOL _____

NAME OF BUSINESS-COMMUNITY PARTNER _____

PERSON COMPLETING QUESTIONNAIRE _____

DATE: _____ PHONE NO. _____

---

1. Please list below or on an attached sheet the partnership activities (with dates, if possible) that have taken place from _____ through _____

2. Please list below or on an attached sheet the agreed-upon-activities (with dates, if possible) that are to be carried out during the next _____ months.

(Information from question 2 will be placed on the Partnership-In-Education Calendar of Events)

Figure 15–4

3. Approximately how many staff members have actually been involved in the activities to date?

_____ From your business-community organization (for business only)

_____ From your school (for school only)

4. Approximately how many staff members do you anticipate will become involved during

the next _____months?

_____ From your business-community organization (for business only)

_____ From your school (for school only)

5. What has been the general attitude of personnel participating in or affected by this partnership?

BUSINESS-COMMUNITY ORGANIZATION (CIRCLE ONE)

EMPLOYEES	Enthusiastic	Interested	Tolerant
MANAGEMENT	Enthusiastic	Interested	Tolerant

SCHOOL (CIRCLE ONE)

STUDENTS	Enthusiastic	Interested	Tolerant
PARENTS	Enthusiastic	Interested	Tolerant
STAFF	Enthusiastic	Interested	Tolerant
PRINCIPAL	Enthusiastic	Interested	Tolerant

6. Have you printed any article in your:

COMPANY NEWSLETTER	Yes	No	
SCHOOL PAPER	Yes	No	(Circle One)

Figure 15–4 (continued)

7. Please send a copy of each article that contains Partnership activity information to:

> Jolene Schulz
> Coordinator Partners-In-Education
> 310 N. Providence Rd.
> Columbia, MO 65201

8. Would you please send a copy of any forms or questionnaires that you have prepared for your employees or staff regarding partnership activities to Jolene Schulz?

9. Please notify Jolene Schulz of any event planned that would be appropriate for news releases and/or pictures.

10. Please notify Jolene Schulz of any event planned that would be appropriate for the Central Office staff and/or Columbia Chamber of Commerce Office staff to attend.

Thank you for completing the questionnaire. Your cooperation is certainly appreciated.

Figure 15–4 (continued)

UP-DATE ON ACTIVITIES

School _____ Business/Industry _____

Date _____ Contact Person _____ Contacted by ___

Activities _____

_____

_____

_____

_____

_____

_____

_____

Date _____ Contact Person _____ Contacted by ___

Activities _____

_____

_____

_____

_____

_____

_____

_____

Date _____ Contact Person _____ Contacted by ___

Activities _____

_____

_____

_____

_____

_____

Reprinted by permission of Partners in Education, Columbia Public Schools, MO.

Figure 15–4 (continued)

SCHOOL PARTNERSHIP PROGRAM EVALUATION OF SESSIONS

TITLE OF PROGRAM: _____

SPONSOR OF PROGRAM: _____

SCHOOL: _____

TEACHER: _____

HOME ADDRESS: _____ HOME PHONE: _____

CITY/STATE/ZIP: _____

_____

PLEASE COMPLETE THE FOLLOWING WITH AS MUCH DETAIL AS POSSIBLE. YOUR INPUT AFFORDS CONTINUED PURSUIT OF EXCELLENCE. IF NECESSARY CONTINUE YOUR ANSWERS ON AN ATTACHED SHEET.

1. What were your instructional goals and to what extent were these goals reinforced by the material presented in this program?

2. How well do you feel the presenter(s) accomplished his or her objective?

    extremely well   well   average   poorly   not at all

    Please support this evaluation with specific examples. What are your suggestions for the presenter's improvement?

3. To what extent did you gain information that will be helpful in future class activities?

    very much   much   some   little   not at all

    What was this information?

4. Specifically, what did you like most about the sessions?

Figure 15–5

5. How might the sessions have been improved? Do you feel your students had optimum involvement?

6. How would you rate the program sessions on the following scale?

excellent   good   fairly good   fair   poor

7. Would you like to participate in this program again next year?

Yes   No

Additional Comments:

_____

_____

_____

_____

_____

_____

_____

_____

_____

Figure 15–5 (continued)

STUDENT EVALUATION OF PARTNERSHIP PROGRAM
SPONSOR OF PROGRAM: _____

Part A.   Answer this part of the evaluation by circling the number according to the following code:

1–strongly agree   2–somewhat agree   3–not sure

4–somewhat disagree   5–strongly disagree

1. I understood the information that the speaker(s) presented.   1 2 3 4 5

2. The speaker(s) presented material that was interesting and informative.   1 2 3 4 5

3. I gained information to help me in my class(es).   1 2 3 4 5

4. The program was well organized.   1 2 3 4 5

PART B.

1. What part of this program did you like the most? _____

_____

_____

_____

2. What part of this program did you like the least? _____

_____

_____

_____

3. What do you feel were the most important things you learned from this program? _____

_____

_____

_____

Reprinted by permission of the St. Louis Public Schools, MO.

Figure 15–5 (continued)

CHARLOTTE-MECKLENBURG SCHOOLS

1250.5
1/84

EVALUATION OF VISIT BY RESOURCE PERSON

Please complete this form after your visit to the school or the school group's visit to your site, then return it to the Community Resource Office in the Teaching/Learning Center, Staff Development Center, 428 West Blvd., Charlotte 28203.

Your Name _____ Topic/Field Trip Location _____

School _____ Date of Visit _____

Teacher _____ Grade/Subject _____

Were arrangements made by the Community Resource Office satisfactory? _____yes _____no

Comments: _____

In retrospect, is there anything you would change about your presentation? _____

_____

From your perspective, is there anything you would change about the student group? _____

_____

In general, was your experience _____excellent, _____good, _____fair, _____poor?

What other suggestions do you have? _____

_____

Thank you for your comments. They help to determine the appropriate educational application of this activity and ways in which our service might be improved.

Reprinted by permission of Community Resource Program, Charlotte, NC.

Figure 15–6

San Francisco School Volunteers

Dear Teacher,

Some of you have had a Corporate Action in Public Schools (CAPS) tutor for several months now; others may have had a shorter time together. We are evaluating the fall semester experience and would appreciate it if you would complete and return this brief questionnaire by January 15.

The CAPS staff will be having informal brown-bag, lunch hour rap sessions with the tutors during the latter part of January, and your comments will be valuable.

I look forward to hearing from you.

Sincerely,

Joanne Dills
CAPS Director

QUESTIONNAIRE

1. Do you feel your students are profiting from the time spent with the released-time tutors?

   Yes ☐   No ☐

2. Do you have a good working relationship with the CAPS tutors?

   Yes ☐   No ☐

3. Do they arrive promptly, follow instructions, and fit into the classroom easily?

   Yes ☐   No ☐

4. Do they make proper use of lesson plans and/or resources available to them?

   Yes ☐   No ☐

5. Do you wish to continue with your current CAPS tutor?

   Yes ☐   No ☐

Please use the back of this page for comments or suggestions which would help us to strengthen the program.

_____   _____   _____
NAME   SCHOOL   LENGTH OF TIME USING CAPS TUTORS

Reprinted by permission of Corporate Action in Public Schools, San Francisco School Volunteers, CA.

Figure 15—7

COORDINATORS REPORT

_____   _____
            (School)   (Period Covered)

_____   _____
       (Coordinator's Name)   (Area)

PLEASE INDICATE BELOW THE NUMBER OF VOLUNTEERS ACTIVE IN EACH AREA AT YOUR SCHOOL THIS PERIOD, AND THE TOTAL NUMBER HOURS WORKED IN EACH AREA. Please list any new volunteers on the back on this sheet. Send this report by school mail to VIPS, Route 10.

ACTIVITIES	NO. OF VOL.	HOURS WORKED	COMPANY
Classroom Teacher Assts.	_____	_____	
Speakers	_____	_____	
Field Trips	_____	_____	
Tutors: Bilingual	_____	_____	
Math	_____	_____	
Reading	_____	_____	
Other (please list)			
_____	_____	_____	
_____	_____	_____	
_____	_____	_____	

Total No. of classes involved   _____

Any noteworthy volunteer news items, achievements, or human interest stories to report from your school?

Any suggestions, requests, or comments?

Figure 15–8

NEW VOLUNTEERS ADDED

NAME	PHONE	BUSINESS

Donations

Funds (Amount)   Purpose

_____   _____

_____   _____

In-Kind (Item)   Purpose

_____   _____

_____   _____

Reprinted by permission of the Houston Independent School District, TX.

Figure 15–8 (continued)

ADOPT-A-SCHOOL

PROJECTS REPORT FOR THE MONTH OF

_____

Signed: PRINCIPAL _____

        ADOPTER COORDINATOR _____

        ADOPTEE COORDINATOR _____

COMPLETED ACTIVITIES NOT PREVIOUSLY REPORTED	PLANNED ACTIVITIES NOT PREVIOUSLY REPORTED

Reprinted by permission of the Jackson Municipal Separate School District, MS.
Figure 15–9

 **San Francisco School Volunteers**

Date _____

_____
Name of Volunteer

_____
Name of Company

_____
Name of School

_____
Name of Teacher
(Optional)

**CORPORATE ACTION IN
PUBLIC SCHOOLS (CAPS)
PROGRAM EVALUATION
QUESTIONNAIRE**

Dear Teacher: Please take a few minutes to respond to this questionnaire regarding the CAPS volunteer project so we can modify and improve the program.

I. EXPERIENCE WITH THE VOLUNTEER   YOUR COMMENTS

_____This is the first time I have worked with CAPS volunteers
_____I have worked with many school volunteers

The volunteers I worked with this year gave assistance in:
_____One-to-one _____ Small group
_____General classroom assistance

Did the volunteer come regularly and on time?
_____Always _____ Usually _____ Very inconsistent

Did the volunteer accept responsibility?
_____Easily and on own initiative
_____With minimal direction needed
_____Needed a good deal of direction
_____Seldom able to assume any responsibility

Did you have time to work with volunteer?
_____Yes _____ No

Did you experience any of the following difficulties working with volunteers?
_____Volunteer would not take suggestions easily
_____Volunteer was critical of your teaching methods
_____Volunteer was critical of your teacher-child relationships
_____Volunteer had attitudes toward children or learning that were different from yours
_____Volunteer assumed too much responsibility in class
_____Volunteer was too strong or direct in approach to child
_____Volunteer was too meek or mild in approach to child
_____Other (describe)

Figure 15–10

253

II. SUPPORT SERVICES   <u>YOUR COMMENTS</u>

Did principal or school coordinator work with you to:

_____Assign volunteers _____ Arrange schedule
_____Orient volunteers _____ Train volunteers

If you experienced problems with the volunteer, whom did you contact?

III. RESULTS

In which areas are CAPS volunteer services most helpful?

_____Tutorial (one-to-one)
      _____Reading
      _____Math
_____English as a second language
_____Changed students' behavior
_____Motivated interest in learning
_____Career role models
_____Small group assistance
_____General classroom assistance
_____Creative projects
_____Other (describe)

Was the volunteer assigned to you compatible with what you requested? _____ Yes _____ No

Would you like a volunteer next semester?
_____ Yes _____ No

Please comment briefly on your experience and attitude about the CAPS Project.

Many thanks for taking the time to complete this evaluation.

Figure 15–10 (continued)

IRVINE PARTNERSHIP IN EDUCATION
QUESTIONNAIRE FOR ORGANIZATIONS

Date: _____

A. Program Selection and Implementation

1. Check the description that best describes the focus of your organization's Partnership in Education program:

_____Adopt-A-School
_____Adopt-A-Program
_____Volunteers

2. Did your Partnership support the instructional program? _____Yes _____ No

If yes, which? _____

3. How did you first learn about the Adopt-A-School program?

_____Barbara Barnes, Director of Irvine Partnership program
_____Media
_____Business associations (e.g., Chamber of Commerce, Irvine Co., etc.)
_____Other businesses
_____Direct contact from Irvine schools
_____Other (please specify) _____

4. Was your company involved in a school program prior to the Irvine Adopt-A-School program? _____ Yes _____ No

5. Check one or two of the following factors that led your organization to choose the school it adopted.

_____Located in area served by the business
_____Prior involvement with the school
_____Recommendation of community member
_____Convenient location
_____School suggested by Partnership director
_____School suggested by school personnel
_____Other (please specify) _____

6. How many of your staff members participated in the school program? _____

7. Were the people who participated

_____assigned to work with the program
_____volunteers in the program
_____a combination (some assigned, others volunteered)

8. Did you provide released time for the employees who participated?

_____Yes _____No

9. When did your program begin actual operations in the school?

_____
(Date)

Figure 15–11

10. How many meetings did you have with school staff before the program began?

_____ Was this sufficient? _____Yes _____No

If not, please comment: _____

_____

11. Who were involved in developing and planning the program? (Check any of the following that apply.)

_____Senior officers/owners
_____Managers
_____Actual volunteers
_____Public relations personnel
_____Training personnel
_____Other (please specify) _____

12. Who identified the objectives for the school program? (Check any of the following that apply.)

_____Principal
_____Organization staff
_____Teachers involved with the program
_____Other (please specify) _____

B. Program Content

13. What activities took place in the program? (Check any of the following that apply.)

_____Tutoring
_____Lectures or panel discussions for students
_____Audiovisual presentations for students
_____Resource materials provided that are not ordinarily available in the school
_____Units taught in class(es)
_____Performances or art exhibits by students
_____Assistance to administrative staff
_____Assistance to clerical staff
_____Other (please specify) _____

14. What difficulties did your organization have in working with the Adopt-A-School program? (Check any of the following that apply.)

_____None
_____Involving organization staff with the program
_____Traveling to the school
_____School staff who were not fully cooperative
_____Maintaining contact with school
_____Students who were not interested
_____Student behavior
_____Differing expectations between the organization and the school
_____Obtaining assistance from the Partnership director
_____Proper program coordination in the school
_____Other (please specify) _____

Figure 15–11 (continued)

C. Program Outcomes

15. Directions: Rate the extent to which you think the program your organization implemented succeeded in the following areas. If the statement is not appropriate for your program, circle DNA (Does Not Apply.)

	Does not apply	Not at all				Very great extent
To what extent do you feel the program accomplished its objectives?	DNA	1	2	3	4	5
To what extent are you satisfied with the program as implemented in the school?	DNA	1	2	3	4	5
To what extent did the school administration cooperate with you?	DNA	1	2	3	4	5
To what extent did the Partnership director cooperate with you?	DNA	1	2	3	4	5

16. Would you like to participate in the Adopt-A-School program next year?

_____Yes   _____No   _____Uncertain

a. If yes, which one of the following would you do? (Check one.)

_____Repeat the same program next year
_____Expand the program for next year
_____Start a completely new program next year

b. If yes, would you wish to continue working with the same school next year?

_____Yes   _____No   _____Uncertain

c. If no, why not? _____

_____

17. What recommendations do you have for the Partnership in Education (Adopt-A-School) program?

_____

_____

_____

18. Describe or attach information concerning the positive activities that have taken place in your partnership program.

_____

_____

_____

Figure 15–11 (continued)

SATURDAY SCHOLARS PROGRAM   NAME _____

SPRING '84 CYCLE: WILLIAMS SCHOOL   RANK _____ COMPANY _____

Please help us evaluate the Saturday Scholars program by completing the following questionnaire. We appreciate your suggestions for improving this program. Thank you for your participation and your assistance.

1. Briefly describe your Saturday Scholars experience.

2. What were the strengths of the program?

3. What were the weaknesses of the program?

4. How do you think this program could be improved?

5. Comments

Please return this form by May 15th to: Lt. J.G. Millard Smith
                                        Student Control Office
                                        Building 520, Room 122

Thank you very much for your cooperation.

Reprinted by permission of Volunteer Programs/Saturday Scholars, Chicago Public Schools, IL.
Figure 15–12

Williams School
Student Evaluation—Saturday Scholars Program

PLEASE ANSWER THE FOLLOWING QUESTIONS ABOUT COMING TO SCHOOL ON SATURDAYS TO WORK WITH THE SAILORS. THANK YOU VERY MUCH.

1. What did you like about the Saturday Scholars program?

_____

_____

_____

2. What didn't you like about the Saturday Scholars program?

_____

_____

_____

3. Do you think your schoolwork improved with the help sailors gave you?

_____

_____

_____

4. Would you come to school on Saturdays to work with a sailor again?

_____

Reprinted by permission of Volunteer Programs/Saturday Scholars, Chicago Public Schools, IL.

Figure 15–13

LOS ANGELES UNIFIED SCHOOL DISTRICT
Adopt-A-School Program

Summary of Activities 1985-1986

Adopter _____   School _____   Reg/
                                                                          Div._____

Company
Coordinator _____   School
                                      Coordinator _____

Title _____   Position _____

Phone _____   Phone _____

When did you meet with the company for the purpose of mapping out Adopt-A-School Program activities? Please list the dates here.

Please respond to each item below by checking in the appropriate column.

DID THE COMPANY OR REPRESENTATIVE(S) OF THE COMPANY:

	NO ACTION	PLANNING ACTION	OPERATIONAL ACTION

1. Strengthen instructional program by providing:

   tutors
   guest speakers
   brochures, pamphlets
   assembly programs
   films
   career day programs

2. Provide awards or incentives for:

   academic achievement
   good citizenship
   good attendance
   other (please explain)

   _____
   _____

3. Participate in:

   School Community Advisory Council
   grade level meetings
   PTSA
   departmental meetings
   other (please explain)

   _____
   _____

4. Provide recognition/appreciation activity(ies) for:

   certificated staff
   classified staff

5. Improve school environment by participating in:

   school pride programs
   school beautification projects
   anti-vandalism programs

6. Promote your school within the larger community through:

   press releases
   in-house publications
   chambers of commerce
   contact with legislators

Figure 15—14

260

	NO ACTION	PLANNING ACTION	OPERATIONAL ACTION

7. Participate in:

   Open House
   Back-to-School

8. Provide (for secondary schools only):

   part time jobs for students
   summer jobs for students
   scholarships

DID THE SCHOOL OR REPRESENTATIVE(S) OF THE SCHOOL:

9. Arrange for media coverage of Adopt-A-School activities:

   television
   radio
   community newspapers
   Adopt-A-School newsletter

10. Include the adopter among those to receive:

    school calendar
    school newspaper
    yearbook
    newsletter
    complimentary tickets to drama/art/music
       festivals or athletic events

11. Do something special for the adopter:

    display student artwork at the company
    design company holiday greeting card
    perform at the company's social events
    host end-of-the-year breakfast/luncheon
    recognize volunteers by celebrating
       birthdays-of-the-month

Please apply the following five Characteristics of a Quality Adopt-A-School Program to your partnership by responding to each of the following:

Check One:

1. The company and school have worked together to establish attainable goals and reasonable expectations. ☐ yes ☐ no

2. The company and school have cooperatively planned activities to enrich the educational program. ☐ yes ☐ no

3. Each partner has established an Adopt-A-School committee which assures continuity of the program regardless of personnel assignment. ☐ yes ☐ no

4. There is open communication and on-going articulation between the company and school which includes an annual review of the program and the development of strategies to renew and nurture the relationship. ☐ yes ☐ no

5. As a result of shared experiences, the company and school better understand each other. ☐ yes ☐ no

OPTIONAL

We welcome additional comments about your partnership. Should you wish to express yourself in greater detail or provide further information, please do so on a separate sheet of paper and attach it to this summary.

DATE: DUE: RETURN TO: The administrator at your region/division who coordinates the Adopt-A-School program

_____
Name of respondent (please print)

APPROVED: William R. Anton,
          Deputy Superintendent

_____
Position

Figure 15–14 (continued)

West Shore School District
ADOPT-A-SCHOOL PROGRAM
E V A L U A T I O N

School: _____

School Representative: _____

Community Organization/Business: _____

Community Organization/
Business Representative: _____

   I. AREA OF AGREEMENT (brief description):

  II. PERSONS INVOLVED:

  III. PROGRAM DESCRIPTION:

  IV. ASSESSMENT:

      A. Value to the School:

      B. Value to the Industry/Organization:

  V. COMMENTS/RECOMMENDATIONS:

_____   _____   _____
Evaluator   Industry/Agency   Date

Reprinted by permission of the Adopt-A-School Program, West Shore School District, PA.
Figure 15–15

PARTNERSHIP ACTUAL MID-YEAR AND PROJECTED END-OF-YEAR IMPACT ON STUDENTS

PARTNERSHIP	ATTENDANCE PROGRAM(S)	TOTALS M-Y	TOTALS PRJTD	HIGHER ED PROGRAMS	TOTALS M-Y	TOTALS PRJTD	ACADEMIC PREP PROGRAMS	TOTALS M-Y	TOTALS PRJTD	JOB PREP/PLACEMENT PROGRAM(S)	TOTALS M-Y	TOTALS PRJTD	PARENT/COMMUNITY OUTREACH PROGRAM(S)	TOTALS M-Y	TOTALS PRJTD
A		0	0		0	0		0	0	Part-time Teller	1	1			
										Shadowships	0	3			
										Get-A-Job Seminar	0	110			
	TOTALS	0	0		0	0		0	0		1	114			
B	In Planning	0	0	In Planning	0	0	Honor Roll	0	75	School Newspaper	5	5			
										Get-A-Job Workshop	0	294			
										Summer Employment	0	40			
	TOTALS	0	0		0	0		0	75		5	339			
C		0	0	Seminars						Job Prep Program	0	150			
				Career Interest Test											
				Speakers											
	TOTALS	0	0		0	0					0	150			
D		0	0	Guest Speakers Series	350	350	Engineer	20	20	Part-time Work	1	1			
				Lectures/Discussions	120	120	Electronic	20	30	Technology Career Day	0	300			
							Class Field			9th Grade Career Awareness	0	300			
	TOTALS	0	0		470	470		40	50		1	601			
E	(CLOSE-UP)	0	5	Contact with hospital professionals	100	100	Family Life Program	100	100	Shadowships	12	12			
				Counseling on higher ed	100	100	First Aid and CPR	40	40	Speakers on Medical Careers	50	50			
				Shadowships	12	12	Hospital Tours	40	40	Jobs	6	6			
							Smoke Out	1028	1028	Jobs	13	13			
							Term Papers	40	40	Speakers on Business and Industry	50	50			
							Test Prep	40	40	Tours	100	100			
							Reading Is Fundamental	300	300						
							CLOSE-UP	5	5						
							Yearbook	250	250						
							P.A.Y.S.	1	1						
	TOTALS	0	5		212	212		1844	1844		231	231			

263

Reprinted by permission of the Tri-Lateral Council for Quality Education, Inc. (now merged into the Boston Private Industry Council), MA.

Figure 15–16

ADOPT-A-SCHOOL EVALUATION
For School Coordinator and Principal

1. In which of the following ways has your adopter helped you this year?

   _____ Student motivation activities and awards

   _____ Teacher appreciation and assistance

   _____ Service projects for school and community

2. In which of the following ways has your school helped your adopter this year?

   _____ Appreciation activities (publicity in newsletters or local media, lunches, thank-you letters from students, etc.)

   _____ Cooperation in adopter service projects

   _____ Public relations efforts (use of adopter logo at school, media contacts for special events)

3. What suggestions would you make to improve the program?

   _____

   _____

   _____

   _____

4. Would you like to continue your partnership with your current adopter next year?

   _____ yes   _____ no

5. Who will be your school's Adopt-A-School coordinator next year?

   _____

Your Name _____

School _____

Reprinted by permission of the Jackson Municipal Separate School District, MS.

Figure 15–17

ADOPT-A-SCHOOL EVALUATION
For Adopter Coordinator and CEO

1. In which of the following ways has your organization helped your school this year?

   _____ Student motivation activities/awards

   _____ Teacher appreciation/assistance

   _____ Service projects for school/community

2. In which of the following ways has your school helped you this year?

   _____ Appreciation activities (publicity in newsletters or local media, lunches, thank-you letters from students, etc.)

   _____ Cooperation in your organization's service projects

   _____ Public relations efforts (use of logo at school, media contacts for special events)

3. What suggestions would you make to improve the program?

   _____

   _____

   _____

   _____

4. Do you plan to continue your Adopt-A-School partnership next year?

   _____ yes   _____ no

5. If so, who will be your coordinator for the program?

   _____

Your Name _____

Name of Organization _____

Reprinted by permission of the Jackson Muncipal Separate School District, MS.

Figure 15–18

GOVERNOR'S PRIVATE SECTOR INITIATIVES TASK FORCE, HUMAN RESOURCES COMMITTEE OF THE CABINET
HARRISTOWN II, 333 MARKET STREET, 9th FLOOR, HARRISBURG, PA 17120, 717-787-6835

COMMUNITY PARTNERSHIP PROJECT SUMMARY

CATEGORIES: ID NUMBER:

PROJECT TITLE: REGION:

ORGANIZATION:

CONTACT: TELEPHONE:

PROJECT BEGUN:

PURPOSE:

NEED:

DIMENSIONS OF PROJECT
   AREAS OF CONCENTRATION:

   TARGET AUDIENCE:

   INITIATORS:

   TIMING OF DEVELOPMENT/IMPLEMENTATION:

   GEOGRAPHIC SCOPE:

   GEOGRAPHIC POPULATION:

   TARGET POPULATION:

   ANNUAL COST OF PROJECT:

   SOURCE OF PROJECT FUNDS:

   COMPOSITION OF PARTNERSHIP:

HUMAN RESOURCE REQUIREMENTS
   PAID STAFF:

   VOLUNTEER ACTIVITIES:

TYPE OF ORGANIZATION:

OTHER ORGANIZATIONS INVOLVED IN THE PROJECT:

Information on this project has been provided by the sponsoring organization. It is made available by the Governor's Task Force to encourage sharing and replication. Its inclusion in the Project Bank does not constitute an endorsement of the project nor has it been possible for the Task Force to verify the information provided.

Figure 15–19

GOVERNOR'S PRIVATE SECTOR INITIATIVES TASK FORCE, HUMAN RESOURCES COMMITTEE OF THE CABINET
HARRISTOWN II, 333 MARKET STREET, 9th FLOOR, HARRISBURG, PA 17120, 717-787-6835

COMMUNITY PARTNERSHIP PROJECT SUMMARY

VOLUNTEER ACTIVITIES: ID NUMBER:

                                                          REGION:

VOLUNTEER SUPERVISION DONE BY:

TYPE OF ORGANIZATION:

OUTSTANDING FEATURES:

PROJECT EVALUATION:

SUBMITTED BY: DATE:

Information on this project has been provided by the sponsoring organization. It is made available by the Governor's Task Force to encourage sharing and replication. Its inclusion in the Project Bank does not constitute an endorsement of the project nor has it been possible for the Task Force to verify the information provided.

Figure 15–19 (continued)

GOVERNOR'S PRIVATE SECTOR INITIATIVES TASK FORCE, HUMAN RESOURCES COMMITTEE OF THE CABINET
HARRISTOWN II, 333 MARKET STREET, 9th FLOOR, HARRISBURG, PA 17120, 717-787-6835

COMMUNITY PARTNERSHIP PROJECT SUMMARY

SUMMARY: **ID NUMBER:**

                                                               REGION:

Information on this project has been provided by the sponsoring organization. It is made available by the Governor's Task Force to encourage sharing and replication. Its inclusion in the Project Bank does not constitute an endorsement of the project nor has it been possible for the Task Force to verify the information provided.

Reprinted by permission of the Governor's Private Sector Initiatives Task Force and the Pennsylvania State Department of Education.

Figure 15–19 (continued)

PART FOUR

MAINTAINING AND EXTENDING SUCCESSFUL PARTNERSHIPS

Maintaining and Extending A Successful Partnership

Thousands of partnerships—limited and extensive—have sprung up all over the country. There is diversity in both the size and quality of programs. Size, if appropriate to available resources, is really no problem; however, the quality of program activities may well determine if a district's partnership is successful or is merely a fad—just another program that is here today and gone tomorrow.

When leaders initiate their partnerships, they concentrate on getting the program started. They do not worry about where the program will be in two years—or five—or ten! However, it is precisely at the time of program initiation and development that consideration should be given to providing a sturdy base upon which to build an effective program for the future. As the leader of a new partnership, you want to ensure the program's immediate *and* future success. Under consideration should be these critical questions:

1. Are the following program components in place?
   - an organizational structure
   - leadership and support staff
   - a program budget
   - tools for recordkeeping as related to program administration and development
2 Are the following program components in their development phase?
   - a process for communication, including networks, procedures and vehicles
   - selected program activities based on priority needs and available resources
   - procedures and recordkeeping forms for program monitoring and evaluation

If answers to these questions are yes, where do you go from here? Guidelines are presented here for partnership leaders; these guidelines can assist them (1) to effectively and efficiently coordinate program components on a daily, weekly, and monthly basis; (2) to retain overall control and understanding of the program; (3)

to facilitate program changes and refinements as necessary; (4) to promote and solidify positive interrelationships between partners; (5) to achieve goals and objectives (illustrated through the successful accomplishment of identified program tasks and activities); and (6) to extend their programs as appropriate to determined needs and available, potential resources.

GUIDELINES FOR GENERAL PROGRAM MANAGEMENT

1. Partnership leaders delegate program tasks and responsibilities to staff and consultants (as appropriate). *All* delegated tasks and responsibilities are approved and monitored by the project director.

2. Check sheets, monthly schedules, calendars, yearly flow charts, and other comparable tools are used to provide clear guidelines to leaders, staff, and partners regarding short- and long-term program planning and development.

3. *Short*, weekly (or biweekly) staff meetings are *scheduled and held on a regular basis* (a) to bring everyone up to date about partnership activities, (b) to issue new assignments (or adjust old ones), and (c) to provide a forum for brainstorming, problem solving, and decision making.

4. Monthly meetings are arranged with the business office to resolve problems related to managing the budget.

5. Be prepared to attend a variety of day and evening meetings, receptions, and events hosted by your board of education, business and community partners, participating schools, central administrative staff, and parent groups. If you can't attend an event, send a representative from the partnership program.

6. Keep superiors consistently advised of program achievements *and* problems. No one likes surprises!

GUIDELINES FOR THE MANAGEMENT OF PROGRAM FUNDS

Briefly mentioned in the general guidelines was the importance of meeting on a regular basis with a business officer to review, discuss, and resolve problems related to management of program funds. At these meetings:

1. Yearly budgets are prepared in consultation with business advice.

2. Necessary approvals and board resolutions regarding special conditions related to budgets are obtained. Such conditions might address the withholding of funds from the partnership's general budget; these funds are then placed in separate accounts for special events, for consultant fees (daily or contractual), or to prepare a final evaluation report.

3. The partnership director requests and reviews monthly printouts of expenditures.

4. Budget changes (transfer of funds, new encumbrances, and so on) are processed in a manner that allows a specified amount of time (for the business office) to expedite budget adjustments *before* additional expenditures are made.

5. Notifications from the business office, regarding adjustments and clarification of accounts and expenditures, receive priority response from the partnership office.

6. The business office is treated as a "partner" and invited to attend partnership events.

GUIDELINES FOR STRENGTHENING COMMUNICATIONS NETWORKS

Since partnerships are a "people" business, there is no program task or activity that does not, in some way, address the area of communications. The following guidelines (in addition to the discussion presented in Section 13) can help leaders solidify communications networks:

1. Refine and adapt procedures and recordkeeping forms to support productive, positive communication linkages.

2. Regularly disseminate publicity regarding program activities (press releases, events, interviews).

3. Schedule ongoing staff training in writing and interviewing skills. Responsibilities for publicity are clearly defined; at the same time, *no* communications about the program leave the partnership office without the director's signature or approval.

4. Change formats for disseminating program information as needed. The partnership's logo should appear on all materials so that audiences become acquainted with and recognize the sender. (*Note*: Many partnerships hold districtwide or schoolwide art contests and choose their logos from student artists.)

5. Request assistance, as appropriate, from both district and partners' public relations-community relations-communications offices and departments. These offices have experience and expertise that can save valuable time and assist you in professionally communicating partnership information; they also like to work with partnership programs—programs that can have a positive impact on public perceptions about the district or partner organizations.

6. When in doubt about the legality or sensitivity of partnership information, *always* check with superiors.

GUIDELINES FOR SOLICITING ONGOING PARTNERSHIP COMMITMENT AND PARTICIPATION

Experienced program leaders know that a large portion of their time must be spent on maintaining existing partners' commitment. Here are some guidelines to follow:

1. Develop special procedures, activities, and materials that encourage partners to continue their support for the program. Two examples of effective materials include a fund-raising form from the San Francisco Education Fund, CA (see Figure 16-1, and note how a return envelope is enclosed with the solicitation); and a letter from the Cleveland Scholarship Programs, OH (see Figure 16-2).

2. Of course, efforts to solicit ongoing program support are well served through reports and evaluations (see Section 15) and through newsletters and other forms of communication (see Section 13).

3. Time and consideration must also be given to problems associated with shaky partnerships (see Figure 16-3 from the Adopt-A-School Program, Los Angeles, CA for guidelines that confront this problem).

4. Procedures and materials soliciting continued commitment should always express program needs as well as accomplishments; if everything is 100 percent, why do you require additional support?

GUIDELINES FOR MAINTAINING ORIENTATION AND STAFF DEVELOPMENT SESSIONS FOR ALL PARTNERS

A discussion of staff development can be found in Section 10. Here are some additional guidelines:

1. The program director supervises the development of orientation and staff training schedules for different groups of participants. These sessions are scheduled in the summer preceding the school year when a calendar of workshops and meetings is distributed to staff, volunteers, and partners. Early scheduling encourages supervisors (of all partners—community organizations, businesses, and the school district) to release their employees or volunteers to participate in these activities; if there should be major conflicts, an early calendar permits flexibility in rescheduling.

2. Volunteers and other staff (from school district and partners) can be effectively trained by the program director, consultants, school district specialists, management from partners, or a combination of the above. What is important is that the partnership's leader determines who will do the training and then supervises or delegates the tasks (*but* monitors the process) associated with staff development. These tasks include (a) securing the site; (b) making hospitality arrangements; (c) developing and disseminating orientation and training schedules; (d) preparing orientation and staff development materials; (e) guiding the trainer; (f) preparing an evaluation

for each staff development activity; (g) collecting, organizing, and analyzing evaluation data; and (h) refining future staff development training based on information from the evaluations.

GUIDELINES FOR ONGOING DEVELOPMENT, IMPLEMENTATION, AND MONITORING OF PROGRAM ACTIVITIES

Sections 14 and 15 provide a full discussion of the development and monitoring of program activities. Following are further recommendations that extend these earlier discussions:

1. The partnership leader selects and solicits commitment from assistants (paid and volunteer and part-time and full-time) who come from the central office, business, civic and community partners, and the school site.

2. Assistants are given orientation or trained as activity coordinators, volunteer helpers, speakers, presenters, and tour guides. The program's leader may be the trainer. If this responsibility is delegated, the partnership's leader still supervises the process.

3. Coordinators are assigned to facilitate program activities. These coordinators do *not* supervise; their responsibilities and tasks support the successful completion of activities. Achievement of problem-solving and decision-making tasks is encouraged through a group peer process.

4. Partnership leaders also supervise the organization and refinement of procedures and recordkeeping forms to complement and support program activities. This is important, since any program can be overwhelmed with meaningless behaviors and paper tasks.

5. Evaluation procedures are developed and used for all program activities to ensure (a) equity in the distribution of available resources and (b) successful achievement of stated goals and objectives.

EXTENDING PARTNERSHIPS: WHAT IS CHANGE?

Over 99 percent of the leaders surveyed through the questionnaire said that once a partnership is established, a good portion of the leader's time is spent searching for fresh resources (human, financial, in-kind) and developing new activities that directly address student and staff educational needs. These leaders view themselves as change agents—with the responsibility of improving the program. In other words, program extension is viewed as an opportunity for improvement and enrichment of already successful, efficient, and effective programs. Viewed in this context, changes related to extension could mean

1. replicating or adapting successful activities in multiple sites.
2. increasing the breadth and depth of activities at the same site.
3. developing new activities at different sites.

4. expanding specific districtwide activities and programs that address such areas as staff development, internships, and resource guides.

5. extending the partnership's clearinghouse capacity.

6. developing auxiliary networks for the partnership, for example, those involving associate or senior partners.

7. providing additional resources so that existing programs could be improved and enriched. The concept of multicorporate sponsorship has become important to many programs.

8. expanding activities (a) for example, from the secondary level to middle and elementary levels—and the other way around, or (b) from adopt-a-school to adopt-a-class, adopt-a-program, adopt-a-student, or adopt-a-teacher.

9. eliciting longer-term commitments from partners.

10. securing resources and commitments from parts of the community that were originally untapped, for example from small businesses, senior citizens, and other nonprofit or civic agencies and organizations.

11. establishing regional partnership networks (especially in rural areas that often have few available partners), whereby resources could be pooled and shared.

12. securing resources beyond local boundaries—at the state and national levels.

13. pursuing partnership arrangements with post–high school institutions: universities, community colleges, colleges, and institutions for technical training.

14. working toward a goal in which all of a district's students, schools, and staff received program benefits.

GUIDELINES FOR EXTENDING PARTNERSHIPS

Planning Is Key

First and foremost, planning for change is the key. Therefore, partnership staffs must be able to answer the following questions *before* extended tasks and activities are planned and initiated:

1. Are changes required in leadership? in partnership policies and/or guidelines? Will additional committees or task forces be needed? Will changes entail the use of legal counsel to avoid entanglements?

2. Does the current partnership format require revision or should new formats be added and the old format(s) terminated?

3. Should there be reassessments of both needs and resources? Which group(s)

should be surveyed? Following the survey, can conclusions be drawn that resources are indeed available to support any program extension?

4. What staffing and role changes and associated responsibilities require implementation? Will additional professional skills and staff time be required?

5. Are communications networks and tools sufficient to handle effective dissemination of increased program information? Will there be a need for more formal public relations strategies?

6. Can existing procedures and staffing resources secure necessary monies and human or in-kind resources to support new activities? Will fund-raising campaigns be necessary? Who will facilitate these campaigns to solicit additional partners and funding—and how?

7. How should budgets be revised to support extended tasks and activities effectively? Can and should carryover funds be used to provide start-up funding for new program directions? How can business administrators and accountants advise partnership leaders to facilitate these changes within existing legal constraints?

8. What procedures and recordkeeping forms must be developed to expedite contemplated changes? Will it be "more of the same" or must alternative procedures and forms be initiated?

9. If your partnership has not established formal evaluation and reporting procedures, should they be developed before extending program activities? If such procedures were instituted, would they provide additional credibility to the program?

Extending the Partnership: Development and Implementation

After answering the questions about planning, staff are ready to develop and implement an action plan. Here are the steps to take:

Step One. Use the suggested action plan outline found in Section 3 (see Figure 3-1) of this handbook to help you structure and organize proposed activities.

Step Two. Review this handbook's preceding chapters for guidelines and strategies that can be used as is, or adapted to initiate, refine, and/or extend existing program components, procedures, materials, and activities.

Step Three. Plans should be developed and implemented, using every available source of *local* expertise and experience. The partnership director monitors the follow-up on leads submitted to the program's office (a) to ensure that no active lead is missed and (b) to prevent the failure that is certain to result if a potential partner is bombarded with multiple requests from the same program.

Step Four. Assistance should be sought from other partnership programs as well as from regional, state, and national resources. A starting point for highly qualified sources can be found in the appendixes of this handbook. All partnerships listed in these appendixes are currently involved in program expansion and improvement and have extensive experience and expertise to share with colleagues. Further discussion regarding the extension of programs and professional skills, through networking beyond the local district level, can be found in Section 17.

The San Francisco Education Fund
1095 Market Street, Suite 719
San Francisco, CA 94103

Yes! I want to continue my support
of the Education Fund.

To help ensure excellence in
public education, I am enclosing
my check for:

☐ $25   ☐ $50   ☐ $100   ☐ $500   ☐ Other

Name _____
Address _____
_____ Zip Code _____

(Please make checks payable to the
San Francisco Education Fund .... Thank You!)

The San Francisco Education Fund
1095 Market Street, Suite 719
San Francisco, California 94103

Attention: Glady Thacher

Reprinted by permission of the San Francisco Education Fund, CA.

Figure 16–1

January 16, 1985

Dr. Clarence Mixon
Executive Director
Cleveland Scholarship Programs, Inc.
1380 East Sixth Street
Cleveland, OH 44114

Dear Clarence:

It is a personal pleasure for me to endorse the Cleveland Scholarship Program. I am impressed by the originators, Roy and Eva Markus, who had the foresight and the imagination in 1954 to implement a cooperative program between students and universities. I am encouraged by the fine work of the CSP counselors who over the years have so effectively guided students through the process of applying to college. Their follow-up services provide universities with a valuable contribution to existing retention efforts.

I am proud that the Cleveland business community has recognized the value of these services and has continued to financially support this program.

A well-planned and administered program, the Cleveland Scholarship Program benefits everyone involved and we can all appreciate this effective interaction.

Sincerely,

William R. Bennett
Director of Financial Aid

WRB:ds

Reprinted by permission of the Cleveland Scholarship Programs, Inc., OH.
Figure 16–2

LOS ANGELES UNIFIED SCHOOL DISTRICT
Adopt-A-School Program
SHAKY PARTNERSHIPS————PROFESSIONAL CONSIDERATIONS

1. Strategies to renew partnerships not meeting expectations.

   A. Intervention by region/division staff to assist principal and company representative to jointly redefine expectations and goals is recommended.

   B. An emphasis should be placed on the mutual benefits of an Adopt-A-School partnership.

   C. New Adopt-A-School coordinators and/or committee members may be beneficial.

   D. Communication from students is particularly effective in motivating companies to maintain and increase support of schools.

2. At what point is a partnership over?

   A. When all five of the characteristics of a quality Adopt-A-School Program are absent from the partnership. (Refer to the enclosed list of characteristics developed at the Lost Angeles Dodgers Stadium Club, September 6, 1984, by region/division Adopt-A-School teams.)

   B. When strategies suggested in Item 1 above have failed.

   C. After repeated efforts by the principal to contact the company have failed.

   D. When it is in the best interest of the school and company to terminate the partnership.

3. How do we exit an Adopt-A-School partnership and still preserve good will?

   A. Regions and divisions must be involved in any action taken to dissolve a partnership.

   B. A letter from the school, with region/division approval, should be sent to the company expressing appreciation for past support and involvement.

   C. The company should be given an opportunity to be involved in other projects at the school even if on a very limited basis. Leave the door open for other assistance.

   D. Offer the company a second opportunity with another school.

Reprinted by permission of the Adopt-A-School Program, Los Angeles Unified School District, CA.
Figure 16–3

Networking at Regional, State, and National Levels

HOW TO CONNECT WITH RESOURCES BEYOND THE LOCAL LEVEL

Survey respondents expressed interest in expanding their networks beyond local boundaries to explore potential sources for additional partners and further technical assistance and expertise related to supplemental programs. Planning and implementation of a network of sources require a thoughtful, concerted effort so that program staff are not forced to "reinvent the wheel" or become involved in tangential, unproductive tasks and responsibilities. The following guidelines should help to place this expansion process within a workable context:

1. Leaders determine the goals and objectives related to program expansion to the regional, state, and/or national levels. This decision is based on assessment of current and future program needs in terms of how needs match *local* available resources; if there is a discrepancy and needs must be met, then the decision to pursue outside resources can be considered.

2. Partnership leaders assign the tasks of researching and developing extended resource networks to staff members, *or* leaders assume these responsibilities themselves. Approval for this decision is solicited from the district's superintendent, board of education and/or the partnership's governing council.

3. A committee, composed of school district, business, and community representatives, is established to support and guide the program's efforts at expansion. A partnership staff person or a member of the partnership's governing council (as appropriate) chairs this committee.

4. A plan is developed and implemented by the committee and includes the following steps:

   • Investigate possible sources of program support—human, financial, in-kind, materials—beyond local boundaries. The appendixes of this handbook provide a starting point for this effort. Instruments used previously in local solicitation campaigns can be adapted and disseminated to explore new levels of potential resources. A checksheet (see Figure 17-1) assists you in developing a source bank (to record and access information regarding potential regional, state, and national partners).

- Coordinate and analyze source information.
- Prepare a list of regional, state, and national organizations whose resources are appropriate to program needs *and* potentially accessible.
- Review data to determine: (a) which organizations will be solicited; (b) what resources these organizations have to offer; *Ask the question: Does the organization to be solicited have the resources to meet determined needs? If not, why are they being solicited? Don't waste time wooing a resource that "might" be needed or that provides a one-time "splash!"* (c) possible services that the program or school district can offer in exchange for particular resources; (d) at what organizational level contact(s) should be made; (e) who will make the solicitation and follow-up; (f) how the solicitation will be facilitated; (g) how the follow-up will be expedited.
- Implement the process outlined above; repeat as necessary. The partnership director monitors the process.
- If partnership arrangements are made with any regional, state, and national affiliates, the program leader and an assigned staff person (depending on the program's size) assume the responsibility for maintaining, solidifying, and further extending the long-term commitment to the local program of these organizations.

IMPORTANT NETWORKS TO KNOW AT THE REGIONAL LEVEL

A partnership's immediate region usually becomes the first target area for pursuit of resources beyond the local school district. It is practical to seek resources within a contiguous area. School districts sometimes form a regional partnership when (a) local resources are insufficient to meet the needs of a specific district or districts within a geographic area *or* (2) large-scale organizations, serving a regional area, are reluctant to provide resources to one school district at the expense of another. The efficient and equitable distribution of resources through regional "pooling" then becomes a more satisfactory arrangement for all partners.

Potential regional partners can be found through personal referrals; through phone and other regional directories; through organizational lists; and through membership and participation in allied public, nonprofit, and private organizations and agencies. Regional sources of support come in many forms, including

- hospitals
- corporate divisions of national companies
- private industry councils and industry education councils
- nonprofit organizations

- foundations
- county offices of state departments of education
- regional federal offices
- cooperatives
- utilities
- professional organizations
- unions
- retail operations (food, clothing, hardware, technology, appliances, furniture)
- factories
- research laboratories

Following are some examples of regional organizations that are partners to school districts.

Minneapolis, MN: *Education Ventures Inc.* is a minigrant program that assists teachers who want to explore and develop new classroom teaching strategies and programs.

New York, NY: *The New York Alliance for the Public Schools* has among its programs:

1. *MENTOR*: a law-related education program where law firms are paired with individual high schools. In the MENTOR program, students learn—through practical experience—about the legal profession and how the courts function, as well as the opportunities and responsibilities afforded by the law. A complete description of the MENTOR program can be found in the *MENTOR Handbook.* This program has been expanded to other cities and states.

2. *Principal as Curriculum Leader*: a staff development program for the City's high school principals and assistant principals.

3. *Go Public!* a public information campaign in support of public education.

4. *Computerlink,* a computerized data bank of resources for the City's teachers.

Washington, DC: *DC Public School/Federal Agency Partners-in-Education* is an organized formal partnership between the city's public schools and federal district government agencies and private industry; each agency is paired with an individual school or program. For example, the *Federal Reserve Board* has a partnership with the DC school district and provides seminars for teachers as well as materials, tours, and lectures for students. The *Department of Education* (DOE) has a partnership with Amidon Elementary School in Washington, DC.

Chicago, IL: the *U.S. Railroad Retirement Board* (another federal agency) has a partnership with a high school. Its program activities use employees from the agency to participate (1) in volunteer tutoring, (2) as classroom speakers, (3) in fund raising for scholarship awards, (4) in arranging for on-site agency tours, and

(5) in conducting computer programming basics workshops and in-service faculty seminars (on personal computer applications).

Boulder, CO: *NBS CARE* (Career Awareness and Resource Education) program provides resources (human and in-kind) that supplement and enrich the mathematics and science curriculum for students in grades 4–12.

NOTE: Other Department of Commerce agencies, in addition to the National Bureau of Standards, participate in regional partnerships.

St. Paul, MN: The *3M Visiting Women Scientists Program* (conducted by the Women Scientists Subcommittee of the 3M Technical Forum) works to encourage career awareness and recruitment of women to the science fields. Activities include large-group presentations and small-group discussions at which students have the opportunity to interact with women scientists.

San Diego, CA: *Partnerships in Education*, San Diego County Office of Education is a countywide program including adopt-a-school, volunteer, clearinghouse, and community school activities focused on the awareness of the world of work, on career opportunities, and on motivation of students to achieve.

Los Angeles, CA: *The Los Angeles Educational Partnership* is a private, nonprofit corporation that works closely with both the Los Angeles Unified School District and the Los Angeles County Public Schools. The corporation acts as a broker between private industry and public education, and partnership activities focus on the following programs: (1) Math/Science Teacher Fellowships; (2) small grants for teachers; (3) public information; (4) linking secondary-level mathematics departments with urban resources; and (5) establishing interdisciplinary humanities programs in Los Angeles high schools.

Harrisburg, IL: *Southeastern Illinois Vocational System* is a partnership between nine rural secondary schools, a regional vocational system, a community college, a correctional institution, and the business and industry of the region. The program provides a broad vocational program, including (1) instruction in advanced courses and vocational training, (2) staff development for teachers, and (3) alternatives for cost-effective site usage for the area's schools.

Greenville, NC: *Teacher Exchange in Rural Schools* is a partnership between East Carolina University and four school districts in which university faculty and public school personnel "change places" to learn more about each other's roles. Orientation meetings, shadowing activities, and program evaluation forms are delineated through a procedural handbook, *The Teacher Exchange Handbook*.

NETWORKING AT THE STATE LEVEL

The next broad ring of partnership networking is at the state level. Potential state partners have their own network of affiliates that include

- state departments of education
- businesses with statewide franchises, offices, or factories
- utilities
- nonprofit agencies and organizations
- state governmental agencies
- state offices of federal agencies and departments
- unions
- corporate headquarters

Following is a selection of state programs that have been cited for their initiatives and expertise in encouraging and supporting the development of alliances.

Harrisburg, PA: The *Pennsylvania State Department of Education and Governor's Private-Sector Initiatives Task Force, Partnerships-in-Education Program.* The State Department of Education's School Improvement Division has responsibility (1) to provide technical assistance, support and recognition—through both central and intermediate units—to partnerships throughout the state and (2) to facilitate and support the development of partnerships between all state departments and agencies and the Harrisburg schools. The state's governor and secretary of education, as well as local chambers of commerce and other business, civic, and community organizations, actively support these efforts.

Indianapolis, IN: *Indiana Partners in Education* (IPIE) is a statewide collaboration between government, business, and education. IPIE assists communities in developing partnerships through general technical assistance and training activities for all partners: business, community, government, and education. The program is actively supported by the governor and is publicly endorsed in the state's new economic development plan, "In Step with the Future."

Columbia, MO: *Missouri Education/Business Partners* (Cosponsored by the Missouri State Teachers Association and the Missouri State Chamber of Commerce) is supporting and encouraging partnerships across the state. One of its successes is the Partners-In-Education Program that pairs schools and business-community partners in the city of Columbia.

Raleigh, NC: Through the *Division of Community Schools*, North Carolina's Department of Public Instruction has developed a statewide partnership program that includes such diverse activities as volunteer services; after-school classes; adopt-a-school programs; adopt-a-grandparent programs; an artists-in-residence program; and building of a swimming pool and a school-civic auditorium at a high school! Valuable materials to consult include (1) *The Community Schools Resource Book*, a complete guide to partnerships across the state; (2) a comprehensive report on the state's Adopt-A-School Volunteer Program; and (3) the "Follow-Up Evaluation of the North Carolina Community Schools Program" (Department of Public Instruction, 1983). *Note*: The State of North Carolina, through its Community Schools Act of 1977, Article 13, encourages increased collaborations, with total community involvement (public *and* private sector), through partnerships.

NETWORKS AT THE NATIONAL LEVEL

Approaching and connecting with national resource networks is often perceived to be difficult, if not impossible, because they appear to be very removed—both geographically and philosophically—from local needs and concerns. In some cases, this may be true. However, many national organizations, businesses, and agencies have already established credibility in terms of

- their willingness to collaborate with school districts at the local level
- their proven support of partnership efforts in the sharing of human, financial, materials, and in-kind resources
- their proactive efforts to strengthen networks linking their organizations *and* associate or complementary organizations and agencies to schools, students, and staff

The following is a sampling, a start, for school districts—an introduction to national resources.

Washington, DC: *National Diffusion Network* (NDN) makes exemplary education programs available for adoption by schools, colleges, and other institutions by funding Developer-Demonstrator projects that provide training, materials and technical assistance to schools and others that want to adopt the programs. NDN also funds state facilitators in each state who serve as matchmakers between NDN programs and schools and organizations that could benefit from adopting the programs. Some NDN programs work closely with community-business partners. Information is available through NDN's *Educational Programs That Work* as well as through their national office (DC).

Washington, DC: The *United States Department of Education* can provide access to national as well as regional and state resources for networking. In addition to giving technical assistance through both central (DC) and regional offices, the DOE disseminates materials that give the local school district access to information related to partnership programs. Particularly useful books are *The Nation Responds: Recent Efforts to Improve Education; Partnerships in Education: Education Trends of the Future;* and *Toward Excellence: Private Sector Initiatives in Education.*

New York, NY: *Mead Data Central* supplies LEXIS/NEXIS training modules that are used in conjunction with the MENTOR program's partnership (NY Alliance for the Public Schools) and are thus focused on law-related education for high school students. The modules, both introductory and advanced, explain the growing use of computers in the law firms for, among other things, automated legal research. Guides, educational aids for students, and complimentary access to LEXIS/NEXIS for instructional purposes are also program components.

Stamford, CT: GTE Corporation, through the sponsorship of the GTE Foundation, supports *GIFT*: a staff development program for secondary level mathematics and science teachers (grades 7-12). The program includes (1) Personal Development Grants; (2) School Enrichment Grants (matching) used in the teachers' schools;

and (3) seminars (by invitation) with GTE scientists, managers, and human resource experts.

New York, NY: *IMPACT II* is a teacher-to-teacher networking program originally funded by the Exxon Education Foundation. The program awards small Developer and Adaptor grants to teachers. Other program components include workshops, a yearly *Catalog of Teacher-Developed Programs*, funding for substitutes (so that teachers can renew developer programs *or* assist adaptors), videotapes for dissemination, and the *IMPACT II Star***, a quarterly sent to all participants involved in the network.

New York, NY: In the *CBS Television Stations Adopt-A-School Partnership Program*, some CBS stations have developed partnerships with public schools in their communities. Through activities that expose students to a range of broadcasting activities, CBS Television Stations expect to broaden students' educational opportunities and, through on-air activities, foster community-business awareness of and participation in partnership programs.

Washington, DC: *Newspapers in Education* (*NIE*), sponsored by the American Newspaper Publishers Association, encourages the use of newspapers in schools to teach (1) basic skills, (2) information relevant to a range of subjects, and (3) basic citizenship. Associated program materials include a manual of publications and training materials and workshops.

Wichita, KS: The *BOOK IT! National Incentive Reading Program* is sponsored by Pizza Hut, Inc. The program's goal is to motivate students (in grades one through six) to read. Each community's program involves the following partners: Pizza Hut, Inc., school districts, teachers, students, parents, and staff from the company and franchise restaurants. Incentives include award certificates for pizza, buttons, progress charts, and class pizza parties.

Washington, DC: *Partnerships Data Net* is a national information resource and referral service to provide information on private-sector initiatives and to support collaboration between the public and private sectors. By electronically linking people and information across the United States, this network acts as a broker to assist in forming partnerships, identifying critical resources, and encouraging an exchange of ideas. Technologies used include electronic mail and bulletin boards, teleconferencing, direct database searches, and other computer capabilities, as well as a direct dial, toll-free number (1-800-8-ACCESS) and a *Partnerships in Education Directory*.

Pittsburgh, PA: *The Public Education Fund* is a national intermediary organization that provides technical assistance and developmental grants support to community organizations, thereby encouraging them (1) to develop structures that can successfully organize and support supplemental programs concerned with educational improvement and (2) to build constituencies for the local public schools. Their report, *The First Two Years: The Public Education Fund 1983–1985*, provides complete information about the fund's activities, past accomplishments and future directions.

Bellingham, WA: *Acres* (American Council on Rural Special Education) *Rural Job Services* sponsors a job referral service that links educators who need jobs with rural agencies that have vacancies. The service operates in every state.

Alexandria, VA: *Future Farmers of America* (FFA) helps prepare high school students for careers in agricultural production, processing, supply and service, mechanics, horticulture, forestry, natural resources, and associated professions. Chapters of FFA are established in public schools; activities include instruction in agriculture, contests, and incentive award programs.

Washington, DC: *Reading is Fundamental* (RIF) is a partnership (of parents, schools, students, business, civic and community organizations, and publishers). More than 7 million books are distributed to and chosen for ownership by 2.2 million young people each year. National RIF provides book discounts and technical assistance to 3,300 local projects to develop their own individual RIF events and activities that strive to motivate children to read for enjoyment and information. One of RIF's popular national activities is the "Reading Is Fun Week," held in late April.

Washington, DC: *Triangle Coalition for Science and Technology Education* is an alliance between scientists and engineers, representatives of business and industry, and educators to share ideas and resources. Activities include (1) building a network of broad-based local alliances to support science teachers and precollege science and technology education; (2) establishing a database of programs that offer assistance in science and technology areas to schools and teachers; and (3) collaborating with business and industry in establishing a minigrant program for funding small projects.

Washington, DC: *MATHCOUNTS* is a cooperative project that promotes excellence and interest in the field of mathematics. The program—focused on the junior high school student—provides: technical assistance to teachers and community organizers; a variety of practice materials, administration handbooks, and promotional accessories; and funding of expenses for state teams to travel to the national competition each year.

Buffalo, NY: *National Association of Industry-Education Cooperation, Inc.* (NAIEC) fosters collaboration between industry and education to further school improvement and economic development at local and state levels. NAIEC activities include: (1) the development of local broad-based Industry-Education Councils, (2) community resources workshops, (3) national clearinghouse activities for industry-sponsored educational materials, (4) job-placement programs and materials, (5) local, regional, and national conferences, seminars, and institutes, and (6) newsletters, a journal, and other publications.

Washington, DC: *The United States Chamber of Commerce* and its local, regional, and state affiliates act as catalysts in support of cooperative activities between business and educational leaders in such areas as (1) career education; (2) the teaching of business and economic principles; (3) staff and curriculum development for teachers; and (4) the development of partnerships at the local level. Two useful publications for partnership leaders are *Business and Education: Partners for the Future* and *Strategy for the 1980s: Business and Economic Education Model Programs.*

Washington, DC: *The National School Volunteer Program, Inc.* (NSVP) serves as an umbrella organization for a myriad of volunteer programs at the local, state, and regional levels, including (1) coordination and facilitation of regional and national conferences; (2) training academies for educational leaders and their partners (community and business); (3) on-site assistance in the design and development of local volunteer programs; and (4) preparation and dissemination of handbooks, pamphlets, and a monthly newsletter (that includes an excellent "Idea Bulletin").

Washington, DC: *National Institute for Citizen Education and the Law* (NICEL) provides nationwide leadership in teaching law in the schools. Partnership activities include (1) linking law schools, bar associations, police, courts, law firms, and other law-related groups with schools (K-12); (2) providing textbooks, filmstrips, and other materials for use in classes; (3) assistance in setting up such activities as mock trial competitions, MENTOR–high school–law firm pairings, and classes where law students teach in schools; (4) training teachers on how to teach law and work with legal partners; and (5) setting up special programs such as its Juvenile Court Alternative Program.

Chicago, IL: *The American Bar Association's Special Committee on Youth Education for Citizenship* is a national clearinghouse-coordinator in law-related education. Activities include (1) seminars for teams of lawyers, educators, juvenile justice officials, and community representatives to highlight teaching strategies and local and state project models; (2) summer institutes for educator-community resources teams from around the country; and (3) the preparation and dissemination of "Building Bridges to the Law," a guide to community involvement for those in the legal field.

Washington, DC: *American Council of Life Insurance's Education Relations and Resources* publishes a manual, entitled "Company-School Collaboration; A Manual for Developing Successful Projects" (prepared by the St. Louis Public Schools) to assist business partners and their staffs to develop and coordinate their partnership programs.

Newark, NJ: *The Mutual Benefit Life Insurance Company* has published reports to assist partnership leaders—particularly those in small businesses, including "The Mutual Benefit Life Report: Corporate Commitment to Volunteerism"; "The Mutual Benefit Life Report II: Small Business Commitment to Volunteerism and Community Involvement"; and, more recently, "Your Small Business: A Big Contribution" (gives small business owners tips on how they can benefit from community involvement).

Salt Lake City, UT: *The National Energy Foundation* supplies energy education materials and instructional programs to help educators incorporate energy concepts into regular classroom instruction, including (1) a resource manual; (2) lesson plans; (3) a Humanities Energy Activity Guide; (4) kits, games, posters and activity workbooks; (5) a newsletter for teachers; (6) a student newspaper; and (7) staff development energy literacy programs.

Washington, DC: *The Young Astronaut Program*, has developed a thematic space program and complementary curriculum materials that address science, math, technology, and related subjects. Activities and materials for elementary and junior high school students include (1) participation in space watches, field trips, and contests; (2) space packages including rocket kits, photo books, and calendars; (3) membership cards, certificates, pins, stickers, and newsletters; and (4) instructions on how to initiate a chapter and how to access the program's computer mailbox for updates on space and program developments.

Alexandria, VA: The *National Community Education Association* (NCEA) works with individuals, groups, and agencies, both public and private, to foster support for and help community education practitioners. Services to members include publications, national conventions, and a wide range of networking activities, for example, the sponsorship of a National Teleconference on Business-Education Partnerships.

ACTION PLAN CHECKSHEET FOR EXTENDING RESOURCE NETWORK

Responsibility _____

1. Source _____

               Regional _____ State _____ National _____

a. Contact:

      Name _____

      Title _____

      Address _____

      _____

      Phone (_____) _____

b. Capsule of Source's Organization:

_____

_____

_____

_____

c. Potential Resources:

_____

_____

_____

_____

d. Status of Commitment:

      No _____ Yes _____ Possible _____

      Comments: _____

_____

_____

_____

_____

_____

Figure 17–1

2. Source _____

       Regional _____ State _____ National _____

a. Contact:

       Name _____

       Title _____

       Address _____

              _____

       Phone (_____) _____

b. Capsule of Source's Organization:

       _____

       _____

       _____

       _____

c. Potential Resources:

       _____

       _____

       _____

       _____

d. Status of Commitment:

       No _____ Yes _____ Possible _____

       Comments: _____

       _____

       _____

       _____

       _____

       _____

Figure 17–1 (continued)

Looking Ahead: How Practitioners View the Future of Partnerships

Partnership leaders were asked the question, "Where do you expect your partnership program specifically and the partnership movement generally to be in 1990?" Following are excerpts from their responses.

The Education Committee is one of seven committees of the Presidential Board of Advisors on Private Sector Initiatives (PSI). It has been this Committee's premise that the interest in private sector involvement in education far exceeds the programs presently in place. Accordingly, the committee has attempted to establish itself as a clearinghouse to exchange information about successful programs, and as a vehicle to provide technical assistance to those who wish to implement programs in their own communities. In this effort, the Education Committee is by no means alone. However, the Education Committee felt that its unique link to the White House might enable it to engage in this work with special effectiveness.

The Education Committee now hopes to further utilize the network which has arisen from its sponsorship of the two National Symposia on Partnerships in Education (1984,85) and its affiliation with Partnerships Data Net, Inc. There is a great American tradition in the area of volunteer support in the field of education, going back to the very roots of our public school system. But as methods and problems become more intricate, there is an increasing need to inform, lest private sector organizations set their sights too low. The Education Committee sees as its continuing role this process of spreading the word.

Thomas W. Evans, Chairman, Education Committee,
Presidential Board of Advisors on Private Sector Initiatives

The potential for highly creative and in-depth program offerings, through partnerships, is tremendous because of the bonding process established through these relationships. When partnerships are one keystone to stable relationships between business, community and public schools, roles of partners can be expanded into multiple arrangements for complementary and jointly sponsored programs beyond the initial one-to-one pairings, thereby reaching a much higher level of sharing and program enrichment.

For example, more companies are coming to the realization that an efficient operation is partly dependent on their employees' pride in the company and their renewed energy due to a change of pace or ability to make a contribution to their community. With this as a motivator, more companies will provide release time for employees to share their professional skills, enriching class subject content . . . under the supervision of a master teacher.

Schools will also begin to acknowledge that student learning is academic rich but experience poor. Students will benefit by having a set of experiences which support their academic preparation such as mentor and community service programs.

Finally, the predicted teacher shortage in the near future is going to require new and creative methods for replacements. If all levels of communities were to serve in instructional roles (i.e., released employees, retired citizens, college interns, etc.), curriculum content would be enriched and teachers would be freed to obtain further training, to visit programs of excellence, to hold parent visitations, and to choose their own community mentor experiences.

Cynthia W. Shelton, Executive Director,
Private Initiatives in Public Education (PIPE), WA

It is a formidable challenge to maintain the initial excitement and enthusiasm generated in the first years of partnership and to fulfill the expectations of all parties involved. During the next five years, I expect to see the pace of collaboration quicken, a logical counterpart to the economic and physical renaissance that is taking place in St. Louis. For these partnerships to be successful and long lasting, teachers, administrators and students must be willing to spend more time in learning how to use these new and invaluable resources.

The business leaders, on the other hand, will have to recognize that the problems which confront us, from the deterioration of the school buildings to low teacher morale to out-dated curricula, have developed over a long period of time and will not be solved in a few years. The business, whatever its size, must make its participation in partnerships in education part of its long-range planning and use its resources at every level—from the chief executive officer to the clerical employee—to address the problems.

Dr. J. Wayne Walker, Director,
Division of Volunteer Services and External Resources,
St. Louis Public Schools, MO

The real reason for industry-education cooperation is to further school improvement and education's role in economic development. This entails the effective and efficient use of industry's volunteer resources in helping education (public and postsecondary) refocus/redesign/restructure its entire academic and vocational program so that it is more responsive to both student and employer needs.

It follows that both the schools and industry (the employment community) need to get organized—establish a broad alliance/mechanism—to undertake this formidable mission. Once organized into an "industry-education council" structure composed of the leaders of the local industry and education communities, both sectors can get down to the substantive areas, that is, the process of joint efforts: cooperative planning, curriculum revision, inservice training of school staff, upgrading instructional materials and equipment, and improving educational management.

We can then anticipate closing the gap between employer expectation and educational preparation. This leads to improving the school-to-work process for students, increasing vocational education's capability to respond to employer training needs, and providing opportunities for entrepreneurship education—all central to a community's economic development

Dr. Donald M. Clark, President and CEO,
National Association for Industry-Education Cooperation (NAIEC), NY

One of the most interesting and exciting things about partnerships is that they are self-perpetuating. So the coordinator's dilemma becomes one of ensuring success by not allowing resources to be spread too thinly-too quickly; by providing a regular forum for liaisons from schools and agencies to hash out difficulties and develop future plans; by giving recognition that is suitable for the community partners; and by offering appropriate inservice orientation and training for school staff on the effective use of these human resources.

The growth, development, and expansion—the vitality—of this movement are to a large extent contingent upon the school system's willingness to continue to provide the coordination, support, and active acknowledgment of program successes *and* failures. Educators must continue to explore ways to effectively involve the community and we must be able to accept and use constructive critique in order to make programs grow. We must take the time to ensure from the outset that both schools and agencies understand that the commitment is one that will not end with the close of a school year.

C. Vanessa Spinner, Director,
Volunteer Services and Training Branch
D.C. Public Schools

In Houston, the school district invites business impact: the expertise, the provisions of positive role models from the world of work, the motivators that business people can be. Moreover, with knowledge and understanding of the constraints on the schools that contributed to decline in achievement, the business community could and, indeed, has helped change the causes.

When excellence in education returns to our schools (as has started to happen in Houston), when our graduates all have acceptable reading, writing, math, and science skills . . . then will the business community continue to be as involved as it now is? I believe it will as the other factors—private enterprise with work ethic and minimal government interventions—will continue to be causes the business community needs to promote.

Will the public schools continue to welcome the influence of the business community? This will depend, of course, on the convictions of state legislatures and elected boards of trustees, but it will depend just as much on the business community's continuing its discreet role of influence by suggestions, examples, and open support.

Terry Chauche, Director, Business/School Partnerships,
Houston Independent School District, TX

On the future of Business/School Partnerships, I would add that a true partnership is a two-way street. We have always stressed mutual beneficiality in inviting and working with the Houston business community. Partnerships will continue and will grow as long as the benefits are mutual.

Additional remarks from Billy R. Reagan
General Superintendent,
Houston Independent School District, TX

The decade of the eighties may well be viewed as the beginning of the evolution of public-private cooperative development, when two previously separate but critical elements of American society interrelated, sharing the need to prepare people, whether students or employees, to be productive citizens in a rapidly changing technological world.

Initially, many partnerships involved short-term, public relations–oriented projects. Increasingly, we are seeing more substantive and sophisticated partnership activities, addressing more challenging business and education issues.

For the past twenty years, interagency cooperation and community involvement in public education have been the main components of community education. Partnerships are one form of interagency cooperation. . . . Joint equipment purchases, sharing personnel, and combining resources in the building of facilities are just a few of the unlimited possibilities that exist.

Even though the impetus may have originated nationally, the state and especially local projects will have the most significant impact on the future of business-education partnership. It may be too early to predict what form these projects will take in the 1990s, since the variety of partnership efforts is likely to, and should be based on the unique characteristics of each community.

Dr. William S. DeJong, Executive Director,
National Community Education Association (NCEA), VA

School-business partnerships are exciting and contain great potential for improving education. That's the good news! The bad news is that the school-business partnership has become the latest fad in education and some school districts are creating partnerships without laying the proper groundwork. The result can be a frustrating and nonproductive exercise for everyone involved. Salem-Keizer public schools have worked hard to develop the firm foundation that is needed to insure a successful and lasting program, for example:

1. We involved the Salem Area Chamber of Commerce in the initial planning for the program and it remains a full cosponsor with us.

2. The activities and resources which are shared between business partners in the Salem-Keizer public schools directly relate to the district's curriculum.

3. Businesses do not enter these partnerships as paternalistic donors; they enter as equal sharers in the duties and benefits.

4. We do not ask businesses to contribute money as a part of this partnership other than the dollars represented in their employees' time and materials and/or equipment which might be used.

Dr. William M. Kendrick, Superintendent, Seattle Public Schools, WA
Former Superintendent, Salem-Keizer Public Schools,
Salem, OR

In smaller communities and suburban areas, partnerships are emerging which capitalize on the concepts of maximizing use of local resources and increasing each other's capacity for change. Set within this context, there are some specific trends for the future. For example,

• Shared staffing will be explored as business identifies needed expertise among teaching staff. At the same time, schools will search for particular expertise from business to enhance their curriculum.

• Teachers and administrators will spend more time with their counterparts in the business world through internships, executive math programs, seminars and information exchanges, and employee loan programs.

• As the number of local service businesses increases and smaller businesses develop as peripheral components of larger industries, K-12 programs and Community Education will develop training modules for youth and adults in entrepreneurial skills to meet local needs in support of the local economy. The partnership concept then becomes an integral component in the formula for attracting or retaining business, and certainly for supporting future economic growth.

Elizabeth A. Bothereau,
Director of Community Education,
St. Louis Park Public Schools, MN

As partnership programs go beyond the exciting courtship period, we must be aware that there are certain dangers if the evolution is to be a positive and long-lasting one. It is very important that the partners have realistic expectations and that the participants not feel used or taken for granted. There must also be mutual benefits and positive results in any voluntary effort. Such programs often have a life cycle, but with proper maintenance, renewal and refinement, the life cycle of partnerships could be extended indefinitely.

Partnerships are definitely *more* than useful public relations or activities that allow people to feel good about themselves. The *BOTTOM LINE IS— PARTNERSHIPS ARE GOOD FOR BUSINESS AND GOOD FOR EDUCATION.* It is extremely important that as the positive results become more evident, institutionalization does not create inhibiting policies and more paper work; we are not complacent; and we do not ignore the team work that was necessary to effect changes and develop successful programs.

Wayne Carlson, Director, Adopt-A-School Program,
Los Angeles Unified School District, CA

A key goal for partnerships in the next five years is to surround them with a strong belief system that they work. As evidence accumulates that today's partnerships are demonstrating educational effectiveness, their reputation for being a peripheral will diminish. In this climate, partnerships will begin to be taken seriously by school district and business leaders who will coordinate strategies to integrate them into the academic schedule. Their planning will include the role of intermediaries such as the San Francisco Education Fund as facilitators and bridging mechanisms of the process.

Gladys S. Thacher, Executive Director,
San Francisco Education Fund, CA

It is projected that the Partnerships in Education effort will continue and grow slowly over the next five years. In addition to the extension of the effort to individual schools, the growth of the number of "district-wide" partners will also be advanced. These relationships link business and non-profit organizations with a number of schools because of a special interest that goes beyond a single site.

Issues regarding the effectiveness of partnership activities, an ongoing review of the things they can and cannot accomplish, the need to present these endeavors as only a part of a strategy for community involvement in the public schools and not as a "quick fix" are all part of an ongoing discussion and planning process that will continue during the next five years.

David Bergholz, President,
Public Education Fund, PA

Single focus partnerships (i.e., cause oriented, jobs, replacement of public monies) have less chance of survival than broader based partnerships that can change with the times, adapt to new situations and add or drop programs or issues. Since partnerships are intermediary organizations, the maintenance of this role is important for survival. Therefore, their ability to be successful rests with their ability to influence and change, *not* to financially support.

Jane C. Burger, Project Director,
Allegheny Conference on Community Development, PA

Pennsylvania has a long and impressive history of partnerships in education. Yet there remains considerable room for innovation, and the future of partnerships will be different from their past. Whether the goal is retraining workers or enriching the education of students, sharing resources allows partners to meet needs that they could not meet as efficiently—and sometimes not at all—alone. For example, as Pennsylvania's reliance on the "smokestack" industries broadens to encompass a more diverse economy, a form of partnership that will be seen more and more often is one that links business and education for the purpose of retraining adult workers.

Recently, the Department of Education and the Pennsylvania Association of Colleges and Universities have begun promoting partnerships between business, schools and institutions of higher education as one means to address the State's concern that the percentage of high school students continuing into higher education has lagged behind the national average. Partnerships provide program and scholarship loan information, help students and parents understand the many other benefits of higher education, and teach students the culture of agriculture and the business of agribusiness.

Dr. Margaret A. Smith, Secretary of Education,
Pennsylvania Department of Education

Our Adopt-A-School program was initiated by the Memphis City Schools in 1979 to bring about a more positive image of our public schools and to make the school system a model of which every Memphian could be proud. In addition, we wanted to enhance and enrich the educational process by utilizing the wealth of human resources to be found in the business, civic, religious, military, governmental, and higher education communities.

The future of Adopt-A-School? Just as in our program, I believe the "sky is the limit." As long as there is a need and educators continue to appreciate the expertise and talents of the adopting groups, we can keep these partnerships solid. Now that partnerships have become the popular thing to do nation-wide, we can borrow ideas from each other to expand our programs and to keep everyone interested.

Barbara S. Russell, Program Director,
Adopt-A-School,
Memphis City Schools, TN

Our Adopt-A-School Program has been largely responsible for the growth of a broad base of public support for our schools. I firmly believe that the future continues to look bright for partnerships in education as programs, such as our Adopt-A-School Program, continue to make a positive impact on public education in communities across the country.

Additional remarks from Dr. W. W. Herenton, Superintendent,
Memphis City Schools, TN

Indiana Partners in Education sees partnership as a phenomenon that needs to grow and change as the future dictates . . . a powerful process that is providing a means of collaboration between diverse entities for mutual gain. These partnerships of the future will:

—*help determine new consumers for education.* The 75% of the community who currently do not participate in public education will be provided with services.

—*provide substantive programming directly related to learner needs,* including retraining of workers who could possibly make multi-career changes during their working lives.

—*support relationships that will develop policy for education on local, state and national levels* . . . organizing active, sustained support mechanisms on behalf of public education.

—*form new enterprises between business, education and the community.* For example, the Center for Community Education and the Small Business Development Center, University of Georgia "married" a concept of vocational education and a community development corporation.

Margaret M. Dwyer, Director,
Indiana Partners in Education,
Margaret M. Dwyer & Associates, IN

Looking into the future of partnerships in education, it appears that the private sector will continue its effort to become more involved with schools, using an increasingly systematic approach to forming these relationships. Partnership goals and objectives will be integrated into the overall objectives of the school system; meet the needs of *and* call on the available resources of each partner involved; and have trained managers who hold positions of relative authority, dedicating full time to the management of the partnership.

The importance of public policy should not be overlooked. One major outcome of the partnership movement will be to involve non-traditional publics in the schools such as seniors, college students and business people. As more become involved in the education of America's children, more support at the local level in terms of tax dollars, bond issues and levies can be anticipated.

Daniel W. Merenda, Executive Director,
National School Volunteer Program, VA

ProEducation . . . The Magazine About Partnerships With Education was created in 1984 to serve as a link between education and the private and public sectors in education partnerships. In our first year of publication, we saw a phenomenal number of creative school-business partnerships being implemented.

We feel that in the next five years there will be at least a doubling or tripling of the number of schools that launch education partnerships. This growth will be nurtured by an increased awareness and willingness on the part of American business—large and small—to become more directly involved in the nation's educational system. Piecemeal, local initiatives can be reinforced through a networking system of data gathering and the implementation of national meetings emanating from corporate headquarters.

A growing number of business people will form coalitions to seek education reform. This "legislative lobbying" will take place both on a state and national level, reinforcing the growing cooperation between pre-collegiate and higher education and American business.

Don Adams, Editor,
ProEducation

Today's established partnerships are working on state-of-the-art programs. Having put program components in place, it is continuous hard work to maintain and to continually refine these procedures. As the partnership network becomes larger, strategies are required to improve communication among all the parties. As more human resources, in-kind donations and financial grants are made by a corporation, we will begin to see large companies establishing national programs through their local and regional offices. Ways of developing "bottom-line" results will need to be established to satisfy the chief executive officers' commitment to these partnerships.

May Ling Tong, formerly Executive Director,
Tri-Lateral Council for Quality Education, MA

Are partnerships worth the effort? As a consultant, working with school administrators and their staffs from around the country, I am constantly struck by their basic optimism—their expression of positive attitudes and productive efforts in the face of professional conditions and bureaucracies that would thwart others—many of whom are highly critical of educators specifically and of education in general.

The willingness to embrace new programs—like partnerships—and make them work is one expression of this optimism. After all, partnerships may represent one more thing to add to or integrate into the already bursting school day. Educators have had "new," "innovative," and "improvement" programs thrust on them before. Administrators, particularly, may be reluctant to burden themselves and their staffs further unless they are convinced that the promise of "partnership" makes educational sense; that is, directly addresses *and* has the potential to support school district educational goals and individual student instructional needs.

Therefore, partners in these alliances will have to be patient and tolerant of educators who appear cautious about their involvement. With time and work, partnerships will become a more normal part of the lives of all partners—educators, businesses, government agencies, and nonprofit organizations.

Dr. Susan D. Otterbourg, Educational Consultant

PART FIVE

APPENDIXES

Local Partnership Resources

Alabama

Dr. Elaine D. Klotz
Adopt-A-School Specialist
Board of School Commissioners of
    Mobile County
1107 Arlington Street
Mobile, AL 36605

Dr. Gene J. Watson
Superintendent
Dothan City Schools
500 Dusy Street
Dothan, AL 36301

Arizona

Karen Sanders, Coordinator
Tucson Educational Enrichment Fund
Community Services
Tucson Unified School District
P.O. Box 40400
Tucson, AZ 85717

Arkansas

Ann S. Brown, Coordinator
Volunteers in Public Schools
School-Community Partnership Program
Little Rock School District
12th and Pine Streets
Little Rock, AR 72204

California

Thomas Silk, Attorney
680 Beach Street, Suite 424
San Francisco, CA 94109

Catherine Pyke, Director
San Francisco School Volunteers
Corporate Action in Public Schools
    (CAPS)
135 Van Ness Avenue, Room 20A
San Francisco, CA 94102

Harvey H. Schwartz, CPA
Hood and Strong, Certified Public
    Accountants
101 California Street, Suite 1500
San Francisco, CA 94111

Gloria S. Curtis, Director
Dedicated Older Volunteers in
    Educational Services (DOVES)
Los Angeles Unified School District
450 North Grand Avenue
Los Angeles, CA 90012

Marilyn Raby
Director of Special Projects
Peninsula Academies
Sequoia Union High School District
480 James Avenue
Redwood City, CA 94062

Wayne Carlson, Director
Adopt-A-School Program
Los Angeles Unified School District
450 North Grand Avenue, Room H-237
Los Angeles, CA 90012

Gladys S. Thacher, Executive Director
San Francisco Education Fund
1095 Market Street, #719
San Francisco, CA 94103

Lin Ishihara, Director
Corporate Action Committee
135 Van Ness Avenue, Room 20B
San Francisco, CA 94102

Jeanne Jehl, Coordinator
Partnerships in Education Program
San Diego Unified School District
4100 Normal Street
San Diego, CA 92103

Barbara Barnes, Director
Partnerships in Education
Irvine Unified School District
5144 Michelson Road
Irvine, CA 92715

Colorado

Ann Fenton, Executive Director
Adopt-A-School in Denver
2320 West Fourth Avenue
Denver, CO 80223

Connecticut

Dr. William R. Papallo
Superintendent of Schools
PROJECT SCIENCE, Stamford Public
   Schools (with CBS Technology Center
   and Holt, Rinehart & Winston)
195 Hillandale Avenue
Stamford, CT 06902

Peter Goldberg, Vice-President
American Can Company Foundation
NYC Join-A-School Program
American Can-Martin Luther King, Jr.
   High School
American Lane
Greenwich, CT 06836

District of Columbia

C. Vanessa Spinner, Director
Volunteer Services and Training
D.C. Public Schools
Federal Partners in Education
415 12th Street, N.W.
Washington, DC 20004

Mattie W. Carey, Director
Associates for Renewal in Education, Inc.
Emeritus Teachers Project
Edmonds School Building
Ninth and D Streets, N.E.
Washington, DC 20002

Etta Green Johnson, Executive Director
Washington Parent Group Fund
1400 Eye Street, N.W., Suite 450
Washington, DC 20005

Ann Winkler, Administrator
Office of Visitor Services
Federal Reserve Board
20th and Constitution Avenue, N.W.
Washington, DC 20551

Florida

Gina Craig, Supervisor
School Volunteers–Dade Partners
Dade County Public Schools
1450 N.E. Second Avenue, Room 227
Miami, FL 33132

George R. Van Wyck, Secretary
American Bankers Insurance Group
American Bankers–Southridge High
   School Partnership (Dade Partners)
11222 Quail Roost Drive
Miami, FL 33157

Georgia

Dr. Boyd Odom, Executive Director
Atlanta Partnership, Inc.
Urban Life, Suite 736-739
University Plaza
Atlanta, GA 30303

Dr. Chuck Fuller
Director of Educational Development–
   Standards
Principals Institute
Atlanta Public Schools
2930 Forest Hill Drive, S.W.
Atlanta, GA 30315

Dr. Lowrie A. Fraser, Coordinator
Adopt-A-School Program
Atlanta Public Schools
Atlanta Partnership of Business &
  Education, Inc.
Urban Life, Suite 736-739
University Plaza
Atlanta, GA 30303

Illinois

Al Sterling, Director
Adopt-A-School Program
Chicago Public Schools
1819 Pershing Road
Chicago, Il 60609

Dr. Frances B. Holliday, Director
Bureau of Volunteer Programs—Saturday
  Scholars
Chicago Public Schools
1819 Pershing Road—6 East
Chicago, IL 60609

Indiana

Andrea Worrell, Executive Director
Partners in Education
Indianapolis Chamber of Commerce
320 North Meridian Street
Indianapolis, IN 46204

Kansas

Shirlene Duncan, Coordinator
Adopt-A-School Program
Wichita Public Schools
640 North Emporia
Wichita, KS 67214

Maryland

Lois P. Parker, Career Education
  Coordinator
Community Collaborative Programs in
  Career Education
Montgomery County Public Schools
850 Hungerford Drive
Rockville, MD 20850

Michael C. Wilson, Coordinator of
  Vocational Trades
Montgomery County Students Auto &
  Construction Trades Foundation, Inc.
Montgomery County Public Schools
12501 Dalewood Drive
Silver Springs, MD 20906

Massachusetts

Betsy Nelson, Executive Director
School Volunteers for Boston, Inc.
25 West Street
Boston, MA 02111

Harold N. Read
Assistant Vice-President and Manager
Personnel Development
Liberty Mutual Insurance Co.
A Partnership for Tomorrow: Liberty-
  Charlestown High School
175 Berkeley Street
Boston, MA 02117

Franklin L. Stafford, Manager
New England Services—Corporate
  Coordinator for Partnership Program
John Hancock Insurance Co.—English
  High School Partnership
P.O. Box 111, John Hancock Place
Boston, MA 02117

Michigan

Dr. James L. Leary, Superintendent
Adrian Public Schools
159 East Maumee Street
Adrian, MI 49221

Minnesota

Darrol Bussler, Director
Community Services
School District #6
357 Ninth Avenue North
South St. Paul, MN 55075

Elizabeth A. Bothereau
Director of Community Education
TwinWest Business-Education
  Partnership Program
6425 West 33rd Street
St. Louis Park, MN 55426

Mississippi

Liz Bullock, Facilitator
Community Resources
Jackson Municipal Separate School
  District
P.O. Box 2338
Jackson, MS 39225

Missouri

Dr. Vincent A. Vento
Assistant Superintendent for Community
  Education
Rockwood School District
111 East North Street
Eureka, MO 63025

Jolene Schulz, Coordinator
Partners in Education
Columbia Public Schools
310 North Providence Road
Columbia, MO 65201

Dr. J. Wayne Walker, Divisional Director
Volunteer Services and External
  Resources
The St. Louis School Partnership
  Program
5057 Ridge Avenue
St. Louis, MO 63113

New Hampshire

Marguery R. Navaroli, Community-
  School Coordinator
Community Collaborative Career
  Guidance Team and Adopt-A-School
  Program
36 Riverside Drive
Nashua, NH 03062

New York

Nydia Ocasio-Gouraige, Director
Join-A-School
Division of High Schools
NYC Board of Education
110 Livingston Street, Room 237M
Brooklyn, NY 11201

Peggy Dulany, Senior Vice-President
New York City Partnership, Inc.
200 Madison Avenue
New York, NY 10016

Dr. Doris Hammond
Senior Volunteers in the Schools
D'Youville College
320 Porter Avenue
Buffalo, NY 14201

Herbert Balish, Principal, Tottenville
  High School and Project Director
Principal as Curriculum Leader Program
100 Luten Avenue
Staten Island, NY 10302

Virginia Hill, Asst. Vice-President
National Community Affairs
Citicon-Citibank—Careers in Office
  Technology
399 Park Avenue
New York, NY 10043

Barbara Probst, Executive Director
New York Alliance for the Public Schools
32 Washington Place
New York, NY 10003

North Carolina

Dianne Avery
Community Schools Coordinator
New Hanover Public Schools
P.O. Box 390
Wilmington, NC 28402

Andrew C. Canady
Assistant Superintendent for Instruction
Onslow County Public Schools
P.O. Box 99
Jacksonville, NC 28540

Beverly T. Mauldin, Community
  Education Coordinator
Mary Boyce, Community Resource
  Assistant
Community Resource Program
Charlotte-Mecklenburg Schools
428 West Boulevard
Charlotte, NC 28203

Ohio

Dr. Leslie Duffey, Supervisor
School-Business Programs
Columbus Public Schools
546 Jack Gibbs Boulevard
Columbus, OH 43215

Bert L. Holt, Director
University, Business-Labor Cultural
  Involvement
Cleveland Public Schools
1380 East Sixth Street
Cleveland, OH 44114

Betty M. Berens, Coordinator
VIP Volunteer Program
Hudson Local School District
Superintendent's Office
77 North Oviatt Street
Hudson, OH 44236

Dr. Clarence W. Mixon, Executive
  Director
Cleveland Scholarship Programs, Inc.
1380 East Sixth Street
Cleveland, OH 44114

Louise Hopkins, Coordinator
School–Business Programs–Adopt-A-
  School
Columbus Public Schools
546 Jack Gibbs Boulevard
Columbus, OH 43215

Joseph H. Chadbourne, President
Cleveland's Teacher Internship Program
Institute for Environmental Education
32000 Chagrin Boulevard
Cleveland, OH 44124

Carol L. Davidow, Coordinator for
  Schools
Partners-in-Education–Cincinnati
  Business Committee and Greater
  Cincinnati Chamber of Commerce
1706 DuBois Tower
Cincinnati, OH 45202

Oklahoma

Robert Zienta
Director of Community-School Relations
Oklahoma City Schools
900 North Klein
Oklahoma City, OK 73106

Saundra Vallejo, Coordinator
Adopt-A-School–Volunteer Services
Oklahoma City Schools
900 North Klein
Oklahoma City, OK 73106

Nancy McDonald, Director
Business-Community Resources
Adopt-A-School Program
Tulsa Public Schools
P.O. Box 45208
Tulsa, OK 74147

Oregon

William Liebertz, Executive Asst. to
  Superintendent
Carla Moyer, Business Partner
  Coordinator, Secondary Schools
Business Partnership in Education
Salem-Keizer Public Schools
P.O. Box 12024
Salem, OR 97309

Pennsylvania

Jeanne Berdik, Program Coordinator
Partnerships in Education
The Greater Pittsburgh Chamber of
  Commerce
3 Gateway Center
Pittsburgh, PA 15222

Gregory Myers, Principal
Burton Elementary School
Hammermill-Burton Adopt-A-School
  Program
1661 Buffalo Road
Erie, PA 16510

Dale L. Baker, Assistant Superintendent
Adopt-A-School Program
West Shore School District
1000 Hummel Avenue
Lemoyne, PA 17043

Jane T. Pelland
Assistant to the Superintendent for
  Partnerships
Lancaster Partners-in-Education Program
225 West Orange Street
Lancaster, PA 17603

Dr. Judith F. Hodgson, Executive
  Director
Philadelphia Alliance for Teaching
  Humanities in the Schools (PATHS)
Suite 400, Suburban Station Building
1617 J. F. Kennedy Boulevard
Philadelphia, PA 19103

South Carolina

Dr. Vance O. Johnson
Assistant Superintendent
Newberry County Schools' Adopt-A-
  School
1539 Martin Street
Newberry, SC 29108

Tennessee

Carl Buckner, Superintendent
Rutherford County Schools
502 Memorial Boulevard
Murfreesboro, TN 37130

Sue W. Boyer, Supervisor
Adopt-A-School Program
Knox County Board of Education
400 Main Street, P.O. Box 2188
Knoxville, TN 37901

Sandy Boone, Coordinator
Adopt-A-School Program
Chattanooga Public Schools
1161 West 40th Street
Chattanooga, TN 37409

Barbara S. Russell, Director
Adopt-A-School Program
Memphis City Schools
2597 Avery Avenue
Memphis, TN 38112

Texas

Toni Brown, Coordinator
Adopt-A-School Program
Fort Worth Independent School District
3210 West Lancaster Avenue
Fort Worth, TX 76107

Kathleen Wood, Coordinator-Producer
Volunteer in Public Schools
Storer Cable Communications, Inc.
2505 Bisbee
Houston, TX 77017

Terry Chauche, Director
Business-School Partnerships
Houston Independent School District
3830 Richmond Avenue
Houston, TX 77027

Larry Ascough, Special Assistant to the
  Superintendent—Communications
Adopt-A-School Program
Dallas Independent School District
3700 Ross Avenue
Dallas, TX 75204

Utah

Adopt-A-School Program
Utah Mountain Bell
250 Bell Plaza
Salt Lake City, UT 84111

Gene Berry, Coordinator
Salt Lake City Volunteer Program
440 East First South
Salt Lake City, UT 84111

Virginia

Jay D. Jacobs, Assistant Superintendent
Department of Career and Resource
  Development
Fairfax County Public Schools
Walnut Hill Center
7423 Camp Alger Avenue
Falls Church, VA 22042

Agenor L. Castro, Coordinator of Public
  Relations
Adopt-A-School Program
Richmond Public Schools
301 North Ninth Street
Richmond, VA 23219

Dr. Arthur W. Gosling
Superintendent of Schools
Arlington Public Schools
1426 North Quincy Street
Arlington, VA 22207

Washington

Dr. George T. Daniel
Superintendent of Schools
Kent Public Schools
12033 S.E. 256th Street
Kent, WA 98031

Cynthia Shelton, Executive Director
Private Initiatives in Public Education
  (PIPE)
1200 One Union Square
Seattle, WA 98101

Wisconsin

Dr. Lee R. McMurrin
Superintendent of Schools
Business-Education Partnership Program
Milwaukee Public Schools
5225 West Vliet Street
Milwaukee, WI 53208

Regional Partnership Resources

California

Peggy Funkhouser, Executive Director
The Los Angeles Educational Partnership
1052 West Sixth Street, Suite 716
Los Angeles, CA 90017

Dr. Gerald A. Rosander
Superintendent of Schools
Partnerships in Education
San Diego County Office of Education
6401 Linda Vista Road
San Diego, CA 92111

Colorado

Kent T. Higgins, Chief
Employment Opportunities Office
National Bureau of Standards
Career Awareness and Resource
  Education (CARE)
U.S. Department of Commerce
325 Broadway
Boulder, CO 80303

Illinois

Jack Rawlinson, Director
Southeastern Illinois Vocational System
112 North Gum Street
Harrisburg, IL 62946

Lawrence D. Smith I, Program Manager
Partnerships in Education
U.S. Railroad Retirement Board
844 Rush Street
Chicago, IL 60611

Dr. Tom Boldrey, Director
Education for Technology Employment
Will County Regional Schools Office
14 West Jefferson Street
Joliet, IL 60431

Massachusetts

May Ling Tong, Executive Director
Northeast Minority Purchasing Council
4 Copley Place, Suite 125
Boston, MA 02116

Minnesota

Corporate Information and Media
  Relations
3M's Visiting Women Scientists Program
P.O. Box 33600
St. Paul, MN 55144

Mary Rollwagen, Program Director
Education Ventures, Inc.
c/o Honeywell Inc.
Honeywell Plaza MN12-5324
Minneapolis, MN 55408

New Hampshire

William A. Southworth, Executive
  Director
Corporate Council for Critical Skills
P.O. Box 2001
Old Wilton Road
Milford, NH 03055

New York

Claire Flom, Chairperson
New York Alliance for the Public Schools
32 Washington Place
New York, NY 10003

Judy Breck, Coordinator
MENTOR
Suite 3600, 180 Maiden Lane
New York, NY 10038

North Carolina

Dr. Parmalee P. Hawk
School of Education
Teacher Exchange in Rural Schools
East Carolina University
Greenville, NC 27834

North Dakota

Larry L. Smiley, Executive Director
Upper Midwest Small Schools Projects
 (UMSSP)
P.O. Box 8158
University of North Dakota
Grand Forks, ND 58202

Pennsylvania

Jane C. Burger, Program Director
Allegheny Conference Education Fund
600 Grant Street, Suite 4444
Pittsburgh, PA 15219

State Partnership Resources

Arizona

Carolyn Warner
Superintendent of Public Instruction
State of Arizona Department of
   Education
1535 West Jefferson
Phoenix, AZ 85007

California

Mary Anderson, Executive Director
The California Roundtable
P.O. Box 7643
San Francisco, CA 94119

Joseph C. Berney
Executive Vice-President
Industry Education Council of California
   (IECC)
1575 Old Bayshore Highway, Suite 106
Burlingame, CA 94010

Colorado

Michael A. Demma, Supervisor
Personnel and Benefits
Fort Collins Business-Education Council
2101 Dover Drive
Fort Collins, CO 80526

Dr. Arvin C. Blome, Assistant
   Commissioner
Federal Relations & Instructional Services
Colorado State Department of Education
303 West Colfax
Denver, CO 80204

Delaware

Margaret McGrath, Executive Director
The Partnership: Business and Education
   of Delaware
P.O. Box 1790
Wilmington, DE 19899

Georgia

Dr. Paul De Largy, Director
Center for Community Education
Small Business Development Center
University of Georgia
Athens, GA 30602

Indiana

Margaret M. Dwyer, Director
Indiana Partners in Education
Hoosiers for Economic Development
   Committee
11 South Meridian Street, Suite 1005
Indianapolis, IN 46204

Kentucky

Alice McDonald
Superintendent of Public Instruction
Kentucky Department of Education
103 Capital Plaza Tower
Frankfort, KY 40601

Massachusetts

Susan Freedman
Coordinator of Community Education
Bureau of Student, Community, and
   Adult Services
Massachusetts Department of Education
1385 Hancock Street
Quincy, MA 02169

Minnesota

Laura Lee M. Geraghty, Director
Minnesota Office on Volunteer Services
Department of Administration, State of
   Minnesota
500 Rice Street
St. Paul, MN 55155

Missouri

Dr. J. A. Kinder, Secretary-Treasurer
Missouri Education-Business Partners
P.O. Box 458
Columbia, MO 65205

North Carolina

Boyce C. Medlin, Chief Consultant
Division of School-Community Relations
North Carolina Department of Public
   Instruction
Education Building
Raleigh, NC 27611

Violet Landreth, Regional Coordinator
North Carolina Regional Education
   Center
P.O. Box 21889
Greensboro, NC 27420

Oklahoma

Dr. Ken Smith
Oklahoma State Facilitator
National Diffusion Network
215 North Boulevard
Edmond, OK 73034

Pennsylvania

Robert Williams, Executive Director
Governor's Human Resources Committee
   of the Cabinet
333 Market Street
Harrisburg, PA 17120

Dr. Margaret A. Smith
Secretary of Education
Pennsylvania Department of Education
333 Market Street
Harrisburg, PA 17126

South Carolina

Robin Burleson, Chief Supervisor
Administrators' Leadership Academy
South Carolina State Department of
   Education
Columbia, SC 29201

National Partnership Resources

FEDERAL RESOURCES

Dr. Charles J. O'Malley
Executive Assistant for Private Education
U.S. Department of Education
400 Maryland Avenue, S.W., Room 4137
  FOB6
Washington, DC 20202

Marlene M. Beck, Associate Director
Winston A. Wilkinson
Special Assistant to the Secretary of
  Education
Private-Sector Initiatives Office
U.S. Department of Education
400 Maryland Avenue, S.W., Room 4169
Washington, DC 20202

Renee L. Anderson, Project Manager
Office of Economic Adjustment
U.S. Department of Defense
3D-968 Pentagon
Washington, DC 20301-4000

Deputy Administrator
Extension Service
4-H Program
U.S. Department of Agriculture
South Building, Room 3860
Washington, DC 20250

Dr. Joseph H. Casello, Deputy Director
Adult Literacy Initiative

U.S. Department of Education
400 Maryland Avenue, S.W., Room 4145
Washington, DC 20202

Frederick J. Ryan, Jr.
Deputy Assistant to the President and
  Director
Office of Private Sector Initiatives
The White House
Washington, DC 20500

William B. Foote, Chairperson
GSA/FSS/SSOC
Steering Committee
U.S. General Services Administration
Office of Federal Supply and Services—
  FM
Washington, DC 20406

National Diffusion Network Program
U.S. Department of Education
Washington, DC 20202-1630

Marion Craft, Senior Program Officer
Cooperative Education, Work Experience
  & Work Study Programs
Office of Vocational and Adult Education
U.S. Department of Education
Reporter's Building, 400 Maryland
  Avenue, S.W.
Washington, DC 20202-5917

BUSINESS AND NONPROFIT ORGANIZATIONS

California

Dorothy Reller, Evaluator
American Institute for Research
1791 Arastradero Road
Palo Alto, CA 94302

Connecticut

Sybil J. Stevenson, Manager
Corporate Contributions
Growth Initiatives for Teachers (GIFT)
GTE Corporation
One Stamford Forum
Stamford, CT 06904

District of Columbia

Linda B. Skover, Manager
Educational Services
Newspaper in Education
American Newspaper Publishers
  Association (ANPA) Foundation
Box 17407, Dulles International Airport
Washington, DC 20041

Ronald P. Simmons
Community Relations Representative
IBM Corporation
1801 K Street, N.W.
Washington, DC 20006

Dr. Dorothy Rich, President
Home and School Institute, Inc.
Special Projects Office
1201 16th Street, N.W.
Washington, DC 20036

Director
Institute for Educational Leadership
1001 Connecticut Avenue, N.W.
Washington, DC 20036

President
American Association of Community and
  Junior Colleges
One Dupont Circle, N.W., Suite 410
Washington, DC 20036

Richard A. Ungerer, President
National Institute for Work and
  Learning
1200 18th Street, N.W., Suite 316
Washington, DC 20036

T. Wendell Butler, Executive Director
Young Astronaut Program
White House Office of Private Sector
  Initiatives
1211 Connecticut Avenue, N.W., Suite
  800
Washington, DC 20036

Jessie Lacy
Director of Program Services
Reading Is Fundamental (RIF)
600 Maryland Avenue, S.W., Suite 500
Washington, DC 20024

Gene DePrez, President-CEO
Partnerships Data Net, Inc.
1111 North 19th Street, Suite 500
Arlington, VA 22209

Eve Katz, Director
Education Relations and Resources
American Council of Life Insurance
1850 K Street, N.W.
Washington, DC 20006

Edmund L. O'Brien and Jason I.
  Newman
Codirectors
National Institute for Citizen Education
  in the Law (NICEL)
605 G Street, N.W.
Washington, DC 20001

Robert Woodson, President
National Center for Neighborhood
  Enterprise
1367 Connecticut Avenue, N.W.
Washington, DC 20036

Maurice E. Weir, Vice-President
Special Projects & Prototype
  Development
Cities in Schools, Inc.
1110 Vermont Avenue, N.W.
Washington, DC 20005

Dr. John M. Fowler, Director
Triangle Coalition for Science and
  Technology Education
National Science Teachers Association
1742 Connecticut Avenue, N.W.
Washington, DC 20009

Holly Stewart McMahon, Director
Government Programs
American Bar Association
1800 M Street, N.W.
Washington, DC 20036

Robert L. Martin, Associate Manager
Community Resources
U.S. Chamber of Commerce
1615 H Street, N.W.
Washington, DC 20062

Florida

Don Adams, Editor
ProEducation
5000 Park Street North
St. Petersburg, FL 33709

Illinois

Vivian L. DeJoode
Membership Development Director
National Association for the Exchange of
  Industrial Resources (NAEIR)
P.O. Box 8076
540 Frontage Road
Northfield, IL 60093

Charlotte Anderson, Staff Director
Special Committee on Youth Education
  for Citizenship
American Bar Association
750 North Lake Shore Drive
Chicago, IL 60611

Kansas

Michael J. Jenkins, Director
The BOOK IT! National Reading
  Incentive Program
Pizza Hut, Inc.
P.O. Box 2999
Wichita, KS 67201

New Jersey

Public Relations Department
Mutual Benefit Life Insurance Company
520 Broad Street
Newark, NJ 07101

New York

The Foundation Center
79 Fifth Avenue
New York, NY 10003

Constance M. O'Hare, MENTOR
  Coordinator
Mead Data Central
200 Park Avenue
New York, NY 10166

Allen Y. Shaklan
Vice President and Asst. to the President
CBS TV Stations
51 West 52nd Street
New York, NY 10019

Ellen Dempsey, Executive Director
IMPACT II
15 East 26th Street
New York, NY 10010

Dr. Donald M. Clark
President and CEO
National Association for Industry-
  Education Cooperation (NAIEC)
235 Hendricks Boulevard
Buffalo, NY 14226

Oklahoma

Richard K. Judy
Public Affairs Representative
Amoco Production Company
P.O. Box 3385
Tulsa, OK 74102

Pennsylvania

Susan J. Ellis, President
Energize Associates
5450 Wissahickon Avenue, Lobby A
Philadelphia, PA 19144

David Bergholz, President
Public Education Fund
600 Grant Street
Pittsburgh, PA 15219

Texas

Jo Ann Swinney, Director
Community Affairs
Tenneco Inc.
P.O. Box 2511
Houston, TX 77001

Donald McGinty, Manager
Employee Relations
Shell Development Company
P.O. Box 481
Houston, TX 77001

Utah

Dr. Dennis W. Cartwright
Director of Program Operations
National Energy Foundation
5160 Wiley Post Way, Suite 200
Salt Lake City, UT 84116

Virginia

Kent Amos, Director of Urban Affairs
Xerox Youth Program
Xerox Corporation
1616 North Fort Meyer Drive
Arlington, VA 22209

Director
National Future Farmers of America
  Center
5632 Mt. Vernon Memorial Highway
P.O. Box 15160
Alexandria, VA 22309

Dr. William S. DeJong, Executive
  Director
National Community Education
  Association (NCEA)
119 North Payne Street
Alexandria, VA 22314

Camy Griffin, Director
MATHCOUNTS
National Society of Professional
  Engineers
1420 King Street
Alexandria, VA 22314

Daniel W. Merenda, Executive Director
National School Volunteer Program
701 North Fairfax Street
Alexandria, VA 22314

Washington

Director
ACRES Rural Job Services
Western Washington University
Bellingham, WA 98225

Resource Publications

*The Art of Making a Successful Slide
   Presentation*
GENIGRAPHICS Corporation
P.O. Box 591, Building 1
Liverpool, NY 13088

Coordinating Your School Volunteer Program
Written by Susanne E. Taranto (1983)
VORT Corporation
P.O. Box 60132
Palo Alto, CA 94306

Corporate Community Involvement and
   Partnerships in Education Directory
Distributed through Partnerships Data
   Net
1111 North 19th Street, Suite 500
Arlington, VA 22209

*The Local Education Foundation: A New
   Way to Raise Money for Schools*
Written by George Neill
NASSP Special Report (May 1983)
National Assocation for Secondary School
   Principals
1904 Association Drive
Reston, VA 22091

*A Nation at Work: Education and the Private
   Sector*
(A report prepared by the National
   Advisory Council on Vocational
   Education)

Published by National Alliance of
   Business
1015 15th Street, N.W.
Attn: Clearinghouse
Washington, DC 20005

*Partnerships in Education: Education Trends
   of the Future*
Contact Marlene M. Beck
Associate Director
Office of Private Sector Initiatives
U.S. Department of Education
400 Maryland Avenue, S.W., Room 4169
Washington, DC 20202

ProEducation
Don Adams, Editor
5000 Park Street North
St. Petersburg, FL 33709

*School-Business Partnerships: Why Not?
   Laying the Foundation for Successful
   Programs*
Written by Santee C. Ruffin, Jr. (1983)
National Association of Secondary School
   Principals
1904 Association Drive
Reston, VA 22091

Index

F

G